Rape and the Culture
of the Courtroom

Negrophobia and Reasonable Racism:
The Hidden Costs of Being Black in America
Jody David Armour

Black and Brown in America:
The Case for Cooperation
Bill Piatt

Black Rage Confronts the Law
Paul Harris

Selling Words:
Free Speech in a Commercial Culture
R. George Wright

The Color of Crime:
Racial Hoaxes, White Fear, Black Protectionism, Police
Harassment, and Other Macroaggressions
Katheryn K. Russell

The Smart Culture:
Society, Intelligence, and Law
Robert L. Hayman, Jr.

Was Blind, But Now I See:
White Race Consciousness and the Law
Barbara J. Flagg

American Law in the Age of Hypercapitalism:
The Worker, the Family, and the State
Ruth Colker

The Gender Line:
Men, Women, and the Law
Nancy Levit

Heretics in the Temple:
Americans Who Reject the Nation's Legal Faith
David Ray Papke

The Empire Strikes Back:
Outsiders and the Struggle over Legal Education
Arthur Austin

Interracial Justice:
Conflict and Reconciliation in Post-Civil Rights America
Eric K. Yamamoto

Rape and the Culture of the Courtroom

Andrew E. Taslitz

NEW YORK UNIVERSITY PRESS

New York and London

NEW YORK UNIVERSITY PRESS
New York and London

Library of Congress Cataloging-in-Publication Data
Taslitz, Andrew E., 1956–
Rape and the culture of the courtroom / Andrew E. Taslitz.
p.   cm. — (Critical America)
Includes bibliographical references and index.
ISBN 0-8147-8229-9 (cloth : acid-free paper)
ISBN 0-8147-8230-2 (paper : acid-free paper)
1. Rape—United States. 2. Adversary system (Law)—United States.
3. Law reform—United States.   I. Title. II. Series.
KF9329 .T37 1999
345.73'02532—dc21   98-40191
                             CIP

New York University Press books are printed on acid-free paper,
and their binding materials are chosen for strength and durability.

Manufactured in the United States of America

10 9 8 7 6 5 4 3 2 1

Contents

Acknowledgments

My heartfelt thanks go to Richard Delgado and Jean Stefancic for their invitation to participate in the Critical America series. Much gratitude to my editor, Jennifer Hammer, for her insights, suggestions, accessibility, and encouragement.

I am also grateful to David Bogard, David Leonard, Keller Magenau, Gregory Matoesian, Robert Mosteller, Aviva Orenstein, and Patricia V. Sun for their thoughtful comments on earlier drafts of this manuscript. My appreciation goes as well to Vicky Byrd, Crystal Collier, Vernita Fairley, Mikee Gildea, Mekka Jeffers, Rikki McCoy, and Dahli Myers for their expert research assistance and to the Howard University School of Law for its financial support of this project. A special thanks to Delphyne Bruner and Sandra Pixley, whose patience and superb secretarial skills helped this book to take shape. Endless praise to Richard Leiter, Iris Lee, and Valerie Railey for being law librarians who relish the search for the unusual.

To my friends Ben, Ethan, and Stefni Bogard; Andrew Gavil; and Nancy Schultz for being there. Most important, to my parents, Saul and Mitzi Taslitz, and my sister, Ellen Duncan, for teaching me persistence and hope, and to my wife, Patricia V. Sun, who makes all things worthwhile.

I have been pondering the ideas in this book for several years, and early versions of some of the ideas in Part I were explored in *Patriarchal Stories I: Cultural Rape Narratives in the Courtroom*, 5 S. CAL. REV. L. & WOM.'S ST. 402–4 (1996). All of the ideas in Parts II and III appear here, however, for the first time in print. Thanks as well to those too numerous to name whose feedback on my earlier work helped in my efforts to make this book worthwhile.

Note to the Reader

Because rape victims are predominantly women, and rapists are usually men, my pronoun usage reflects that reality. Similarly, because most prosecutors and defense counsel are men, and even women lawyers trying rape cases usually mirror male lawyers' ways of speaking, I refer to prosecutors and defense counsel by the pronouns "he" and "his."

Introduction

"SHIRLEY ROBINSON, TAKE THE STAND!" My ears hurt as the court clerk bellowed my witness's name, showing not a hint of the appropriate tone one might expect in calling a rape victim to the stand. But no one else seemed bothered by his demeanor or saw anything unusual in the routine of assembly-line justice in Philadelphia's juvenile courts.

Shirley (a pseudonym) rose slowly from her chair. She wore a long, polyester blue dress; like most crime victims, she was not a woman from comfortable economic circumstances. Luckily, she was dressed modestly, unlike some rape victims, especially younger ones, who would dress in clothes for court that were both inexpensive *and* revealing, unless I had convinced them in advance that juries expected greater modesty from "real" rape victims.

The judge glowered at Shirley. There was no jury, for juveniles were not entitled to one. Judge K. was not known for his warmth and was, indeed, the judge before whom I would have liked least to try any rape case. Since all my efforts at judge shopping had failed, I had had no choice. I swallowed my concerns, and, with the judge's permission, asked Shirley to tell us what happened on the night that brought her to court.

Shirley testified that she had been at choir practice at her church and had participated in a Bible study group that same night. It was a cold, January night with snow from a few days before still on the ground. Leaving church about 9:30 P.M., she had started walking the five blocks to her apartment, where she lived alone. She walked quickly, knowing that the streets were not safe, although she had made this nightly trip from church many times with no incident. This night, however, Tony, a teenage male from her church, also African American, started walking beside her. "Hi, Shirley. Why don't I walk you home to make sure you get there safe?"

Shirley testified that she kept up her pace but turned to look at the boy beside her. She did vaguely recognize him from church, but they had never spoken before. "No thank you," she said, "I'd rather walk home alone." "But I think you need company," he said, then swiftly covered her mouth with one hand and grabbed her waist with the other.

She tried to scream, but his hand muffled any sound. She could barely breathe. Much larger than she, he dragged her into a nearby alley, saying that he would snap her neck if she didn't shut up and that she would enjoy it. Shirley stopped trying to scream. But she cried, loudly, and he slapped her hard, saying, "Don't cry. I'm just going to make you a woman." Then he ripped off her panties and hurt her. She bit her lip in an effort not to scream or cry. When he was done, he told her how much he had enjoyed himself, promised to call her next week, and said he hoped she'd let him sit next to her in church.

Afterward, Shirley sat still awhile crying, terrified. Then she bolted, running for home. When she got there, she called no one, just hugged her pillow, crying. She showered, douched, and tried vainly to sleep. For several days, she called in sick at work. Finally, four days after the incident, fearing venereal disease, she saw a doctor. The doctor urged her to see Women Organized Against Rape (WOAR), a local rape victims' support group, which she did. WOAR urged her to see the police, which she also reluctantly did. Driving around the neighborhood with the police, Shirley saw Tony, pointed him out, and the police arrested him.

Tony was indeed much larger than Shirley. But in court he was very young (barely seventeen) and clean-cut, with closely cropped hair, a nice suit, and a sharp, bright expression. In contrast, Shirley was obviously older (about forty), less self-assured, heavier-set than many, with her makeup a bit askew.

Shirley recounted her ordeal clearly, despite the defense's objections, which slowed her down and even rattled her a bit. But she had no apparent motive to lie, and her chances of having made a mistaken identification were small because she knew Tony from church. I felt good about the case.

I also knew that with the testimony of my expert on the behavior of rape victims, I could show that Shirley's delayed report of the incident was very common for a rape victim. Of course, some aspects of her story might sound far-fetched to those unfamiliar with the realities of rape (e.g., "Why rape someone you know, who could identify you?" "If it was rape, why would the rapist expect a date and look forward to seeing you in church?" "Wouldn't cold winter ground be too uncomfortable, even for the rapist, to engage in sex?"). Yet I knew from experience that the details

Shirley recounted were all too common, and I knew that the judge had presided over enough rape cases that he should know that too. In any event, why would she go through the humiliation of a rape trial where she had no motive for revenge, for covering up an unwanted pregnancy, or for any of the other standard fictionalized motives created by defense attorneys?

The judge, I hoped, had to see that too.

I was wrong. Defense counsel did not try to portray Shirley as a liar or a fool but as a crazy woman. She believed everything she said, he argued, but it was all fantasy from the imagination of a prudish, sexually repressed woman looking for sexual release. The seemingly bizarre elements were indeed bizarre. Then he asked a series of questions—over my strenuous objections of their irrelevance—that stunned me. In all my preparations, I had never anticipated that a rape victim's *lack* of sexual experience would be used against her, but that is precisely what happened:

Q: You claimed to have been raped, once before, didn't you, when you were 16?

A: I was raped before, and yes, I was 16.

Q: And wasn't that also at night, on the street, near the church?

A: I was coming home from choir practice, and . . .

Q: Just answer the question, please.

A: Why? I've tried to forget that. What does that have to do with this?

By Judge: Just answer the question.

A: Yes, it was near the church, at night.

Q: And you claimed he covered your mouth and dragged you into an alley?

A: Covered my mouth and dragged me into an abandoned building.

Q: And you claimed there as well that he ripped off your panties and raped you?

A: He did.

Q: He was never convicted of rape, was he?

A: No.

Q: It never happened, did it, Ms. Robinson?

By me: Objection, Your Honor. He's harassing the witness, it's irrelevant, as is this whole line of questioning.

By Judge: Overruled. Answer the question.

A: Yes, it happened.

Q: Ms. Robinson, you've never had voluntary, consensual sex with any man?

By me: Objection, Your Honor. The rape shield laws prohibit inquiry into a victim's prior sexual history, except for certain narrow exceptions not applicable here.

By defense counsel: (at side bar, out of Ms. Robinson's hearing): The rape shield laws prohibit inquiry into prior sex acts offered to show that a victim was, for example, promiscuous and that her present sex acts were therefore consensual. I am seeking to admit evidence of the *absence of sex acts*, the *absence of promiscuity* by a girl who very much wanted sex but was too shy, too plain to find it. So she fantasized it.

By Judge: Overruled. Answer the question, Ms. Robinson.[1]

The questioning deteriorated even further into a broad-ranging inquiry emphasizing Shirley's few boyfriends, her sexual inexperience, and her church's strong ban on premarital sex. When defense counsel was done, the judge called both lawyers into his chambers.

Judge K. spoke plainly. "Mr. Taslitz, I'm having some doubts about this woman," the judge declared. I replied,

> Your Honor, almost 40 percent of all rape victims, whether they were attacked by strangers or by acquaintances, have been raped more than once. These repetitive rapes may be similar merely because the victim may be more vulnerable to certain types of assaults than others. For example, the only similarities in this case involve the rapist's opportunity to commit the crime. Shirley had regularly participated in evening Bible study classes and choir practice at that same church, walking home alone by the same path, for more than twenty years. She was easy prey, her movements predictable, her isolation easy. And a rapist's ripping off his victim's panties is so common as to be irrelevant as a similarity. I remind Your Honor that there are key differences too: the first rape involved a sixteen-year-old girl dragged into an abandoned building, the second a forty-year-old woman in an alley.[2]

"I'm still not convinced," Judge K. responded.

Defense counsel immediately argued that Judge K. should then simply enter a not guilty verdict, there being no need to hear from further prosecution witnesses. The judge waved off my protests and instead offered me a Hobson's choice: Either he would take defense counsel's suggestions or I could agree to a court-ordered psychological examination of Shirley to determine whether she lived in a world of sexual fantasy. Judge K. would permit no independent examinations. "A partisan waste of time," he declared; it would be the court psychologist or no one.

I silently weighed the alternatives. No court psychologist could reliably offer such an opinion under these circumstances. Only a psychologist specially trained in forensics and character assessment is equipped to offer opinions as to a victim's character and ability to distinguish fantasy from reality. And before such a psychologist can make such a determination, he or she must evaluate written personality tests, patient observations, medical and other records, interviews with family, friends, teachers, coworkers, and neighbors. The psychologist must also review the empirical data on both the existence of the trait in question and on psychologists' ability in general accurately to identify that trait.[3] Furthermore, the opinion requested—whether Shirley lived in a world of sexual fantasy or reality—skated dangerously close to being an opinion on the ultimate issue: whether she was telling the truth. "Lie-detector" test results are commonly excluded from criminal trials precisely because technicians, like psychologists, are generally not very good at determining ultimate issues.[4] Moreover, the examination would humiliate Shirley. I would have to tell her that the judge thought that she was hallucinating, that being twice raped only served to convince Judge K. that she was crazy, and that her only chance for a conviction was to let a psychologist decide. Also, Judge K. had to have a motive for his suggestions. Perhaps he wanted to escape public censure for a not guilty verdict by pointing to the psychologist's report for "evidence" of Shirley's instability.

Logic told me to say no to the examination but that would certainly mean losing the case and would, in any event, take the choice from Shirley. Shirley's choosing, however, would add to her pain and her sense of responsibility if the case were lost, all at a time when she would likely not be thinking clearly. Yet if I denied her the choice, I would deny her autonomy, as had her rapist and defense counsel, further destroying her dignity.[5]

I chose to leave it up to Shirley, who chose to undergo the thirty-minute examination that day. We recessed for her to do so.

In the afternoon, the psychologist's report came back. As I feared, it said very tersely:

> Subject fantasizes about sexual events. She comes from a religious and family background that represses sexuality, yet she has a strong libido. Being

shy, she finds herself unable to satisfy that libido in even modest ways, so she obtains release in fantasy. The most salient example of her fantasizing was her unsubstantiated report of a rape 24 years ago, a rape suspiciously similar to that which she now alleges here.

The judge would not permit me to call the psychologist to the stand for cross-examination. Judge K. simply took the bench, told Tony that he was on "probation" for six months, and, if he stayed out of trouble, his case would be dismissed. Then the judge called the next case, leaving me to explain to Shirley.

But why did I find myself having to explain anything to Shirley? She was, in my mind, a highly credible victim of a heinous crime, with no motive to lie and no history of mental illness. What had gone wrong?

An easy explanation was that we had had the bad luck to appear before a nasty, irrational, and sexist judge. Indeed, Judge K. was all those things, and he was, moreover, the only judge I had appeared before who had ordered a mental health examination of a rape victim. Nevertheless, the judge's reasoning was fairly typical of decision makers in rape cases. Despite several decades of a renewed women's movement and increasing attention to the problem of rape, judges and juries continue to be skeptical of rape, demanding greater proof than for many other types of crimes and demonstrating deep suspicion of victims.

In the usual robbery case, for example, the victim's identification of the defendant alone results in conviction. This is so even if the lighting conditions were poor and the time for observation brief. The victim's testimony is rarely corroborated. There are usually neither fingerprints nor bruises nor eyewitnesses. Still, juries are convinced by the victim's word alone, despite empirical data showing high error rates in such identifications.[6] Rarely is the robbery victim portrayed as deranged or a liar.

But rape is different. With rape, the victim's truthfulness is almost always challenged: she is covering a pregnancy, hiding an affair, seeking revenge for advances spurned. Or the problem is her character: a slut, drug addict, "nut" case, or congenital liar. Consequently, we demand corroboration in the form of physical evidence of force, prompt report, eyewitnesses, and tributes to pure character. Yet, the majority of rape cases leave no wounds, not even bruises or scratches. Moreover, many women are so shocked, ashamed, and fearful that they long delay reporting the crime.[7] Furthermore, rape is most often a private act, taking place in parked cars, homes, and the dark places of public streets. As for purity of character, few possess it. How many of us, after all, have never lied, even about small things? Never engaged in a minor sexual transgression, perhaps as a teenager or in a vulnerable moment? In any event, even if character evidence is deemed relevant—and it is not—rape juries magnify it, giving it far more weight than it deserves.[8]

Feminists, of course, have made these arguments for years, scoring major victories in rape law reform.[9] Corroboration is no longer required by law, juries may not be instructed to view victims skeptically, and evidence of a victim's prior sexual acts is often excluded. The reforms had these goals: shifting the trial's emphasis from the victim's character to the defendant's conduct, and increasing rape report and conviction rates. In some jurisdictions, the reforms have indeed bred progress toward these goals, but the progress is modest, and in many more jurisdictions it is nil. This is so because police, prosecutors, judges, and defense counsel have used their discretion to circumvent these reforms. Prosecutors often require corroboration before even bringing a case, judges admit evidence of prior sexual conduct as relevant, and defense counsel either ignore rape shield laws (which limit inquiry into prior sexual conduct) or find legal ways—a focus on a victim's clothing, the crowd she hangs with, her body language—to disparage her character.

Why do they do this? Because they know that juries demand corroboration, speculate about a victim's character, and hypothesize about motives for her to lie. And they often do so with no conscious malice. Even liberals, feminists, the kind and the compassionate simply find that absent corroboration and given any hint of the "abnormal," they just do not believe the victim, for her story makes little sense, and his story seems sound.[10] And women jurors, although better on this point than men, generally feel the same way.[11] The behavior of police and prosecutors now becomes more understandable: they are reluctant to spend scarce resources on cases where juries will not convict.

Why do these attitudes persist, and is the law capable of changing or overcoming them? This book seeks to answer both these questions, answers that must begin by understanding the power of stories.

The human mind reasons not so much as a computer reasons but more as the Brothers Grimm reasoned. We think in terms of stories. Indeed, artificial intelligence researchers trying to duplicate human thought processes are programming computers to tell tales.[12] Jury research similarly reveals that jury reasoning is story-based. Juries convert evidence into familiar stories, filling in gaps in the evidence where needed to craft a coherent tale. Whom jurors believe turns on the consistency of each witness's testimony with the plausible stories that juries create based upon their preexisting stock. These stock stories come from experience and culture, tales learned from the Bible, children's tales, television, radio, books, magazines, and movies. Stories create our world of meaning; they are the lens through which we view all of life's events.[13] Many of these stories tend to channel the political and economic power that our society most values to men and to privilege male perceptions of reality. These are the "patriarchal stories" for which Part I is titled.

Two types of patriarchal stories are important to rape cases: first, stories about rape itself, about when and why it happens, and to and by whom; second, gender-role stories about the sexes' similarities and differences, motivations and needs, strengths and weaknesses. These tales, commonly patriarchal in nature, shape rape-jury deliberations.

Most obviously relevant are television and movie accounts about alluring young women just "asking for it" and ultimately, therefore, getting "raped." The dual message: only vixens get raped, and when it happens it really is not rape anyway because they really want and deserve it. But the media also feature tales about older, less "attractive" women, spurned or desperate for affection, lying to get what they need or to fulfill their fantasies.[14] Media images of rapists matter too, most depicted as crazed beasts, hyperviolent, hypersexual strangers leaping from the cover of night. Men not fitting this image are, in the public mind, not capable of rape.[15]

Perhaps even more important, however, are the stories that have nothing to do with rape but portray women as hypersexual, selfish liars. While the rape tales are often obvious in their message—for example, the Bible's portrayal of Potiphar's wife, spurned by Joseph and thus vengefully, falsely claiming rape[16]—the gender-role stories can be more subtle. In James Barrie's *Peter Pan,* for example, sexually jealous Tinkerbell, the fairy "slightly inclined to embonpoint" (plumpness), lies in an effort to kill or sicken Peter's "girlfriend," Wendy; better Wendy dead than in Peter's embraces.[17] In stories like these, which we will review, cultural images of the respective sexual characters and roles of men and women are carefully forged.

But gendered stories are not the only ones. Race and class matter, too. Notably, black women, for example, are often portrayed as oversexed, lazy welfare queens, whores with babies. Their stories of sexual violation are thus particularly unlikely to be believed, and empirical data bear this out.[18]

Shirley's reception by Judge K. now becomes clearer. An overweight, older woman, Shirley was not the kind our cultural stories portray as the object of rape. Yet she was black, so her outward appearance must have masked sexual need. Moreover, she claimed a brutal rape on a dark street, yet the police found no bruises, cuts, or eyewitnesses. Her story seemed odd, for reasons noted earlier, not at all like the media stories of rape. Furthermore, Tony's image was not a rapist's. He was young, bright, good-looking, "normal." Surely he could have had many prettier, younger women than she. So she must be lying or fantasizing, reasons the "rational" fact-finder—including both Judge K. and the court psychologist. That the psychologist, the supposed "expert," was drawn into an opinion far beyond his expertise, particularly demonstrates the power of cultural rape tales.

This does not necessarily mean, of course, that a different fact-finder would have reached Judge K.'s result nor have done so in the same fashion. But it does mean that the chances of a jury's acquitting or failing to reach a verdict in circumstances like Shirley's are high, even with a kindly, compassionate judge at the helm. Judge K. just made overt what is more often covert.

Patriarchal stories are not the whole problem, however. Another barrier stands in the way of a fair rape trial: the adversary system itself. That system is based on competition. It assumes that a battle between warring adversaries will yield truth.[19] It requires vicious verbal warfare.

Many men are taught to view language as a tool, indeed a weapon, to obtain desired goals; for many among them, this competitive, adversarial use of language is second nature. Not so for most women, who are taught to use language to build relationships, strengthen emotional bonds, and mediate disputes.[20] This language difference is not universal; individuals display much variation and women sometimes use words to wound, men to heal. Moreover, both sexes can learn to change.[21] But, on average, men are socialized to be both more practiced at and pleased with linguistic combat than women.

These differences are magnified in rape cases because of the emotional trauma that makes battle hard, the expectation that women in public settings will adopt "feminine" language styles, and the patriarchal quality of the stories women often bring with them to the trial.

Nor does the prosecutor's presence make it all "fair." Shirley was able to tell me a more complete, sincere, and plausible story in private preparation sessions than on the stand. This was so because in private she could speak in her own fashion. But at trial she had to recount a brutal experience following male linguistic combat practices and arcane rules that laypersons find difficult to fathom. Her answers, for example, naturally bred objections. Or her fear forced me to ask questions that helped to draw out her story but that were, again, objectionable. These objections threw off her pace, while the debate and hostility surrounding them frightened and confused her. Although broad, open-ended questions ("What happened?") that elicit long, narrative answers would have been most natural for her, the law frowns on such questions. This is so because a lengthy answer may reveal matters to the jury before the defense can object. But for Shirley this format was unnatural, strained, and confusing. Moreover, defense counsel on cross used leading questions, innuendo, body language, and tone of voice to cast doubt on Shirley's answers in ways that fed the stereotypes of patriarchal tales. A witness like Shirley, unaccustomed to verbal combat and courtroom language games, faces linguistic Armageddon, no matter how skilled the prosecutor.

What, then, can the law do? Rape law reform, despite some modest successes, has largely failed. But this has been so because the reformers did not appreciate the storied, linguistic nature of the problem. Cultural tales in particular tip the scales toward the defense in a rape case, muting the victim's story. But equalized storytelling resources can unmuzzle the victim. Possible changes include ethical rules prohibiting lawyerly appeals to race- and gender-based stereotypes; evidence rules permitting evidence of prior sexual aggression by a defendant; new jury selection procedures to screen for those with especially patriarchal views; stronger and less discretionary rape shield laws; and prosecutorial strategies revised to appeal to story-based reasoning. All this can be done subject to safeguards that respect both traditional fair trial protections for defendants *and* voices of victims.

But those voices can be heard only if both what and *how* women speak is changed. The rules that mark our adversary system are justified by a free-market metaphor: lawyers compete to offer a better (more persuasive) product (information), each hoping the jury will buy his or her side's arguments. Information is sold in exchange for a verdict. Like any market, the justification for this unbridled competition is that an "invisible hand" moves the self-serving parties toward socially beneficial results.

But where that justification is absent, where markets fail, state intervention is necessary. Adversarial language rules lead to market failure in rape cases. Women are disempowered, their voices silenced, patriarchal tales validated, rape legalized. Jurors' decisions end up based on distorted, incomplete information in a courtroom market that ignores externalities (costs not borne fully by the parties creating them)[22] such as heightened gender inequality, impaired dignity, and wounded trust and reciprocity between the state and those it is obligated to protect. The terms of the courtroom linguistic exchange must thus be altered, the market regulated to reflect more equally female, as well as male, speaking styles. Minimizing objections, permitting extended narratives, cabining the rat-a-tat of traditional cross-examination, and enabling women to speak after their own fashion are among the sensible changes this book advocates.

This book's critique, while drawn from rape cases, may, however, have broader implications. If adversarial market failure in the sense used here is more widespread than simply in rape trials, then a feminist evidence law may well teach broader lessons about the adversarial system. A system controlled by the parties can be feminist rather than adversarial, can respect dignity while taking account of storied reasoning and the roles of context and power.

Patriarchal Stories

Part I examines how cultural narratives about gender and sexual violence shape trial outcomes. Our everyday cultural preconceptions about sex are embodied in, and created by, stories. Chapter 1 summarizes the psychological research demonstrating how jurors go about constructing a story of a specific case from broader cultural tales. The chapter then reviews the principal themes from cultural stories that juries use in crafting a case-specific story of "rape" or its absence.

Chapter 2 illustrates jurors' use of these story themes in three rape trials, two of which were infamous—the Mike Tyson and Glen Ridge rape cases. These illustrations demonstrate how cultural narratives undermine justice for rape victims.

Chapter 3 closes by recommending changes in legal rules and strategy to cure the distorting effects of cultural rape narratives.

1

Cultural Rape Narratives

Storytelling Theory

God made man because he loves stories.[1]

Storytelling theory, which is supported by a significant body of empirical data, holds that juries deliberate by constructing stories based on the evidence presented to them at trial. This means that the story of a case must be told in such a way as to satisfy a jury's needs for narrative coherence and fidelity.[2]

Narrative coherence concerns whether the story "hangs together." That requires determining whether the story has structural coherence; material coherence, which involves comparing and contrasting with more familiar stories in a search for problems, counterarguments, and missed issues; and characterological coherence, which addresses the central feature of all stories, character.

Narrative fidelity is demonstrated through the logic of "good reasons." Good reasons are the means by which jurors decide if the story of a case is accurate, conforming to the jurors' sense of reality. Good reasons fuse logic and values. Thus, narrative fidelity may, for example, include whether relevant facts have been omitted or distorted, whether the connections of facts to conclusions are reasonable, and whether values implied by the facts of the case are confirmed by the jurors' own experience.

The example of Ms. B illustrates the application of these principles outside the context of rape.[3] Ms. B was charged with knowingly possessing nine stolen welfare checks. The prosecution's undisputed evidence showed that six checks, made out to different payees, were given to Ms. B by her boyfriend's good friend, Scott. Ms. B deposited the checks, which supposedly had been endorsed to Scott, into her account. One check was returned unpaid and her account charged accordingly, but Scott made good her loss. He subsequently deposited three more checks. The prosecution's theory is that Ms. B "must have known" that the checks were stolen, but Ms. B testified that she did not in fact believe that the checks were stolen; she believed Scott's story that the checks had been given to him in payment for a debt, and he needed her assistance because he had no bank account of his own.

Standing alone, this evidence would probably lead a jury to reject Ms. B's story and convict her as charged. Her story lacks narrative coherence because it is inconsistent with jurors' preexisting stories drawn from their own experiences. It seems implausible that Ms. B would believe Scott when one of his checks previously bounced, all the checks were made out to different payees, and he claimed that he lacked his own bank account. In the stories that jurors hear and experience, honest people do not behave like Scott.

Narrative fidelity is also weak because facts are clearly missing; surely Ms. B and her boyfriend must have talked about Scott's request. Moreover, most jurors would assume that Scott is dishonest, and that associating with dishonest people violates fundamental social values favoring honest behavior. That Ms. B is the kind of person who would associate with Scott suggests that Ms. B is also dishonest, a defect of character, thus reflecting back on narrative coherence. Ms. B is, therefore, not someone to be believed.

An expert character witness—a psychiatrist—could testify, however, that Ms. B's personality is characterized by an unusually high degree of passivity and dependency. These conclusions would be supported by the psychiatrist's recounting relevant portions of Ms. B's life history, interviews, tests, and other data collected during her evaluation. Because Ms. B is dependent on others to satisfy her emotional needs, the psychiatrist would opine, she is compliant and generally avoids conflicts that threaten the stability of her emotional attachments. Consequently, in situations like this one, her dependence on her boyfriend and desire to please him would likely lead her to want to please her boyfriend's good friend, Scott. Like others with her personality traits, Ms. B would rely on denial and repression to keep out of her consciousness any anxiety-provoking thoughts that might threaten her emotional connection to her boyfriend. Thus, doubts about Scott's honesty and, by implication, about her boyfriend's character, would be repressed. Her unusual gullibility in situations of this kind would therefore explain her behavior.

The psychiatrist's testimony seeks to improve the narrative coherence and narrative fidelity of the defendant's testimony. Narrative coherence is improved by suggesting an alternative story line that may make sense when placed in light of the defendant's life experiences: she did what she did because her life story molded her into someone especially eager to please and to believe in those she loved. Although her reaction may seem extreme, jurors' own stories likely include actions motivated by the desire to help those close to them and the refusal to believe bad things about such people. Moreover, Ms. B can then be seen not as dishonest but, rather, as a sad dupe of her loved one and his friend, who have taken advantage of her.

Narrative fidelity also improves by adding this type of information. The jury need not wonder about missing facts, such as conversations between Ms. B and her boyfriend, for the jury is presented with other facts to fill the gap: facts regarding the experiences, feelings, and motivations of Ms. B that help to explain her behavior in a way that does not require the jury to condone dishonesty. Although jurors may not especially admire someone who is gullible, they will not condemn her as harshly as someone who is dishonest. Without the psychiatrist's evaluation, however, it is unlikely that the jury would give Ms. B's full story even passing consideration.

Ms. B's tale teaches several lessons central to understanding the significance of storytelling for rape trials. First, jurors judge the credibility of courtroom stories by comparing how they square with standard cultural ones.[4] In Ms. B's case, those stories concerned how honest people behave. In a rape case, the stories will concern how "proper" men and women behave and to whom rape happens.

Second, cultural stories and storytelling rules are so powerful that we will listen to other stories, those contradicting the culturally pervasive ones, only if we are first convinced that the familiar tales are inadequate. Even then, however, new tales must create a common bond of understanding by appealing to old ones.[5] Narrative change is therefore both difficult and incremental. The psychiatrist sought to provide plausible alternative explanations for Ms. B's behavior other than her dishonesty. Offering jurors new psychological information made it more possible for them to be open to a new tale. Nevertheless, the new tale still relied on older stories of fools duped by love.

Similarly, with rape cases, we cannot simply bemoan cultural tales that oppress women and paint a rape victim as incredible. Instead, we must work toward incremental change in rape stories. We achieve such change by pointing out weaknesses in the application of some cultural narratives to a particular case and by giving jurors new information. But the new tales we craft must still be rooted in old ones. Careful study of existing cultural rape tales is therefore necessary.

Additionally, stories and scripts imply certain labels and vice versa. Once Ms. B is portrayed as behaving in some ways that are consistent with dishonesty, jurors may label her "dishonest." But if jurors accept that label as correct, they will attribute all that goes with that label to the labeled item, thus shutting their eyes to the unique aspects of Ms. B's case.[6] Only by using the psychiatrist to suggest a new label—"dupe"—could we move jurors toward a broader vision.

Thus, in a rape case, if jurors accept the label "slut," they will view the rape victim in all ways and circumstances as a "slut," therefore by definition consenting to sex. Alternatively, if jurors have already accepted a particular script, say the "wild teenage party," jurors may label a teenage girl attending such a party a "slut" because that label is associated with the party script. Again, jurors end up moved toward an overall story of consensual sex.

Finally, we must distinguish between the "incident narrative" (that of the "narrative experiencer") and the "courtroom narrative" (that of the in-court legal storyteller). These two levels of story are connected to each other and to broader cultural versions.[7] If Ms. B's incident narrative involves the Dishonest Woman, she will be seen on the stand as fitting the tale of a Crook-Seeking-to-Shift-the-Blame. Correspondingly, the cultural story of the "Lying Woman" in a rape case may help to craft a courtroom story of the vengeful, spurned woman, lying on the stand to reap her retribution. But, by definition, if the "victim" is lying when she says on the stand that she did not consent, then the "true" rape incident narrative is one of consensual, not forcible, sex. The tales jurors craft in rape cases thus flow from prevailing cultural rape stories. Like any good story, cultural rape narratives' power turns on their effective use of story themes.

Narrative Themes

A story theme is a recurrent pattern of human intention. It is the level of story concerned with what the characters in the narrative want and how they pursue their objectives over time. It is at the level of theme that elementary-school children most clearly apprehend the meaning of stories.[8]

"Cultural rape narratives" are the culturally pervasive tales of proper intergender sexual behavior that affect the crafting of courtroom and rape narratives at trials. Rape need not, therefore, necessarily be a part of these themes. Four themes, Silenced Voices, Bullying, Black Beasts, and A Little More Than Persuading, matter most at real-world trials.

Silenced Voices

Women, like children, should be seen and not heard. Like children, women who do speak up and make noise are "bad," annoying, unworthy, and, if they make excuses for their noise, lying. This overriding theme of female silence as the mark of a good woman expresses itself in numerous variations in our general sexual culture and our conceptions of rape. A woman need not literally be silent. She may speak if her voice soothes, entertains, informs, or otherwise serves male needs. What she may not do is express her own needs or views, whether for sex (even if far short of intercourse), power, political gain, or economic achievement.

So strong is this theme that women who do speak are themselves seen as violent, aggressing against men. Accordingly, a woman who expresses a need for sexual attention and physical freedom while refusing to "go all the way" with a man is a "tease." She is, on the one hand, consenting to intercourse because she surely knows that her behavior can lead only to that inevitable result, and we are all responsible for the foreseen consequences of our actions. On the other hand, she is heading toward that outcome by using her enormous sexual power to torture the male, whom she knows has an uncontrollable need to possess her once she expresses her sexuality. She is thus both consenting to intercourse and deserving of some punishment for her vicious behavior; therefore, she is not really raped. Alternatively, a woman who instead of first voicing sexual needs, responds to an expression of male need with a firm "no," or refuses to acknowledge or respond to the male's efforts—in short, a woman who clearly communicates her own desire not to have sex—is viewed as "aloof" and hence equally aggressive, assaulting male prerogatives and feelings. If she had demurely expressed virginal fear or reluctance and by indirection or flight sought to stave off male advances, then her action would be acceptable. But a clear expression of her own wishes is unacceptable, angry, and deserving of punishment.[9]

Even after the sexual act, a woman who cries rape, who speaks of her violation, her assailed dignity, and her physical and emotional pain, is to be distrusted, for she breaks the rule of silence. It is not that every sexual act is seen as consensual—"real rapes" occasionally happen—but that true speech by a woman is so unusual that it is to be greeted with suspicion and with presumptions of lies based on nefarious motives rather than acceptance.[10] Here too, both rape itself and the justice system's reaction to rape silence the victim, returning her to her appropriate, quiescent state.[11] Sociologists have long recognized that such silencing is the hallmark of an oppressed group; others have found an association between the degree to which a society silences its women and the prevalence of rape.[12]

The instructive fairy tale *The Little Mermaid*—its most recent incarnation is as a Disney movie—effectively illustrates the theme of female silence.[13] Ariel, a young mermaid, falls wildly in love with Prince Eric, a young land-dwelling male. Ariel believes she can have Eric's love only by becoming human. She approaches Ursula, the local Sea Witch, for help. But the Sea Witch, fat and ugly in her natural form next to Ariel's thin, classic beauty, sets a price. Ariel can have legs in place of her fishtail only by giving up her voice. To Ariel, this sacrifice is even greater than it would be for most because she has a beautiful singing voice. Indeed, she met Eric by saving him from drowning, and in the whirling wind and water what he remembers most about his savior is her tender song.

Ariel worries about how she will make Eric love her without a voice, but she expects to do so by dint of her great beauty. She agrees to pay the price; to give up all that she has known, her life in the sea and her voice, for his love.

The Sea Witch, of course, transforms herself into a beautiful, thin, young woman, hiding her true appearance, and takes control of Ariel's voice, which she keeps in a locket around her neck. Using these tools, she then systematically goes about seducing Eric, all for an evil purpose. Eric, believing the Sea Witch's voice to be that of his savior, agrees to marry her. The plot is ultimately foiled, with Eric falling in love with Ariel when she regains her ability to sing. The story ends happily, with Ariel forsaking the water to live on land with her new-found love.

The messages are striking. Ariel must silence herself to get her man. She is expected to win him by her beauty alone, not directly expressing her needs. We are led to believe that Ariel is almost able silently to get Eric's love, were it not for the nefarious deceptions of the Sea Witch. Ariel ultimately prevails when her voice returns, but it is the soothing power of her song, her voice as an aspect of physical beauty, not the content of her words or making her needs known, that enables her to get her man.

The Sea Witch, of course, is not silent. She is sexually aggressive, alluring (after a spell makes her so), direct, and goal-oriented. She uses both words and physical manifestations of her desires, in addition to Ariel's voice, to entice Eric. Her words are literally power, casting spells to help her achieve goals. But she is a liar. Her beauty is a mask and her song is stolen; they cover up her repellent appearance and evil heart. Ariel, the muted beauty, is thus the Good Woman. The Sea Witch, the woman with voice, is the Lying Woman, cold and deadly.

These images of appropriate sexual role-playing carry over into tales about rape. The woman who breaches silence is the woman who gets (and deserves to get) raped, or is lying about it. The woman who is silent is ultimately safe.

The 1960 movie *Where the Boys Are*, while offering some conflicting images and some women who play at sexual aggression, ultimately embodies precisely these themes.[14] Four college "girls" go to Florida for spring break clearly looking for guys. Their sexual aggression consists mostly of putting themselves in the right place at the right time to be approached by men. "[T]hree remain virgins and end up with steady boyfriends," but one, Yvette Mimieux, "goes all the way with the first guy she meets, then takes up with his best friend, whom she shamelessly chases."[15] By the end of the film, however, she is the in-shock victim of date rape, wandering through traffic aimlessly until hit by a car. The message: Mimieux brought this on herself by her overt expressions of real sexual desire.

Television programs as well have long played on this theme. Among the most infamous was *Police Woman*, in which rape victims were consistently young and "asking for it" by engaging in professions that required at least the semblance of an overt expression of sexual desire:

nude modeling, stripping, or pornographic acting.[16] An officer on the show commented that one victim was "not exactly the kind of chick who'd have to have her arm twisted."[17] The remark reflects an important message of this theme: women with voice suffer grave character flaws. Their voice is not the result of the situation—a need to work in an out-of-the-mainstream profession to survive, or a cry of rape because the rape is real—but, rather, of flawed character. Flawed character in turn is a superb predictor of their behavior. When a woman speaks of rape, therefore, her protest against the act is viewed as suggestive of a character flaw. Furthermore, if she has voiced nonpatriarchal needs, desires, and viewpoints in the past, then her character impairment is serious. She must be lying; she was not the kind, after all, "who'd have to have her arm twisted."

More recent media images continue these same themes. Even a movie like *Thelma and Louise*, touted as a feminist classic, reinforces messages of silence. The two women are in very bad, even abusive, relationships with men.[18] They decide to take a weekend trip on their own, without their men. Early on, the women stop at a bar. Thelma starts drinking and ultimately engages in some very close dancing with one of the barflies. The two stroll out to the parking lot, where the barfly begins kissing Thelma. He then presses for more and, when she resists, starts to or does (it is unclear whether penetration is achieved) rape her. Louise shows up, points a gun at the rapist, and orders him to stop. He complies but then makes a vicious comment about women and rape. Louise, who has herself been raped, shoots and kills him. The two women flee, fearing that the law will never believe their story or excuse their actions, and begin what others view as a crime spree. They both become freer, happier, and more open about their own thoughts, needs, and desires. Ultimately, however, the law catches up with them, and they see only one way out: driving their car into a canyon to their deaths.

The film was hailed as feminist because the women wreak revenge on their male oppressors and truly give voice to their desires.[19] But note two messages at work. First, Thelma was raped precisely because she drank, danced, touched, and otherwise gave voice to her sexual needs; the wiser Louise avoids this fate by her more circumspect behavior. Second, when the two women fight back and their voices grow louder, they face death.

Press coverage of sex crimes similarly contributes to linking the breach of female silence to rape. The press tends to report not representative but, rather, lurid rapes. Lurid rapes are (1) those that tend to outrage the public because of their extreme violence; (2) those that victimize the particularly vulnerable, such as very elderly women; and (3) those whose victims can be painted as "vamps," deserving of their fate.[20] Among the factors that lead the press to paint the victim as a vamp is whether "she in any way deviated from the traditional female sex role of being at home with family or children."[21] Reframed, a woman who voices career goals, independence from male expectations, or, worst of all, sexual interest may be depicted as a vamp. And the rapist may be painted as the boy-next-door who has been victimized by his loud neighbor.

An example is the *New York Times* reportage of the "whirlpool" assault of a fourteen-year-old girl. Fifty boys circled her in a municipal swimming pool, tore off her suit, and inserted fingers into her vagina. The accompanying photo was of the girl in a bikini, laughing and embracing her boyfriend. Similarly, in the "Big Dan gang rape case," in which six men assaulted a woman on a pool table while others cheered them on, newspapers reported charges that she was a prostitute. There was no evidence to support these charges other than rumormongering neighbors who resented her revealing the crime in their community. Early press coverage of William Kennedy Smith's case also portrayed the victim as wild: driving fast cars, going to parties, skipping classes, and having affairs. Her independence of mind was portrayed as sluttishness, while Smith's sex life was largely ignored. Later, when evidence of prior sexual assaults committed by him was offered (but not admitted) at trial, those allegations were indeed covered. Yet stories generally continued to show him happily playing with puppies and emphasized his fine medical skills and public service, and for the most part his own taste for partying and wild driving, as well as allegations that he impregnated a woman out of wedlock, were not written about. What mattered most was evidence that the victim had voiced a desire for more than marriage and motherhood.[22]

Lawyers recognize the significance of voice versus silence at trial. Among the most common defense strategies in rape cases in which consent is raised as a defense are these: (1) continual questioning about the details of a rape to locate inconsistencies or revisions; (2) stressing delay in reporting the crime; (3) revealing a preexisting sexual relationship; and (4) seeking to undermine the general character of the victim by, for example, emphasizing hitchhiking, excessive drinking or smoking, wearing seductive clothing, and bad language.[23] The last two strategies fit the expression of voice, an expression of sexual desire or of "unwifely" needs or interests.

The second defense strategy, the failure to report the crime promptly, is an interesting play on the silence theme. Our cultural narratives teach women that muting and silence are sex-appropriate behavior. Further, women are taught that rape is avoidable and so, when it happens, it is partly their fault. They also know (at least implicitly) of the suspicion with which female voice is treated and thus fear being both blamed and disbelieved. Their initial reaction to rape, then, is often fully consistent with cultural expectations: silence.

If the woman ultimately regains her voice and reports the rape, however, her initial silence is offered as evidence that she lies. She is ordinarily expected to be mute, yet she is expected to and must speak promptly and loudly, and in anguish, if there is a "real" rape. This is because of another theme we will soon meet: real rapes are committed by bullies, and it is all right to defend yourself against a bully. But the woman is now in a Catch-22: if she speaks, she will face skepticism and have the burden of proving that she found voice only because of the exceptional circumstance of bullying; if she is silent, the silence will be evidence that any later speech is not credible. She will be judged by the cultural themes of silence and voice, not by the natural psychological reactions to rape or an informed understanding of its causes and circumstances.[24]

The first of the defense techniques, emphasizing inconsistencies and revisions, is a variation of the second. A woman's first words about a rape may offer accounts that help to make things normal again. The words seek to smooth social relationships by minimizing the harm, and cultural expectations lead the victim to engage in self-blame. In short, the woman engages in denial and suppression of her experience, pain, and needs, muting her voice. As she heals, she may regain that voice, telling more coherent, detailed, and honest stories. Yet the result of early muting is inconsistencies, and the suspicion facing her voice in the first place leads jurors to a greater willingness to accept lying as an explanation. Jurors focus on inconsistencies rather than consistencies, on perceived inappropriate character rather than the psychological and political circumstances of her situation.[25]

This analysis reminds us of the significance of the relationship between the courtroom narrative (the legal storyteller's version of postincident events, including at the trial) and the rape narrative (the narrative experiencer's interpretation of the rape event itself). Defense counsel draws on themes of breached silence to craft a courtroom story of the lying woman, thus by definition revising the rape narrative to one of consensual sex. Silence versus voice are thereby manipulated by defense counsel to mold these narratives in ways that are consistent with these cultural narrative themes.

Bullies

We live in a "cult of masculinity,"[26] a cult of aggression. The term refers not so much to the quantity of aggression, although there is ample evidence that at least physical aggression (violence) is primarily a male domain,[27] as to the differing meanings men and women give to aggression.

For most men, aggression, whether physical or verbal, is instrumental, a way of controlling others, attaining social or material benefits, dominance, and self-esteem. For most women, aggression is expressive, a release of frustration or anger, viewed as a loss of self-control and a danger to relationships. So conceived, female aggression is more likely to be private, angry, and a source of guilt. Male aggression may be unconnected to anger and more often is public; it is a necessary prerequisite for attaining self-esteem, social dominance, and closer male bonding. This is not to say that there are no limits on acceptable male aggression. To the contrary, for public aggression to serve as an instrumental means of distributing social and economic resources rather than social chaos, it must be governed by rules. And one overriding rule is that excessive public aggression directed toward an opponent who has no real chance of winning is bullying and hence unacceptable.[28]

Several corollaries follow from this analysis. First, because aggression is by definition seen as a necessary, even desirable, aspect of male behavior, a great deal of aggression, including the physical version, will be tolerated before the aggressor is deemed a "bully."[29] Second, because aggression is about attainment, men tend to talk of aggression in terms of winning and losing, the language of games. The great male fear is of losing. Third, because much of life is seen as a game to be won or lost, men tend to look upon female behavior, even crying, as gambits in a greater contest rather than as sincere expressions of views or powerful emotions.[30] These notions carry over to sexual relationships, and there combine with notions of masculinity that involve explosive sexuality, sexual success, independence from relationships, physical toughness, and loss of empathy.[31] The result: many men deem aggression to be an essential ingredient in masculinity and consider many of their sexual contacts to be free of "force" because the aggression component is part of fair gamesmanship, not bullying. But many women's "take" on the same conduct is that it involves unwanted force.[32] Additionally, men assume that women with whom they interact understand both the game of sex and its rules. It follows that men often assume consent, a kind of assumption of the risk, from certain female behaviors, such as heavy drinking, attending fraternity parties, or willingly accompanying a dominant male (a "stud") to his quarters. These men do not, therefore, view the consequent intercourse brought about by their use of physical force as rape. Finally, men believe that the ultimate victory is one won by verbal aggression and fear of their prowess and skill, which make physical violence unnecessary.[33]

The notion that these male rules for aggression are partly learned through stories has been enormously well documented and is obvious in our everyday lives. Movies like *Rambo* and *The Terminator*, and their television equivalents, send clear messages of the instrumental value of male violence. My favorite movie that illustrates this point is *Back to the Future*.[34] In it, teenage Marty McFly, son of a wimpish loser forever bullied by the successful macho jock Biff, travels back in time to 1955. Marty meets his wimpy dad, then a youth, and tries to teach his dad to fight for his woman (Marty's future mom) in a contest with Biff. When Biff attacks Marty's mom in a parking lot, dad at last finds the strength to punch Biff senseless, forever changing history. When Marty returns to the present, he finds his dad is a sophisticated, confident, and successful businessman in a much-improved marriage, and Biff is a weak, toadying, sycophantic failure. A single punch changed an entire family's future, bringing good fortune to the victor and disaster to the loser.

Messages need not be carried solely by movies and television. The instrumental view of male aggression as part of male sexuality is widely acknowledged to be taught freely in books and by word-of-mouth.[35] The tales fathers tell sons, older brothers tell younger ones, and both boys and men tell one another instruct in the rules of the game. The fraternity is the clearest example of sex as a game. Fraternity brothers exchange stories about "riffing" and "beaching." "Riffing" is the skill of getting sex from a woman through talking, dancing, and drinking. Brothers frequently tell riffing stories with slapstick humor and sadism. "Beaching" is engaging in sex with a woman while knowing, indeed hoping, that one's fraternity brothers are watching through an opened window. "Pulling train," gang bangs with women rendered unconscious or unable to resist through alcohol, are also viewed as ways of scoring manliness points. All these activities are often recounted in fraternity house minutes. Moreover, fraternity brothers fill new recruits with these tales as part of the socialization process, teaching them that the women were at fault for drinking and that they knew what they were getting into, and hence were not raped. But the very public nature of it all, the exchange of tales true and false, and the close "scorekeeping" show that it is all a game played to aid male bonding ("teammates"), to compete for social dominance, and to practice the competitive use of aggression that will be key in the males' future wider world, a world in which women are just pawns.[36]

Although many adult males might publicly frown on such behavior, especially once they are past young adulthood, they might secretly be proud of their sons for "scoring" in this manner.[37] More important, even many women—who may be future jurors—accept the logic that instrumental aggression is part of male sexuality, that we all know the rules of the game, and that women who choose to play the game have not been raped, even where significant male aggression was necessary to overcome the woman's "reluctance."[38]

The second corollary of the theme of "bullying" requires us to remember the common assumption that there is a close connection between character and behavior. Accordingly, only bullies bully. Because bullying sex is the popular definition of rape, it follows that only bullies rape. Additionally, character traits are assumed to be "cross-situational"; if you are a bully, it permeates all situations, all spheres of life.[39] Males shown to be limited to acceptable levels of aggression in many life spheres are accordingly neither bullies nor rapists. But rapists are true and consistent bullies, "psychopaths lurking in dark alleys waiting to pounce on any likely victim and inflict their uncontrollable desires upon her."[40] Fictional movies and television programs contribute to this image, but many of the tales supporting this subtheme come from the news media. The news media tend to focus on stranger rapes, rather than acquaintance rapes, and often paint the stranger rapists as inhuman monsters.[41]

One of the most infamous stranger rape cases to receive this treatment was the Central Park jogger or "wilding" case, in which thirty-six youths raped a jogger.[42] A *New York Post* story was typical of the coverage:

> New Yorkers learned a new word for fear yesterday. It's called "wilding"—a street term even high-ranking police officers hadn't heard before. Like something out of *A Clockwork Orange*, packs of bloodthirsty teens from the tenements, bursting with boredom and rage, roam the streets getting kicks from an evening of ultra-violence. . . . . [L]ike an animal, which has caught the scent of blood, the mob—buoyed by the excitement of the chase—gets of out control.[43]

While there were racial themes promoting the story's emphasis (the victim was white, the suspects African American), the rape images were the common ones in the press: Jack-the-Ripper, snarling animals, hate-filled, lust-enslaved thugs, the insane, wolf packs. These are the rapists, not the boy next door, not the "good doctor"—the William Kennedy Smiths of the world—the neighbor, the boyfriend, parent, or teacher. To win an acquaintance rape case, the prosecutor's task becomes clear: paint the rapist as a monster, a beast, or, at the very least, a bully. However, this has two downsides as a strategy. First, most rapists are not beasts, with situations mattering far more than most people realize.[44] Second, in some cases there is another theme available, which, when used by prosecutors, is particularly evil—the bully as black: the Black Beast.

Black Beasts

WALKING PHALLIC SYMBOLS

But suddenly we struggled round a bend, there would be a glimpse of rush walls, of peaked grass roofs, a burst of yells, a whirl of black limbs, a mass of hands clapping, of feet stamping, of bodies swaying, of eyes rolling, under the droop of heavy and motionless foliage. . . . It was un-earthly, and the men were—No, they were not inhuman. Well, you know, that was the worst of it—this suspicion of their not being inhuman. It would come slowly to one. They howled and leaped, and spun, and made horrid faces; but, what thrilled you was just the thought of their humanity—like yours—the thought of your remote kinship with this wild and passionate uproar. Ugly.[45]

This description of blacks as animalistic, only remote kin of mankind, from Joseph Conrad's classic novel *Heart of Darkness*, embodies a white image of long standing, one particularly powerful in the case of black males. More precisely, an image of animals in heat, strong, violent, rutting, or, in James Baldwin's description, "a kind of walking phallic symbol."[46] Conrad captures this white fear and fascination that the wild thing that whites paint the black to be lurks in truth in the white heart. The image has deep roots in American culture and, while perhaps taking its most overt form in the Deep South, has had an equally powerful, if more subtle, grip on the northern imagination.[47] This image of blacks as in a "state of savage promiscuity" is learned "through jokes, anecdotes . . . mores and folklore."[48]

In the era of lynching, fear of black sexuality was often a primary motivation for brutalization of black males. Castration often accompanied lynchings, making the southern obsession overt. The courts abetted the lynching, often applying special rules to cases charging black-on-white rape, allowing juries to consider the respective races of defendant and victim. A black defendant/white victim combination alone entitled a jury in some courts to draw the inference beyond a reasonable doubt that the defendant intended rape. This instruction was based on the assumption that black males "always" want to rape "only" white women.[49]

The classic illustration of the grip of this image on the American mind is the Scottsboro case in the 1930s. In a fight between groups of black and white youths stealing a ride on a train, the blacks had "got the better of it." Shortly after, a posse stopped the train, rounded up nine black teenage males and two young white women. Then somebody said something about rape. The two young women, having been found alone on the train with the black teenagers, took up the story of rape. One later wrote to a friend that no rape had taken place, but twelve days after the accusations, the teens were convicted of rape and sentenced to death, even though they had had virtually no competent representation at trial. After numerous appeals and three major Supreme Court opinions, the Scottsboro defendants were released, none having spent fewer than six or more than nineteen years in jail. It was the viselike squeeze of the bestial image on black throats made manifest.[50]

Frantz Fanon, writing in the 1950s of the white preoccupation with the black male as "beast and penis," used a word-association test to measure the fears of his white psychiatric patients. In 60 percent of the replies, the patients associated the word *Negro* with "biology, penis, strong, athletic, potent . . . savage, animal, evil, sin." The sociological inquiries of Roger Bastide echoed these conclusions, and more recent studies have revealed continuing images of black males as lazy, violent, dangerous beasts.[51]

Great Western literature, from *Othello* on, has perpetuated this image. Among the most offensive of the modern works is William Styron's *The Confessions of Nat Turner*, in which he converts Turner from a religious zealot and antislavery rebel into a "sexual pervert," driven by his obsession with "beautiful white girls with golden curls."[52] Even white friends of black equality perpetuate the image, recasting it into a purportedly more positive light: the "good barbarian."[53] Jack Kerouac and Norman Mailer wrote wistfully and romantically of black sexuality. Mailer's black man "subsisted for the Saturday Night Kicks, relinquishing the pleasures of the mind for the more obligatory pleasures of the body, and in his music . . . [giving] voice to . . . the infinite varieties of joy, lust, languor, growl, cramp, pinch, scream and [the] despair of his orgasm."[54]

The news media contribute to the image. The Central Park jogger case, magnified by race the image of rapists as bullies and animals: the suspects were all black or Hispanic. Reporter Pete Hamill began by painting the suspects as typical African American kids, which, to him, meant coming from a world of crack, welfare, and knives "to smash, hurt, rob, stomp, rape" the white enemy.[55] More damning, however, was later press coverage that painted them as middle class, even privileged youths who attended parochial schools and lived in buildings with doormen. This fed the notion that class, age, and upbringing were irrelevant, because black lust would surface, even among the better off and accomplished. The alternative press ultimately debunked these images, with the fact that many of the suspects were among the most notorious of troublemakers. The mainstream press's willingness without even minimal reportorial investigation to "broadstroke all black men as a wolf pack and wilding animals" provoked justifiable anger in the black press.[56]

Rose Finkenstaedt has concisely summed up the theme revealed by the totality of these images:

> The stereotype of the black brute has engendered fantasies not only of the over-endowed properties of the Negro male and female but also of their gross performances. It was—and still is—commonly believed that the black had "larger . . . sexual organs," as a psychologist recorded; the black was looked on as "an inexhaustible sex-machine with oversized genitals and a vast store of experience." Their wild, unrestrained passion, their "always controlling force," was presumably for the white woman. As Ishmael Reed observes, "Everybody knew that all black men did was rape white women"; or, as Langston Hughes poeticized, ". . . a tall white woman / In an ermine cape / Looked at the black and / Thought of rape."[57]

One final point. The usual presumption is that a suspect is *not* a bully but, rather, a victim of the Lying Woman. But this presumption is turned on its head when there is a black defendant and a white victim. Reversing usually powerful patriarchal presumptions suggests a deep-seated white male fear of black male sexuality as a challenge to white male power, including white men's control over white women.[58] That fear evaporates, however, and the presumption of the Lying Woman returns with a vengeance, where the victim is a black woman.

NO SOUL TO BE OUTRAGED

Elizabeth Iglesias has articulated a trichotomy of American female imagery: "mother, virgin, whore."[59] It is a trichotomy that reflects American society's predominant image of white women. White America, however, views black women as constituting not a trichotomy but a unity: the whore.

The "Mammy" may also have been a central image of the black woman in the past, but that image has in many ways faded, giving way to the "welfare queen," the oversexed, greedy, animalistic, lazy black woman who breeds children for cash; spends endless free time in drunken sexual encounters; and is unworthy of her children, or even of feeding at the public trough. The image changes in film to the overt prostitute, streetwalker, or druggie selling her wares for a fix.[60]

"The image of the black mother and whore thus merge in the white mind into one. And the black virgin is nonexistent, an oxymoron, in white mythology."[61] The image, of course, draws on earlier historic images from the antebellum plantation of white boys using black women like blow-up dolls, to post-Reconstruction rape of every handy black female, a story of abuse justified in the white mind in part by the woman's perceived bestial needs. The unitary white image of black womanhood then grows from whites' general view of blacks as "animals, outside of the providence of God."[62] White men, believing in the prodigious sexuality of black women, often crave them wildly and view them as evil temptresses, the kind of desire to be expressed behind locked bathroom doors, like "a kid . . . look[ing] at dirty pictures."[63] The black woman may be viewed as the ultimate test of a white male's masculinity. For example, in the words of one white rapist, "[W]ell, I've made it with a black girl . . . I feel so good. I was so afraid that I wouldn't be able to satisfy a black woman. But now I know I can."[64] The result, of course, is to render black women virtually nonrapable by definition. This is precisely what the empirical data suggest.[65] The virtual nonrapability seems to manifest itself in media coverage as well in even the most extreme cases. For example, the press almost wholly ignored the story of a gang rape of a black woman who was thrown from a three-story New York building mere days after the Central Park jogger rape.[66]

Nell Irvin Painter has summarized this lengthy historical imagery powerfully and concisely:

> Overdetermined by class and race, the black-woman-as-whore appears nearly as often as black women are to be found in representations of American culture. Mary Chestnut, in her Civil War diary, pities the virtuous plantation mistress surrounded by black prostitutes anxious to seduce white men and boys. The stereotype that averred there were no virginal black women over the age of fourteen was prevalent enough in the 1890s to mobilize black club-women nationally against it. The figure of the oversexed-black-Jezebel has had amazing longevity. She is to be found in movies made in the 1980s and 1990s—*She's Gotta Have It*, *Jungle Fever*, *City of Hope*—in which black female characters are still likely to be shown unclothed, in bed, and in the midst of coitus.
>
> Mammy, welfare cheat, Jezebel, period.[67]

The logical conclusion of this unitary image in the white mind is "that no Negro women can be raped because they are always willing."[68] And the counterpart, noted Chester Himes, to the ever-sexually-ready black temptress was her unworthiness, for the white male "turn[ed] to Negro women because in them they saw only the black image of flesh, . . . possessing no mind to condemn, no soul to be outraged, . . . no power to judge or accuse."[69]

A Little More Than Persuading

The final theme to be examined here is "rape as seduction." This too is a variant on bullying. Rape as seduction assumes that violence can be and often is part of consensual sex. Further, "[w]omen are culturally conditioned to silence and chastity. The need for the heroine to function as the ideal woman—chaste, pure, and passive—prevents her from enunciating and acting on her desire; so she must be taken."[70] Violence toward women, accordingly, helps a woman to have what she really wants and is not rape at all. As romance novels consistently teach us, even a woman's fear has an "erotic edge," thus "merging fear and desire."[71] Even if "no" does not always mean "yes," "no" often means both "yes" and "no" at the same time. Such equivocation, then, entails not rape but seduction. Correspondingly, "[t]he absence of equivocation, unequivocal resistance, marks rape."[72] Bruises, blood, a valiant, brutal but losing battle—these help to mark rape, to mark the bully.

Sigmund Freud's brief discussion of rape in *The Psychopathology of Everyday Life* has, in the view of many, both reflected and contributed to these popular narratives. Freud compared the roles of the unconscious in suicide and in rape:

> The case is then identical with a sexual attack on a woman, in whom the attack of the man cannot be warded off through the full muscular strength of the woman because a portion of the unconscious feelings of the one attacked meets it with ready acceptance. To be sure, it is said that such a situation paralyzes the strength of a woman; we need only add the reasons for this paralysis. Insofar the clever sentence of Sancho Panza, which he pronounced as governor of his island, is psychologically unjust (*Don Quixote*, vol. ii, chap. xlv). A woman hauled before the judge a man who was supposed to have robbed her of her honour by force of violence. Sancho indemnified her with a full purse which he took from the accused, but after the departure of the woman he gave the accused permission to follow her and snatch the purse from her. Both returned wrestling, the woman priding herself that the villain was unable to pos-

sess himself of the purse. Thereupon Sancho spoke: "Had you shown yourself so stout and valiant to defend your body (nay, but half so much) as you have done to defend your purse, the strength of Hercules could not have forced you."[73]

Although it has been argued that this passage suggests that unconscious desires are irrelevant to the question of rape—it is conscious desires that matter—what is remembered in the popular mind is Freud's point that "a conscious desire to repel a man's assault is subverted by an unconscious impulse to meet it with encouragement."[74] And to the popular mind those "unconscious desires" can render violence to be seduction, not rape. Even well-known legal scholars have accepted this popular theme. For example, Glanville Williams generally rejected relying on subconscious desires to prove a criminal's mental state because such desires are difficult to prove, may not be deterred by the threat of criminal sanctions, and, given their concealment from awareness, are involuntary. Yet, in his *Textbook of Criminal Law*, he concluded:

> That some women enjoy fantasies of being raped is well-authenticated, and they may welcome a masterful advance while putting up a token resistance. . . . If . . . the woman failed to use all means open to repel the man, including shouting for help, the jury may well think it unsafe to convict him.[75]

One further aspect of this blurring of the rape/seduction distinction is the woman's violence. Specifically, a woman is often viewed as an "aggressor provocateur . . . an overpowering temptress/temptation, a species of rapist."[76] A woman may, by her own appearance, flesh, dress, and makeup, assault the man.[77] When the man responds with violence, he acts to defend himself by stopping the provocateur from torturing him when she knows no torture is necessary, for her body bespeaks her need; she wants it too. A man who acts in self-defense is no bully, no rapist.

These themes are well illustrated by the Victorian novel—later slavishly followed in a 1979 Roman Polanski movie of the same title—*Tess of the D'Urbervilles*.[78] Tess is the eldest child of a once-great family, the d'Urbervilles. Tess's immediate family, however, now lives in near-poverty, having lost its main source of income, a horse. When her father discovers that he is a descendant of "the ancient and Knightly family of the d'Urbervilles," he sends Tess to visit a wealthy local family of similar name to "claim kin," hoping that that family will help Tess's own. Tess does so, ultimately working at the wealthy purported relatives' farm. While there (and dependent on the d'Urbervilles), she is relentlessly pursued by Alec d'Urberville, and repeatedly rebuffs his physical and verbal overtures. One night, he lures her, when she is most exhausted, into a wood, despite her protests. When she collapses in sleep, he awakens her, "taking her" in a scene that is hinted at but not described. Although some have asserted that what happened was clearly a rape, which Thomas Hardy could not describe because it would offend Victorian sensibilities, many critics have recognized Hardy's elision of the scene as purposeful ambiguity, a blurring of the seduction/rape line. One critic put it this way:

> In Alec, [Tess] senses both her creator and her destroyer. It is the attempt to do justice to the extent and range of the feelings that makes Hardy so calculatedly ambiguous about the nature of their encounter in the Chase; it is both a seduction and a rape. If it were merely a rape, then there would be no sense in Tess's profound feeling throughout the novel that her whole being has been invaded by Alec, so that in one sense she belongs to him, belongs because he brought to consciousness her own sexuality. If it were simply a seduction, there would be no sense in Tess's equally profound feeling that her past with Alec is a nullity. We could say that as a woman, Tess feels it to be seduction in the way the strawberry scene hints at; as an individual person, she knows it was rape: "There were they that heard a sobbing one night last year in The Chase."[79]

Note this critic's distinction between persons and women (nonpersons). For the person in Tess, this was rape; for the woman, mere seduction, a distinction that itself plays into images of women as irrational, animalistic, and dangerous. Hardy adds to the ambiguity by having an "objective," third-person narrator describe Tess's own thoughts: "She had dreaded him, winced before him, succumbed to adroit advantages he took of her helplessness; then, temporarily blinded by his ardent manners, had been stirred to confused surrender awhile."[80] The picture drawn is of protest giving way to deeper desires, followed by regret, but it is not one of rape.

A later scene here is particularly helpful. Two field-women observe Tess playing with the soon-to-be-dead child of her "union" with Alec. One of the women says:

A little more than persuading had to do wi' the coming o't, I reckon.
There were they that heard a sobbing one night last year in The Chase.
. . . *Well, a little more or a little less,* 't was a thousand pities that it
should have happened to she, of all others. But 'tis always the comeliest!
The plain ones be safe as churches—hey, Jenny?"[81]

"A little more than persuading," but perhaps a little less than rape,
was involved. It is thus arguable that Hardy's view is of rape as "an extension of seduction." "A little more or a little less" complicates the
reading. Two possible interpretations are most supported by the text:
first, that the women are skeptical about the events, perhaps more than
persuading but perhaps not; second, that the difference between rape
and seduction is really no difference, either one being worthy of pity
and sorrow; "the little more that is added to seduction is too trivial to
bear mention; it is no longer a question of the violence within sexuality.
Rape and seduction collapse into each other—at best, the project of
separating them out . . . is a fruitless one."[82]

The continuing power of this theme of confusion between rape and
seduction is demonstrated by an experiment Robert Garcia conducted
with a law school class.[83] Two students, respectively playing the roles
of prosecutor and defense counsel, presented eyewitnesses (peeping
neighbors) to a sexual encounter between a man and a woman in an
apartment. The facts on which the presentations were made were based
on a scene from the movie *Last Tango in Paris*. The remaining students
served as the jury, and all concluded that despite the use of force and
violent language, there was no rape. This result particularly surprised
Garcia because the student jury consisted of female law students who
had studied rape, rape trauma syndrome, and rape myths, and who
were politically progressive. They came from varied backgrounds, a
profile that suggested to Garcia, as a former trial lawyer as well as a
professor familiar with the relevant empirical studies, an ideal prosecution jury. When the students watched the film of the scene itself, however, all agreed beyond a reasonable doubt that there was a rape. The
students, when confronted with a video of the events, were able to see
the violent acts as rape, but when facing the more realistic trial situation of testimony about those acts, they were led to acquit by narrative
themes that blurred rape and seduction. "A little more than persuading," perhaps a little less than rape.

Competing Narratives

Skeptics may argue that patriarchal themes are fading away, falling victim to the competing feminist narratives now permeating public consciousness. The narratives are presented in television talk and news shows, university rape awareness programs, college classrooms, congressional debates, textbooks, and novels. Moreover, growing female economic and political power give women a stronger voice and accompanying awareness of their own needs and power, with which to lend the lie to patriarchal themes. Women may be no more likely than men to accept the feminist political claim that rape is a prop of patriarchy, yet both sexes now widely recognize that women are neither at fault for their own abuse nor deserving of suspicion because they cry rape. The four themes undergirding patriarchal narratives may still grip some reactionary minds, but these themes are otherwise rapidly falling into the dustbin of history. The first part of this book might therefore have been more appropriately titled "Patriarchal Stories: A Historical Retrospective of Midtwentieth-Century Attitudes Toward Rape."

The skeptics are mistaken in thinking that patriarchal narratives are losing ground to feminist narratives in the American collective subconscious. They ignore the empirical data on jury attitudes and the politics of denial that show that patriarchal narratives have a continuing—and growing—credibility.

The Empirical Data

A comparison of American attitudes toward race and toward rape highlights the flaws in the skeptics' reasoning. Racism skeptics, making claims similar to those made by rape skeptics, have argued that individual racism is on the decline. What racism does persist is either so socially unacceptable as to manifest itself subtly and covertly or is institutional, the result of social processes that make it difficult to end racial disparities long after we have abandoned racial hatreds and stereotypes. One of the most recent and sophisticated studies of racial attitudes has exploded these assumptions.[84] Paul N. Sniderman and Thomas Piazza's study concluded that large percentages of whites are still perfectly willing to express negative stereotypes about blacks to strangers (that is, to the interviewers involved in the study). The study found that 61 percent of whites believe most blacks on welfare could get a job if they really tried; 43 percent believe blacks are worse off than whites primarily because blacks do not try hard enough to better themselves; 42 percent agree that blacks do not take care of their own property; 36 percent believe that blacks have a chip on their shoulder; and 22 percent believe that blacks are more violent than whites. This does not mean that attitudes have not changed at all. For example, only 6 percent agree that blacks are less intelligent than whites. Nevertheless, whites are widely willing to denigrate blacks as a group on some critically important assumed traits. Significantly, for those same traits, blacks are in every case at least as likely, sometimes more likely, than whites to accept negative stereotypes about blacks.

But, when whites are asked not to reveal their general attitudes toward blacks but, rather, how whites would treat individual blacks in particular situations, there is a curious shift in outcomes. In certain circumstances, whites choose to treat blacks the same as and, sometimes, even better than similarly situated whites, albeit often ironically reaching this stance precisely because of the negative white stereotypes about blacks. Thus, conservatives judge both black and white "not very dependable" laid-off workers in specific factual scenarios as equally undeserving of government assistance. Consistent with their ideology, conservatives viewed both undependable blacks and undependable whites as undeserving but, curiously, viewed dependable black workers as more deserving than dependable white workers. Apparently, whites were willing to treat the blacks better precisely because the whites viewed "dependable" blacks as so unusual as to be especially deserving of government help. Whites may therefore be willing to treat individual blacks as well as or, in some respects, better than similarly situated whites. But whites, on the other hand, are more willing to stereotype any individual black male, because of his race, as undependable, lazy, or violent, eventuating unequal treatment. Interestingly, these results are consistent across age and income. Only one factor, education, significantly reduces the likelihood of white stereotyping of blacks. Education has a modest effect on conservative white's attitudes and a dramatic effect on white liberals' attitudes, leading some theorists to conclude that an educated electorate is critical to battling modern racism.

Striking similarities and important differences are revealed in similar social psychological studies of attitudes toward rape.[85] On the one hand, a survey conducted of university students as recently as 1991 found that almost one-quarter agreed that women frequently cry rape falsely, that rape is often provoked by the victim, and that any woman can prevent rape if she really wants to do so. Further, almost one-third agreed that some women ask to be raped and enjoy it, and if a woman says "no" to sex, she really means "maybe" or even "yes." These numbers arguably underestimate how widespread these beliefs are because university students are more likely to hold progressive views about rape than are the less educated, suggesting that an even larger percentage of the populace than revealed by this study is likely to admit to patriarchal views. Moreover, the percentage holding but unwilling to admit to such views is likely to be larger still.

On the other hand, these numbers suggest a decline in student misinformation about rape from the late 1970s to the mid-to-late 1980s. Even more important, these numbers show significantly smaller percentages of reactionary views toward rape than Sniderman and Piazza found toward race. Both the declining trend and the smaller percentages of reactionary views on rape relative to race arguably suggest that feminist views about rape have indeed made significant inroads.

This superficially heartening conclusion fails when confronted with the very different results obtained when, rather than exploring general attitudes toward rape, researchers examine how people evaluate rape victims and suspects in particular fact situations. These studies reveal that greater evidence of the increased use of male force, of strong and early onset of female resistance, of sustained physical injury, and of an encounter between strangers increases the willingness to define conduct as rape. However, arguments that the woman provoked the rape, that her ambiguous behavior suggested her sexual desire, and that she, or she and he, consumed alcohol decrease the likelihood that people will find that there was a rape. Moreover, although many people see attractive victims as more seductive, they also see less attractive victims as more blameworthy, perhaps because of the perception that unattractive women must have "wanted it" because they "couldn't get it elsewhere." Even normal behaviors (e.g., visiting a bar) were often perceived as provocative, while merely careless behaviors, like hitchhiking and not locking one's car, also lead to greater attributions of victim responsibility. A rapist's attractiveness also diminished his likelihood of guilt, and a sexually active victim was assigned more responsibility. In striking contrast to race, therefore, moving from research on general attitudes to research on how people view individual rape victims in concrete situations adds more, not less, support to the notion that patriarchal thinking is still widespread and powerful, and therefore apt to lead to the continuing unequal and humiliating treatment of rape victims.

At trial, these results are likely to be far worse. First, men are much more likely than women to hold reactionary attitudes toward rape; to define an ambiguous sexual encounter in a scenario as not rape; to derogate rape victims; and to attribute blame, fault, and responsibility to those victims, especially on the basis of their character—that is, a woman's sexual history, appearance, and seductive behavior are more likely to be perceived by men as reflecting deep-seated character traits, and thus likely to be repeated in the situation in question. But women are more likely to perceive the very same factors as situational and therefore less likely to be repeated. Other recent research suggests that men often do not see their aggressive sexual behavior as force, and women think the use of force obvious.[86] Yet at least one-third to almost one-half of any jury is likely to be male.[87]

Second, as with the study of race, although reactionary attitudes toward rape diminish as education levels increase, jurors are often likely to have had only a limited education. An all-male jury whose members have at most a high school education is a rape prosecutor's nightmare.[88]

Third, juries in possession of uncertain and limited relevant information are more inclined to draw on stereotypes and cultural stories as aids to their decision. Moreover, subjects in rape-attitude studies have largely been educated students who may want to appear enlightened to researchers, factors that may result in seriously underestimating the hold of patriarchal tales. The few field studies that observe real-world trials, sometimes followed by participant interviews, reach conclusions strongly supporting the continuing power of traditional rape views in the more representative situation of an actual trial. However, some of these studies are older than many other surveys and experimental studies.[89]

Finally, even if "only" one-quarter of the population, as the 1991 survey suggested, believe that women frequently lie about rape, that is more than enough to hang a jury working under a unanimous-decision rule. To illustrate, three aggressive jurors (25 percent of the twelve) with strong personalities advocating a not guilty verdict may be able to turn the tide in a particular case. Yet, as we have seen, every trial dominated by such androcentric reasoning and discourse both reflects and re-creates patriarchal values. This, in turn, renders real change in social attitudes toward, and in the justice system's treatment of, rape victims an ever-more-distant dream.[90]

The Politics of Denial

Apart from the social science data, numerous reasons suggest that patriarchal tales continue to have a tenacious grip on our imagination. Notably, even if in 1991 only one-quarter to one-third of surveyed university students were willing to admit to reactionary attitudes toward rape, the number is probably significantly higher today, is certainly higher among the adult intelligentsia, and is likely higher still among the general populace for a simple reason: the Deniers' assault on feminism has made it increasingly socially acceptable to display such attitudes. The Deniers are those who deny the existence of patriarchy—and therefore deny that rape serves any social function—or admit the existence of patriarchy but deny that it is both avoidable (for it is part of our biological nature) and evil.[91] The Deniers' assault includes both high-brow (Camille Paglia) and low-brow (more popular) batterings of feminism. Television appearances, best-selling books, and the general attacks in the media and by the Republican Party on changing women's roles have made the dinosaurs walk again. Increased skepticism toward women who behave in nontraditional ways is in many quarters no longer neanderthal but backed by perceived solid intellectual arguments and a social and political commitment to "family values." The trend in rape attitudes is heading in the wrong direction.

This conclusion is not altered by recent amendments to the Federal Rules of Evidence that make it easier to admit evidence at rape trials of prior sexual misconduct by rape defendants. Some have argued that passage of the amendments shows the widespread adoption of feminist attitudes toward rape by members of Congress who would not move in that direction unless their constituencies held progressive views toward rape. The flaw in this argument requires understanding the distinction between what I will call "political feminism" and "cultural feminism" (the latter not to be confused with a school of feminist philosophical thought by the same name). "Political feminism" is the power of even a progressive (here, feminist) minority, if well organized, to effect some change on certain issues by deal making. Here the deal was "[Y]ou support letting in prior acts of sexual misconduct, Mr. President, or you won't get the swing votes for your crime bill." Certainly members believed that a vote on such a fairly narrow and technical issue would not harm them politically and could be presented to the public as consistent with commonsense justice: "When a man is proven to have raped in the past, a jury has a right to know that; no coddling for criminals, I say; that's what I promised you when I ran for Congress, and that's what I voted for!" But that does not mean that either the representatives or their constituents have seen the feminist light. By that reasoning, the widespread legislative adoption of rape law reform at both the state and federal level during the 1970s—the result of an organized, grassroots feminist movement—would have evidenced progressive nationwide change in popular attitudes toward sexual assault. Yet, as we have seen, that simply is not so. We (Americans) are not yet cultural feminists.[92]

These and other modest legislative reforms, and the previously documented judicial reluctance to move any reform too far, probably reflect instead what Richard Delgado has called the "homeostatic" function of law. Law is naturally conservative; it relies on precedent and background assumptions, and seeks interpretations consistent with those assumptions. Legal change is, accordingly, generally incremental. It is just enough reform to look good to large segments of the public, to preserve the system from collapse, and to make everyone feel proud, but not enough reform as to wreak radical change. Because of that, the nature of legal training is likely to perpetuate historically dominant cultural tales that have previously penetrated the law and are a brake on rapid change in the master narratives. Patriarchal rape tales will not give up the ghost easily.[93]

If patriarchal rape tales no longer hold sway, then what explains the failure of rape law reform? The only other reasons advanced are that judges, consciously or not, undermine the force of reform by restrictive interpretation; that defense attorneys ignore the reforms and are rarely disciplined for doing so; that social attitudes prevent juries from accepting the reforms; and that legislatures have made reforms too narrow.[94] But if judges, for example, continue to admit evidence of prior sexual misconduct of victims, they do so because they continue to see such evidence as relevant. If defense counsel continue to draw on narrative themes such as breached silence and rape as seduction, they do so because they expect these themes to work, and case outcomes suggest that they do. If jurors remain skeptical where there are no bruises or corroborating witnesses on a "date rape," they do so because these matters still resonate with them.

In short, all "alternative" explanations to cultural tales are not alternatives at all: it is precisely such tales that mold and are molded by the attitudes that underlie all other interpretations. A combination of patriarchal stories and law's homeostatic function offers the real explanation for the failure of rape law reform.

The power of this explanation holds true for many of the most enlightened of jurors. We can reason only by stories, and absent the most careful intervention to substitute other tales, we are bound by the dominant cultural narratives. Thus, an educated white male may know that a woman's being sexily dressed does not mean she deserves to be raped and that "no" means "no." Yet, in a real case involving a real defendant's freedom, where the woman wore a low-cut dress and drank, and the accused says that she did consent and offers some motive for her lying, the motive seems plausible, the dress and drinking seem relevant, and the chances for miscommunication seem clear. Suddenly, perhaps reluctantly, the well-educated, progressive white male juror has a reasonable doubt. And he has the doubt not because he rejects feminist insights—he may even endorse many of them—but because he must first judge credibility and determine the "facts." The defendant's tale simply seems more plausible than the woman's precisely because the former matches cultural rape stories. It was precisely this process of patriarchal-narrative interpretation that seemed to be at work in the three recent real-world rape trials of David Forshile, Mike Tyson, and the Glen Ridge jocks.

2

Cultural Rape Narratives in the Courtroom

This chapter brings the above cultural rape themes into the courtroom by briefly illustrating how they applied in three real-world trials. The easy, typical cases have not been selected, for the application of the themes to such cases should by now be self-evident. For example, an alleged "date" rape by a white premed student of a white coed, after the two had been dancing and drinking into the wee hours of the morning at a fraternity party, invokes obvious themes of breached silence, lack of bullying, and rape as seduction; these are themes that are likely to result in an acquittal. Change the white to a black coed and the chances of acquittal rise further.

This chapter focuses on three more-atypical cases that illustrate the power of these themes. One case is an acquittal under circumstances where it is probable that the jury believed at least part of the victim's story. The other two cases, both well known, are convictions: the Mike Tyson and Glen Ridge rape cases. Cases where the prosecution prevailed (in the latter case, we will see, "prevailed" is actually quite an exaggeration) are included to illustrate the very unusual circumstances often needed for these themes to work for the prosecution: a rape by a powerful, black male prizefighter literally trained to wound, certainly physically capable of killing with his bare hands even a strong opponent; and a gang rape of a mentally retarded young woman. Both cases illustrate the intense pain and humiliation these dynamics cause for victims, even in relatively successful prosecutions.

Raped Twice

A Frail Psycho

Audrey Savage was a fifty-four-year-old psychotherapist taking two years off from her practice to travel and write.[1] About 5'7" tall, 150 pounds, with short curly hair and blue eyes, she was told by many that she looked as if she were in her early forties. While visiting the British Isles, she "did things tourists did not normally do": talked to cockneys, listened to unknown musicians in out-of-the-way pubs, attended concerts with London's punks, and discussed politics with England's most active labor enthusiasts. She had been taught to be independent and to work hard. These traits showed in her willingness to travel alone, leaving her lover behind in the States.

Near the end of her stay, she took a bus to Llandudno, a town in Wales, armed with camping equipment. She pitched her tent on a peninsula called Ormes Head, a quiet, grassy area full of sheep and mountain goats that jutted into the Irish sea. On her last night camping there, a voice from the dark told her it was dangerous for her to be there because there were crazy Welshmen about. The voice belonged to a small, wiry, sandy-haired man with a stubbly beard, wearing a black sweater. She asked him to leave, but he refused, continued to warn her of danger, and asked her for water. She gave him water on the condition that he leave, which he did. She was frightened but thought it better to stay put rather than follow him in the direction he went, toward the clearest exit from the area.

The man later returned, while she was zippered in the tent, and started ripping at the zipper and demanding that she let him in. Rather than be trapped in her small tent with him, she exited the tent and tried to get him to leave. He responded with repeated slaps, jerking her head to the right, the left, then back again. Blood dripped from her swelling nose, and he lunged at her jeans. She knew, based on her psychotherapeutic training, that he was a "nutter" who would kill her if she did not cooperate.

"Are you going to rape me?" she asked. He did not answer, continuing to tear at her clothes, so she said, "Wait . . . I'll take them off," which she did. She grabbed her sleeping bag when he told her to get down, so at least she would be protected from the thistles on the ground. Even then, she thought to herself:

I know what they would say. They would say something like this: what woman who wasn't asking for exactly this would have been out there camping alone in the first place? Why wasn't I home, under the protective care of my husband? Why wasn't I in my woman's place, taking care of my house and children, or my garden and dog, if I had no house and children? What right had I to travel alone to another country to camp alone on the Welsh countryside, this Great Orme? Since I had refused to stay in my proper prison, I was only getting what I deserved.

He did his deed, and finished mercifully quickly. She put her jeans back on, but he soon ordered her into her tent. To avoid that, she asked to sit outside and talk, which they did for about an hour. Most of his conversation made little sense. Finally, he started talking about imminent broken arms and crushed feet and ordered her back in the tent, again grabbing at her clothes. She took them off once more, but this time he was flaccid and gave up. He fell asleep, holding her in a vise-like grip. She spent the night planning her escape.

In the morning, she said she had to catch a bus, and he insisted on walking her there. He said, "I'm glad you stopped fighting me last night. You saw how I was." They passed a public toilet, and she went in, leaving her things with him outside. As they resumed walking, they passed two bobbies on the street. She thought about screaming but, wanting nothing more than to get on her bus and get away, continued toward the bus station. When they arrived, he asked for something to write on and wrote his name for her, "David Forsythe." He said, "I'll be famous one day." He then demanded money, which she gave him. The bus arrived and she fled. Later, she notified the police.

The offender, whose real name was David Forshile, was eventually caught. At trial, his appearance was completely different. He was clean, his hair was neatly cut, and he wore a suit. When the police had questioned him, he had given a rambling, bizarre statement, denying a rape but admitting to intercourse. "Q. Did you force her to have sex? A. Not me. She wanted it. I could tell." He also admitted to using some force for reasons that were confusing. Savage's testimony and that of the detectives who took the defendant's statement made up the bulk of the prosecution's case. The defense cross-examination of Savage stressed her failure to leave when the defendant first left her alone, not calling out to the bobbies when she had a chance, chatting with him for over an hour, pulling out her sleeping bag for comfort, and taking off her own clothes.

The defense case consisted of the defendant, who was by now a good deal more coherent, a psychiatrist, and another detective who had interviewed the defendant. The focus of the defense was primarily consent. The defendant testified that he knew his "luck had gone up" when she invited him back to her tent. She was the aggressor, he said, stressing how frail he was at the time and how any woman could have resisted him. He admitted slapping her at one point, in what he made sound like a lover's quarrel, and pushing her, but, "I pushed her away, 'Oh? Come off it,' just joking-joviality." No insanity defense was raised, but a psychiatrist did testify that the defendant was a sometimes-delusional schizophrenic, suggesting that even if Savage had not consented, the defendant might have believed that she did.

Defense counsel's closing statement, however, mentioned the defendant's psychiatric problems in only a single sentence. Instead, the focus again was consent. "If she had been so frightened, why did she not pack up her things immediately and leave the area? Why did she stay, believing, as she says, that a man was near whom she was afraid might hurt her?" Moreover, later "she could easily have run to the road and gotten away" but did not because of worry about her equipment. "Doesn't it seem strange that a woman who believes her life to be in danger would worry so much about her equipment . . . ?" The defendant was not a rapist but a lover, defense counsel argued:

> [T]hey spend an hour outside the tent talking. She claims she has just been brutally raped, but she still spends an hour sitting on the hillside with him chatting about the this and that. And this is before she invites him inside the tent to sleep away the night. . . .
>
> And throughout the night, they sleep, wrapped together with their arms around each other.
>
> And even if she deluded herself into thinking it was rape, he certainly did not think so. She called him back. She came out of the tent with nothing on her but her shirt. She was pushing him. She willingly took off the rest of her clothes and lay down on the ground, asking for her pad to protect her, then invited him to sleep away the rest of the night. He certainly would have been rightfully confused about her intentions, especially given his mental health at the time of the alleged incident.

The verdict: Not guilty of rape; guilty of "indecent assault."

More My Enemy Than the Man Who Raped Me

What explains the jury's verdict? Several possibilities offer themselves: first, the jurors believed she did not consent but also believed any man would have the right to believe she did; second, she did not consent, and he knew it, but she deserved it, and a compromise verdict would send her that message; third, she did not consent, but he, because of his mental health problems, was unaware. Any of these explanations fits into, and shows the power of, cultural rape narratives.

At first blush, the case might look like a strong one for the prosecution. Savage was white, a respected professional woman, and, in the stereotypes of our culture, neither so attractive as to look like a "tramp" nor so unattractive as to breed whispers about how "she had to want it. She has to get it where she can." Moreover, she had been pushed and slapped, and the defendant admitted he did so, suggesting bullying. The classic image of the rape bully is the psycho, jumping from the bushes in the dark,[2] an image that fit Forshile precisely. Furthermore, it was hard to see what reason Savage would have to lie. She was beyond childbearing years and thus unlikely to have faced a pregnancy that she would have had to explain to her lover. There was no evidence that she had contracted a venereal disease nor any other reason to think she feared being caught in infidelity, and would need to explain it away. Even the assertion that the defendant was incapable of knowing of her nonconsent rang hollow if you believed her story (and there was no reason not to). He had repeatedly slapped her to the point that she gushed blood. He had intimated much worse harm to come, broken arms and crushed feet, and had lunged at her tent and clothes. Perhaps most important, the next day, he praised her for not resisting him because not cooperating might have been dangerous for her. Even if delusions altered his memories later, his actions and words at the time bespeak an awareness of her nonconsent.

Yet several themes worked strongly against Savage. She was an independent, professional woman, economically self-sufficient, and apparently so independent that she could go alone to a park in a strange country at night and camp. She was a woman willing to vacation apart from her lover, to leave for a place where she was free to do as she liked, to visit a world of punks, to sleep in the wild with no male protection. Such a woman violates all the rules on silence: economic, social, and sexual. She was a standing invitation to men, "open season." And she looked so young for her age, a woman with the vitality, vibrancy, and eroticism of youth. Yet she violated another rule of silence: if she was telling the truth, she was required to speak at her first opportunity—to the bobbies—yet she had not. She was, therefore, the Lying Woman. She either wanted it or deserved it, consenting in deed if not in soul.

The bully theme was problematic too. Forshile was a "psycho," but a frail one: thin, ill, and weighing less than one hundred pounds. Savage was observed with little in the way of injuries, at least no injuries inconsistent with the usual force to be expected in much consensual sex.[3] The bully corollary, the fine line between rape and seduction, thus came into play as well. She probably consented, perhaps later regretting it. Alternatively, her professional status may have hurt her. She cooperated, she said, because her professional training told her he would be dangerous if she did not. But any man would then be entitled to interpret her "cooperation"—her taking off her clothes, getting comfortable on a sleeping bag, not screaming and struggling against his nightlong embrace, and being willing to chat and listen—as consent. The defendant must have thought so, for otherwise why give her his name, or a name close enough to his real name so that she would have something real to remember him by?

The last possibility, that he was so delusional that he could not be aware of her nonconsent, is the classic Catch-22. If you are a seemingly "normal" white man, you are, in all likelihood, not a rapist. But if you are a "psycho," you cannot know of your victim's nonconsent and, once again, you are not a rapist. The bully theme works yet another time to narrow severely the social definition of rape and excuse a wide range of abusive conduct.

Savage indicated an awareness of the cultural themes that led to Forshile's acquittal: "Out of what culture does rape emerge?" she asked. She described defense counsel as "more my enemy than the man who raped me." Her verdict on the rape trial: "Twice Raped," once by Forshile, once by society.

Mike Tyson: Embracing the Beast

Desiree's Tale

Mike Tyson embraced the image of the beast. He played directly into white tales of dangerous carnal black desires. His defense: he was so famous and such an animal that any woman who came up to his room, including Desiree Washington, the woman he was charged with raping, had to know precisely why she was there.[4]

Desiree Washington's tale was of an innocent betrayed. She was a star high school student and stereotypically beautiful and was a participant in the Miss Black America contest. Her father had long been a huge Tyson fan. Consequently, when Tyson visited the contestants and asked Washington out, saying he liked her because she was a "nice, Christian girl," she jumped at it and said yes. When he neither called nor showed up, however, she got ready for bed. To her surprise, he called at about 1:30 A.M. She said it was too late, but he said that he would be gone in the morning, so she agreed to meet him at his limousine to go out.

When she got to the limo, he said he had to get something from his room, and encouraged her to accompany him for the brief stop. Once in the room, they chatted, and he was friendly. But he abruptly changed his tone, declaring, "Oh, you're turning me on." She responded that she did not do one-night stands, and he called her "just a baby." She was uncomfortable but did not sense danger.

She excused herself to use the bathroom. When she returned, he had stripped to his underpants. She went for her purse, saying it was time to go. But Tyson was much faster. He quickly stripped off her outer jacket, bustier, shorts, and underpants and told her not to fight. She told him to leave her alone, expressing fear she might get pregnant and repeated that she did not do one-night stands. She complained that he was not wearing a condom, but he answered that he did not need one; they would just make a baby.

He tried putting his penis in her vagina, but it hurt, and she started crying. He then twisted her like a pretzel and licked her vagina for lubrication. She hit him, saying that Tyson had said he respected her and thought she was a good, Christian girl. He ignored that, calling her "[O]h, Mommy," and continued hurting her further. He asked whether she wanted to get on top, but when he moved to let her do so, she tried to escape. He resumed his original efforts, pulled out, and ejaculated outside her.

When she got back to her room, she told her roommate that Tyson had "tried" to rape her, unable to admit to herself that she had been raped, and then cried. Within twenty-three hours, she had reported the rape to police and her parents. Shortly thereafter, she went to Methodist Hospital.

Tyson's Tart

There were several factors working in Tyson's favor. Most important, Washington was a black woman, invoking the theme of overpowering female lust. Although Tyson, as a black male, might be viewed as a beast, too, in the white stories such beasts attack only white women. What the beasts do to black women those women like anyway.

The theme of animal sexuality was reinforced by Washington's being young and attractive. Moreover, she went to a man's room at two o'clock in the morning, clearly invoking themes of breached silence. She had a motive to lie too: Tyson was wealthy, and crying rape might be a quick way to make some serious money. Moreover, Tyson had claimed Washington seemed fine until he brushed her off after the act. Angry at being treated like a one-night stand, she cried rape. Indeed, had she really been raped, would she have had the strength to complete the pageant? Yet that is what she did. Further, Tyson offered witnesses who testified that Washington had been friendly with Tyson before the rape. Moreover, Washington admitted she had taken the time to change her panty shield when she went to the bathroom in Tyson's hotel, hardly the behavior of a woman fearing rape. The picture seemed a clear one of the Lying Woman.

Two problems plagued Tyson: first, he warmly embraced, even magnified, his image as a lustful beast; and second, Washington's behavior, conduct, character, and background were radically disconnected from the image of a hypersexual whore.

The Beast Awakes

Even Tyson's defenders early on fed the media images of Tyson as a quintessential black stud. One of the officers in charge of investigating Washington's charges put it this way:

> I've got an eighteen-year-old black victim who leading black spokesmen are trashing. I saw some professor from some small southern school on television explaining that what Mike Tyson did to Desiree was part of some black dating ritual. It's normal, he said, for black men to treat black women this way.[5]

Tyson, rather than seek to overcome white cultural images of black men, sought, instead, to magnify them. His lawyer stressed repeatedly that Tyson was an octopus, publicly feeling female breasts and buttocks everywhere he went, including at the Miss Black America contest. Every woman knew what he was about, and Washington was no exception.

Tyson's behavior before and at the trial matched this image. At a press conference, Tyson was heard saying to a friend, "I should have killed the bitch." On the stand, his usual soft-spoken manner snapped at least once, revealing an angry face of a large, powerful man. He was, testified one witness, routinely disrespectful of black women and black leaders. His testimony at trial, moreover, seemed scripted for an actor playing a role. This impression was reinforced when he became obviously rattled and uncomfortable once the prosecutor departed from the expected routine. And, he admitted to the court that he had lied to the grand jury twice; at trial, he said he had flatly asked Washington, "Want to screw?" as his way of asking for a date, something he had denied to the grand jury. He also told the grand jury that his bodyguard, Dale Edwards, had been in an adjacent room in the suite at the time of the alleged rape and heard what really happened. At trial, however, he admitted this was not so; he had just "assumed" Edwards had been there.

The physical evidence seemed to confirm Tyson's bullying, something rare in a "date" rape. Washington had two small vaginal abrasions—one an eighth of an inch wide, the other three-eighths of an inch long, making her wince with pain when the doctor had inserted a speculum. Such injuries, testified a prosecution expert, are virtually unknown in consensual sex cases but occur in 10 to 20 percent of all rapes. Even the defense's own expert, called to say that such injuries can come from consensual sex, admitted he had seen such injuries only two to three times in twenty thousand examinations. Her panties were also torn at the waistband, consistent with her testimony that Tyson ripped her clothes off. Additionally, blood on the panties matched the site of the injuries she described.

Tyson was, therefore, an admitted liar and beast. He reinforced, rather than rethought, precisely those themes likely to lead to his conviction.

Captivated by Innocence

Much about Desiree Washington contradicted standard cultural tales. "[J]urors were captivated by her beauty, innocence and integrity." She was small and slight compared with the 260-pound Tyson. She bore the scars and blood of the bully. She was a good student and churchgoer, with a father who revered Mike Tyson. When she testified, she made clear that the thought of publicly attacking a black man in court troubled her deeply. Her image, then, was of a good, somewhat innocent kid who had been misled. Except for her arguable lapse of judgment that night, she presented little apparent threat to the patriarchal order.

Moreover, her demeanor and relatively prompt reporting of the incident matched what was expected of a victim. She returned from Tyson's room to his limo. The limo driver had done a practicum at a mental health counseling center, where she attended women who had been raped and beaten. She thought Washington fit the profile, her eyes "frantic, dazed, and disoriented," her clothes and hair mussed, looking scared. And she kept repeating: "I don't believe him. I don't believe him. Who does he think he is?" She reported the rape quickly to her roommate (saying that he tried to rape her), then called 911, the hospital, and her family. Her 911 call, which was played for the jury, was powerful and fully consistent with her tale in court. It included her fears that no one would believe her or that people would think that she was just after money. Consistency, as we have seen, is something jurors expect if they are to convict in a rape case. Movingly for the jury, she explained how, like a little girl, she had to sleep with her mother for many nights after the pageant to shield her from nightmares.

Greed rang hollow as a motivator as well. When Tyson had first called Washington, she had asked her roommate to come along, but the roommate had refused. It would be hard to set up a rape blackmail scheme if there had been an eyewitness. Moreover, Tyson had offered her a substantial sum of money to drop the charges, which she had refused. At trial, little more than speculation supported greed as a motivator, speculation that contradicted Washington's deeds and demeanor. However, some have argued that there were a host of procedural errors at trial that prevented Tyson from countering this image.[6]

Once Tyson made the decision to embrace the image of the black beast, to go beyond that image and admit, and even celebrate, abusive behavior toward black women, Washington's race began to matter less. At that point, her actions and injuries fit well the bullying theme to which Tyson was tethered, pushing the incident over the thin line from seduction to rape. Washington followed many, though not all, of the rules of silence too. By day's end, the jury had decided there was a beast who needed caging, a rare, very rare verdict, where a black woman has cried pain.

Lolita Returns

Easy Prey

Seventeen-year-old Betty Harris had a tested IQ that measured at only 64, putting her in the lowest 1 to 2 percent of the population.[7] At that level, she was considered "trainable mentally retarded" and to have the social judgment of an eight-year-old. Betty was naive and trusting; anyone who was nice to her became her best friend. She deeply wanted to be accepted as normal and would do much to achieve that acceptance. She also lacked the knowledge of how to say no to a request or demand for sex.

That ignorance cost Betty dearly on March 1, 1989. On that date, Christopher Archer asked her to come to the Scherzer family's basement. When Betty refused, Christopher offered her a prize if she complied: a date later that night with Christopher's brother, Paul. He then put his arm around Betty, a gesture she perceived as "romantic," and walked her to the Scherzers' basement.

"It was set up like a movie," Betty later told the jury as she described the arrangement of the chairs there. Christopher, Paul Archer, Kyle and Kevin Scherzer, Richard Corcoran, Peter Quigley, Bryant Grober, and a half dozen of their football teammates were among the "audience." All the youths had known Betty since childhood and knew that she was mentally slow, a matter of lore in that part of the Glen Ridge, New Jersey, community; she was the one "everybody teased."

First, Grober removed his jeans and underwear, while Christopher, Kevin, and Peter told Betty to remove her clothes; either Christopher and Grober undressed her, or she was induced to do so. Grober then pushed her head down to his penis and "received fellatio." The audience cheered, "Go further, go further!" Grober slunk away but managed the energy to call out, "finger yourself." Christopher then inserted his fingers into her vagina.

Then Kyle Scherzer put plastic bags and Vaseline on a broomstick and forced it into Betty's vagina. Other implements followed, most importantly a thirty-three–inch-long bat with a two-inch-diameter. A tormentor screamed, "Whore!" while the cheering continued. A dirty dowel followed.

Next, Christopher Archer and Kevin Scherzer both sucked Betty's breasts. Betty then masturbated Richard Corcoran, Christopher and Paul Archer, Quigley, Grober, and Scherzer.

Betty was then told to keep the matter secret or her mother would be told and she would be expelled from school. She was frightened, but ultimately she did tell a counselor, asking, "How do I say no if this happens again?" That report ultimately led to criminal charges, primarily against four of the participants.

Not one of the defendants denied the basic details of their "predatory perversion." The act was vile, reprehensible, disgusting, and the essential facts were uncontested, so convictions should have been certain. But although the events were unchallenged, the interpretation of those events was contested. Startlingly, the youths' main defense was that this functional eight-year-old had consented. One of the gang said simply, as is done concerning so many "normal" girls, "She wanted it."

Nabokov's Nymphette in New Jersey

The defense argued that Betty was a "Lolita," the teenage seductress of the much older, more sophisticated Humbert Humbert in Vladimir Nabokov's novel of the same name.[8] The argument was not only that Betty enjoyed "it," and therefore consented, but that she instigated and controlled it. When defendant Paul Archer took the stand, he described Betty as "totally in control . . . she made all the advances. She was the one doing everything. It was all her idea." The defense went so far as to argue that Betty voluntarily inserted the broom into herself, in addition to asking for help from the defendants because she could not masturbate with the bat unassisted.

Her mental impairment, the defense argued, made her all the more a Lolita. "Let me tell you," argued one defense attorney, "in that condition she had feelings for sex, her drive, if you like, for sex. Her brain and her stomach and her genital signals are greater than normal. Obsession. One word. Obsession." This same defense attorney sought to rely on alleged seductive demeanor and dress to prove his point: "There are some girls who are Lolitas," he said. "Do you know Lolitas, fourteen, fifteen, and dress-up like they are eighteen and nineteen, to entice and attract?"

To prove their case, the defense drove trucks through the holes in New Jersey's rape shield statute, which then read in relevant part: "Evidence of previous sexual conduct shall not be considered relevant unless it is material to negating the element of force or coercion." The trial court apparently considered much evidence of prior sexual conduct "material to negating . . . force or coercion." Thus evidence was admitted that Betty took birth control pills before the incident; that she used the words "penis," "dick," and "blow job"; that on the day of the assault she put her hands between Grober's legs; and that she once exposed her breasts in a high school music class. The defense insinuated that she was a flirtatious female, who propositioned classmates for sex, repeatedly engaged in conversations with sexual themes, and was touched on her breasts in a classroom at least once.

Betty's testimony, read in its entirety, painted a picture of a confused, frightened child who wanted acceptance but also wanted to say no, a picture supported by expert testimony. But her testimony also contained some significant inconsistencies and changes; she hesitated, displayed a confused understanding of what the trial was all about, and seemed to agree easily to whatever she was led to say on cross-examination.

All four defendants were convicted of conspiracy to commit aggravated sexual assault and aggravated sexual conduct. Christopher Archer and Kevin Scherzer were each found guilty of first-degree aggravated sexual assault, meaning penetration of a mentally defective person with a bat, broom, and dowel. Archer and Scherzer were also convicted of assault, using force and coercion.

But the defense arguments largely hit home. All four defendants were acquitted of forced fellatio, fellatio by a mentally defective person, improper touching of Betty's breasts, and forced masturbation. It can be inferred from interviews with the jurors that they believed she had consented (or at least had a reasonable doubt about whether she consented) to all but the insertion of the objects; concluding, as to the latter, that "[n]o human being would submit to that, period."

The Power of Cultural Narratives

The verdicts in the Glen Ridge rape case demonstrate the extraordinary power of cultural rape narratives. Aspects of the verdicts made little sense. For example, the jurors clearly believed that Betty did not consent to the insertion of objects like the bat and broomstick. Yet some of the events that the jurors believed were consensual, the sucking of Betty's breasts and forced masturbation, took place after the insertion of the objects. Does it really make sense to believe that Betty would engage in acts to which "no human being would submit" and then happily engage in fondling and masturbation? Moreover, the jurors readily agreed that

Betty was mentally defective and that the defendants knew, or at least should have known, this fact. That was in part why they convicted the defendants on charges involving inserting the objects. Nonetheless, the jurors acquitted the defendants of engaging in fellatio performed by a mentally defective person. More important, they apparently believed that she was mentally impaired but not so impaired that she could not consent to a wide variety of group sex acts while a "movie" audience watched. Only inserting the objects went "too" far.

Luring a far weaker victim, a mentally impaired child, into a public gang bang; taking advantage of her known need for acceptance and willingness to submit to extreme demands; laughing at her, taunting her, ordering her to finger herself; loudly chanting, "Go further, go further"; and pushing her down to fellate a participant were all acceptable violence, well within the bounds of "consensual" sex. Her obvious breach of the silence codes—birth control pills, publicly exposed breasts, alleged prior sex acts, and lewd behavior—combined with her infirmity and her "animal-like" need confirmed these impressions. The jury may have even believed the defense's line that Betty was a seductress, thrilled to be invited there and then leading the boys along. Only when the boys got too caught up in the excitement of the moment, starting to use large and painful implements, did the incident cross the line from consent to bullying, from seduction to rape. Yet, so strong were Betty's needs, and so inconsistent her denials (another silence theme), that she quickly rebounded, willingly masturbating her tormentors. From seduction to rape, from rape to seduction, an easy and endless patriarchal loop.

3

A Fair Fight

Some feminists have instinctively recognized the importance of cultural stories in rape trials. They have also recognized that trial experiences and results can reinforce cultural tales. One suggested solution, consequently, has been to reject patriarchal themes in court and craft entirely new feminist themes that thereby contribute to the formation of more liberatory tales as part of the path to a more egalitarian society.[1]

But this solution underestimates the power of cultural tales in the courtroom and the importance of catharsis and retribution. The empirical data reviewed here strongly suggest that jurors rarely deviate from cultural themes. Although weaknesses in those themes can be identified partly by exposure to new ones, modifications to cultural tales are likely to be gradual—employed to fill gaps and correct incoherence rather than to replace old stories with radically new ones. Success in a rape trial therefore requires fitting into, or at least analogizing to, general cultural themes. Indeed, it is for that reason that such themes have been developed here with some care.

But fitting into stereotyped themes creates a tension with individualized justice—the victim's need, and the law's demand, that the individual situation, thoughts, and feelings of these participants, not the normal or reasonable participant, be considered. This tension can partly be resolved by seeking subtle modifications to cultural tales that do not sharply deviate from accepted themes. For example, rape trauma syndrome testimony (the idea that many rape victims subsequently behave in an identifiable manner different from that of a woman who was not raped) seeks, in a storytelling framework, to convince jurors that there are psychic and behavioral bruises that are as real and objective as physical ones. Bruises are expected if there was true bullying (a common cultural rape theme), a necessary prerequisite for a cultural finding of rape. Rape trauma syndrome testimony thus raises the chances that the victim's unique story will be heard, but does so by fitting the victim into the recognized, stereotypical theme of bullying.[2]

I am not suggesting that prosecutors can or should accept existing themes wholesale. To do so usually works against the prosecution, and sometimes, as in appealing to images of black males as beasts, is so extraordinarily reprehensible as to unquestionably breach the prosecutor's duty to "do justice." [3]

On the other hand, ignoring cultural themes will not work either. For example, in Desiree Washington's situation, she had breached some rules on silence (going to a man's room at two o'clock in the morning, for example) and, because of her skin color, faced the theme of the black seductress. The prosecutor went to great pains to paint Washington as no threat to the patriarchal order, and as obeying most rules of silence, such as modesty, gentle femininity, and sensitivity to the role of woman as quiet nurturer. This was done with dignity, without demeaning Washington or distorting the evidence. Similarly, evidence of following other silence rules, such as prompt reporting, and of physical and psychological marks of bullying, were stressed.

I admit that this tactic offends me. It tells the jury that following the silence rules is indeed necessary for a finding of rape. In Tyson's case, I was equally offended by the images of the black male as rapist. But those images were invoked by the defense, not the prosecution. Indeed, as I have argued above, it would be flatly wrong for the prosecutor to appeal to the black rapist theme at trial. Yet the prosecutor had no choice, if he were to win the Tyson case, but to treat Tyson—as an individual—as a bully. Because race speaks volumes on its own, this line is a difficult one to draw: How do you prove that Tyson was a bully because he was Mike Tyson, not because he was a black male, while many white jurors will at least subconsciously already have invoked the black male rapist theme upon seeing Tyson's skin? Yet if this line is not drawn, especially in the more common situation of intraracial rape, rapes of black women will go unavenged.[4]

Unavenged is, perhaps, a bit imprecise, but I use it here as a shorthand for lack of retribution. The need for societal and individual retribution is great when society's deepest moral codes—largely embodied in its criminal law—are violated. When the justice system fails to achieve adequate retribution, respect for that system and for the rule of law breaks down, and social conflict and tension escalate. In the case of rape, the victim feels abused, disregarded, raped again. Reported rapes decline. However, rapes (because of the uncertainty of conviction, even if the rapist is caught) may rise and female fear will rise, thus reinforcing patriarchal values. The feminist solution of simply rejecting or ignoring patriarchal tales, thereby raising the rate of acquittal, thus plays into the hands of the patriarchy.[5]

This solution is the lesser of evils—using patriarchal themes rather than having them used against you—it relies on a difficult ethical balance. I strike the balance as I do because the prosecutor must still stick to the credible evidence. In Desiree Washington's case, portraying her as no threat to patriarchal values was done by simply emphasizing some true aspects of her experience and not others, and crafting those aspects into a coherent story. That is an unavoidable task in any trial, rape or otherwise, and does not stretch the bounds of the prosecutor's personal or professional ethical codes too tightly.

Caution is necessary in stressing the need for prosecutors to use patriarchal themes. Prosecutors must not too easily dismiss rape cases because they do not fit the ideal patriarchal tale. That is precisely what is happening now, and because so many tales stray from the ideal, many cases simply die at early stages of the pretrial process. Rather, the challenge for prosecutors is, with the evidence they have, to fit even weaker cases as much as possible into existing cultural themes; to persuade jurors to modify those themes slightly while rebutting defense efforts at crafting patriarchal tales; and, only to the extent necessary, to risk crafting relatively new themes. A brief illustration: one approach is to view as a myth the belief that a true rape victim promptly reports the crime. A more effective strategy is likely to be to convince the jury that delayed reporting is a symptom of psychological pain, of a bruise inflicted by a bully.[6]

Storytelling theory also suggests, however, that legal change accompany strategic change. Once again, I find my civil libertarian instincts troubled by what I see as necessary but difficult solutions. Most significant, Congress recently passed a statute creating new rules 413-415 of the Federal Rules of Evidence. These hastily adopted rules permit, in a criminal case in which a defendant is accused of sexual assault, the admission of evidence of another offense—or offenses—of sexual assault, which "may be considered for its bearing on any matter to which it is relevant." These rules are extraordinary. They radically change the historic bar on character evidence being offered to prove present conduct. Even worse, perhaps, they ignore the empirical data. These data require us to know more than that a defendant committed one prior sexual assault before we can say that the earlier assault made it more likely that he committed the later one. We need, at a minimum, to know about any similarities and differences between the two assaults or circumstances. Moreover, one prior sexual assault is simply too small a sample from which to make reliable character judgments. We need to know far more about a defendant's history of sexual violence to judge him a predator likely to harm again.[7]

Nevertheless, a core of truth is behind the new rules. What storytelling theory teaches us is that patriarchal tales are of enormous power, weighing heavily in favor of the defense. This power disparity is so great that it is very difficult for the victim's story even to be heard. Unequal power needs to be redressed so that both sides have a fair opportunity for their competing tales to be heard by the jury. It may, therefore, be necessary to level the playing field by imposing different evidentiary rules on the prosecution and the defense in rape cases. The federal rape shield statute keeps out most, but not all, evidence of prior sexual conduct by the victim precisely because such evidence is given undue weight by the jury. A woman's prior sexual conduct may have little to do with whether she consented in this case, yet jurors will often find such conduct determinative, precisely because the conduct breaches codes of silence. Despite rape shield statutes, we have seen that victims' stories rarely get adequate consideration. Admitting evidence of a defendant's prior sexual conduct, evidence of his bullying, may thus help jurors to listen to the victim's tale.[8]

The adopted rules go too far because they are unsupported by the empirical evidence. But the United States Judicial Conference, while opposed to changing the existing rules, had suggested an alternative to Rule 413 if Congress insisted on change. The Judicial Conference's proposal would permit exclusion under other rules of evidence (for example, hearsay or undue prejudice under Rule 403) and would require the court to consider those factors that the empirical data show to be key: temporal proximity, frequency, and similarity of the prior acts to the present ones, relevant intervening events, and surrounding circumstances. This proposal properly balances competing interests. Some asymmetry is retained—exclusion of the victim's prior sex acts but admission of the defendant's but only where social science suggests the defendant's earlier behavior has significant probative value. Moreover, unfair jury prejudice against the defendant is far less likely than would be true for nonsexual crimes precisely because it is so difficult, given existing patriarchal themes, to convince jurors of defendant bullying, yet so easy to convince them of victim seduction. Although I, like most lawyers and law professors, originally viewed with fright the proposals for change of this nature in the character evidence rules, storytelling theory has convinced me of the need for limited change, and no more, like that in the Judicial Conference's proposal.[9]

Additionally, changes may be needed in the rules of professional responsibility. Some states have adopted, and the American Bar Association is considering, proposals to modify the rules of professional conduct to bar discriminatory behavior or the manifestation of bias or prejudice by lawyers in the course of certain activities (limited in some states to activities connected with representing clients, if the discrimination is based on race, gender, ethnicity, or other specified categories). I have proposed elsewhere that a similar rule—if limited to intentional conduct designed to intimidate or to gain a tactical advantage, or to a course of conduct that harasses a litigant, witness, juror, court officer, or other opposing attorneys (even if unintentional)—will survive First Amendment scrutiny. Such a limited rule might discourage at least the most rude and abusive uses of patriarchal themes by either side (for example, a prosecutor's argument that no white woman would ever consent to sex with a black man) at trial.[10]

Changes in jury selection procedures in rape cases are needed as well. Some changes suggested by the empirical data—for example, excluding men and certain members of minority groups from juries because they are more likely to accept patriarchal tales—are both unconstitutional and morally offensive because they rely on invidious group stereotyping.[11] However, there is empirical data suggesting that more individualized inquiries, which do not rely on invidious group comparisons, can be helpful. These inquiries rely instead on the study of individual personality traits.

For example, there is some evidence that men with macho personalities and persons of either sex with rigid or dogmatic traits assign more responsibility to rape victims. Other research focuses on "internals" versus "externals." Persons with an "internal" orientation believe that individuals can and do exert control over life events, while externals believe that fate or chance controls. Those scoring higher on personality tests as internals assign more blame to rape victims. Additionally, those who readily endorse rape myths are more likely to define forced sex on a date as rape. On the other hand, those who reveal greater empathy toward rape victims, as measured by the Rape Empathy Scale, are more willing to attribute responsibility for a rape to the assailant. By contrast, individuals who accept more traditional stereotypes and attitudes toward women set up very stringent criteria for defining rape and are less likely to see rape victims as traumatized by the experience.[12]

What these data suggest is that prospective jurors in rape cases could be required to participate in pen-and-pencil and perhaps other tests for personality traits and attitudes that make them likely to be more accepting of cultural rape tales. Privacy protections, requiring that this information not leave the courtroom, could be built into the relevant authorizing rules or legislation. Perhaps persons refusing such testing should be dismissed as potential jurors. The names and purposes of the tests, for example, Rape Empathy Scale, should, as far as possible, be kept from the potential jurors to minimize the effect of such factors on test results.[13]

At the very least, this procedure will enable counsel to make more intelligent use of peremptory strikes (the right to strike a specified number of potential jurors without giving a reason). Of course, the advantage accruing from the new information provided by these tests will be available to both the prosecution and defense counsel. Moreover, given the defense advantage of being able to draw on cultural rape narratives, it would be absurd to bar a prosecutor from striking a person who has, by these tests, been identified as someone with such high scores that it would be unlikely that he or she could loosen the grip of patriarchal tales. Accordingly, prosecutors should be able to strike for cause persons scoring so high on those personality traits and attributes as to make them likely to fall prey to the metaphors and myths of patriarchy. How high is high enough, and whether that judgment will be left to judicial discretion (based on a weighing of a wide array of case-specific juror data rather than simply on test scores) should be worked out by crafting court rules on the subject informed by consultation with qualified psychologists familiar with the experimental data and methodology, and with input from the judiciary, prosecution, and defense counsel. At the very least, handbooks should be drafted to guide judges in the intelligent exercise of discretion, much like the handbooks drafted to aid trial judges in case-specific admissibility questions regarding scientific evidence.[14]

Storytelling unavoidably limits and shapes how we determine what is real in a trial, meaning what happened at some point in the past. But language is the tool by which stories are shaped, both in the wider culture and in the courtroom. It is by examining the detail of everyday gendered language use and of language use in the courtroom that we can better understand what further and far more radical changes in patriarchal evidence rules are needed to achieve justice in rape trials.

PART II

Lawyers' Language
in the Courtroom

Part I examined courtroom language at the macrolevel, arguing that cultural rape narratives shape the kinds of stories told at trial. Part II shifts the focus to the microlevel, the linguistic tools that trial lawyers use to craft appealing narratives.

Chapter 4 lays Part II's groundwork for understanding how lawyers use these tools in court by reviewing how men use similar tools to maintain their dominance in everyday life. Interruptions, silence, word choice, and aggressive questioning are used by men in public settings to mute the female voice. The chapter explores why and how these tactics work, the impacts of race and class, and whether male-female differences in language tactics are rooted in biology, socialization, or the preexisting unequal distribution of social power.

Chapter 5 explains how the male view of language as a tool for domination is re-created in rape trials by evidence rules and courtroom customs. It illustrates the male view of language by examining lawyer-witness exchanges from several real-world trials, including the infamous William Kennedy Smith case. Chapter Five further demonstrates how cultural rape narratives combine with male-biased evidence rules to stack the deck heavily against the victim so that only a radical reworking of the patriarchal assumptions of modern evidence law can make the game fair. The task of Part III will be to articulate that alternative feminist evidentiary vision.

4

Gendered Language

In 1990, linguist Deborah Tannen's book *You Just Don't Understand: Women and Men in Conversation* made the best-seller list.[1] Tannen argued that there are fundamental differences in the ways that men and women communicate, indeed in each sex's understanding of what is the whole point of communication in the first place. Tannen illustrated her thesis with this story about Josh and Linda, a husband and wife:

> When Josh's old high-school chum called him at work and announced he'd be in town on business the following month, Josh invited him to stay for the weekend. That evening he informed Linda that they were going to have a houseguest, and that he and his chum would go out together the first night to shoot the breeze like old times. Linda was upset. She was going to be away on business the week before, and the Friday night when Josh would be out with his chum would be her first night home. But what upset her the most was that Josh had made these plans on his own and informed her of them, rather than discussing them with her before extending the invitation.[2]

There are at least three ways to interpret this exchange.

Way one (Tannen's way): Josh, like most men, has been socialized to see himself as part of a hierarchical social order. He believes, therefore, that we all negotiate for status, to be "one-up" or "one-down" on others.[3] Language is Josh's tool in these negotiations. He therefore prefers "report talk," talk as a way of exhibiting knowledge, solving problems, and otherwise preserving his status and independence in a hostile world. Josh also assumes that others, including his wife, share his worldview. Consequently, for him, checking with his wife would mean seeking her permission. That permission would make him feel like a dependent child or underling.[4]

Linda, like most women, has been socialized to see herself as part of a web of connections, seeking intimacy and community. Unlike Josh, Linda therefore seeks to stress similarities to, and equality with, others. She prefers "rapport talk," talk as a way of exchanging secrets and troubles, avoiding standing out, and stressing equality. Linda would have appreciated the discussion itself as evidence of involvement and communication. She thus perceived Josh's failure to check with her as a severing of bonds.

The problem between Josh and Linda, indeed between men and women generally, is, in Tannen's view, one of miscommunication across two cultures. If Josh understood Linda's need for talk as intimacy, he would not have minded consulting her. If Linda understood Josh's need for independence, she would not have viewed his failure to consult her as an assault on their mutual bond.

Way two (Tannen's critics' way):[5] Tannen's notion that men and women are socialized into essential differences in communication styles is nonsense. That notion looks to past wrongs, distracting attention from current power imbalances. Moreover, if male-female differences are essential ones, rooted in our personalities, then change must come slowly, perhaps with the next generation. Furthermore, the emphasis on miscommunication urges individuals to change, ignoring the need for institutional and collective action. Additionally, Tannen's two cultures/communications-style approach assumes the best of intentions from all parties. But male communication "styles" in fact reflect and reinforce male status and power. There is no reason to believe that men will easily relinquish that power. To ignore current power imbalances in favor of "miscommunication" is like saying that

> Black English and Oxford English are just two different varieties of English, each valid on its own; it just so happens that the speakers of one variety find themselves in high-paying positions with a lot of prestige and power of decision-making and the others are found more in low-paying jobs, or on the streets and in prisons.[6]

Under this "social constructionist" view, Josh ignored Linda because it never occurred to him that she should have any say about what he does in his own home. Linda is the subordinate, and she better well understand that. That this is so is demonstrated by a thought experiment. Imagine that Josh had a male roommate instead of a wife. Would Josh have behaved the same way? The social constructionist's answer is no. Moreover, if Josh had so behaved, his male roommate would never have let him get away with it. Josh need not be pushy or macho to prevail. He rules subtly, by his silent refusal to consult Linda.

Way three (the middle way):[7] Both Tannen and her critics are right. Socialization does matter, albeit because it teaches us gendered social roles and status, not because it fundamentally shapes our personalities. In our hierarchical world, those social roles and status serve as cues to elicit linguistic differences that in turn reinforce women's subordination in many settings. Josh and Linda, therefore, need both consciousness-raising *and* reform of the institutions of work and marriage. Those reforms should, however, show due respect for what is good in each linguistic style, including the potential of Linda's style to promote a more caring and trusting world.[8] Indeed, Tannen has rejected her critics' views of her as an essentialist. Instead, she considers herself a social constructionist sensitive to the influence of socialization, a view consistent with this "middle way."

But Josh and Linda's plight, while a helpful illustration, is far less important than how gendered linguistic differences play out in public settings. Because public settings provide the greatest opportunity for status seeking, it is in public contexts—meetings, seminars, and lectures—that report talk most thrives. Understanding the pervasive implications of this observation in our everyday lives sets the stage for appreciating how male linguistic rules disadvantage many women in the public setting of most interest here: rape trials.

Feminine Silence

The popular image of women is of chatty female gossips boring stoic men.[9] The image is typified by the hit 1960s sitcom *Bewitched*, in which Abner Kravitz is the husband repeatedly condemned to pained silence while his wife, Gladys, speculates breathlessly about Samantha, the witch next door.[10] Yet despite this image, the ideal set for women has long been one of silence, not moderation. "Silence," it was said, "gives the proper grace to women."[11] It may indeed be true that women talk more than men on average in private, intimate settings. But the data show fairly consistently that it is men, not women, whose talk dominates the public arena, or at least the most status-and-power-enhancing public speech.[12]

Several mechanisms may be at work here, all of which are connected to the themes in the Josh versus Linda example. There is thus some evidence that women do the "interactional shitwork,"[13] helping men to speak more. For example, a woman might raise many topics, but the male-selected topics are more likely to survive. That same woman might pepper her speech with minimal responses ("Uh-huh," "Yeah") designed to express interest in what the male speaker has to say. Although this woman expresses interest, prods the man, and fills polite spaces, the male responds with status-enhancing information and directives.[14]

Deborah Tannen focuses on the discomfort that relational women might feel in an agonistic, male-dominated public setting:

> Knowing you are likely to be attacked for what you say, you begin to hear criticism of your ideas as soon as they are formed. Rather than making you think more clearly, you doubt what you know. When you state your ideas, you hedge in order to fend off potential attacks, making your arguments appear weak. Ironically, this is more likely to invite attack from agonistic colleagues than to fend it off. When you feel attacked, emotion does not sharpen your wits, but rather clouds your mind and thickens your tongue, so you can't articulate ideas that were crystal clear before. Speakers with this style find their creative juices flowing in an atmosphere of mutual support but stopped up in the face of ritual opposition.[15]

Other theorists posit a very similar thought process, but one based on social status rather than communication style. Simply put, lower-status individuals (women) feel less competent relative to higher-status individuals (men) and are thus less willing to contribute to discussions involving those of higher status.[16]

This does not mean, however, that women do not move toward "male" styles in public settings. They do. But they retain much of the "feminine" style, even when in positions of authority because the high status of their position is moderated by the low status of being female.[17]

Another mechanism at work is skewed perceptions. Regardless of a woman's actual talking time, her contribution is "systematically judged as greater than that of a male speaker."[18] Indeed, women in mixed-sex groups who receive but a small share of total talking time perceive that share as fair, and the men complain of being silenced. Two factors are at work here. First, we have a "perceptual bias" or cultural tendency to judge high-pitched speakers as faster talkers. Second, we have a gendered-perceptions bias in which we devalue female speech. Women may thus be silenced by males without anyone's recognizing that this is so.[19]

Yet another mechanism at work is the "antagonistic elicitation," a comment or question designed to elicit a response but done in a challenging manner. Men are far more likely to use this strategy than are women. Men are therefore more willing to offer directly conflicting accounts of events, to criticize even minor differences, and to insult speakers. Men often see such antagonism as bonding rituals; women are more likely to view these tactics as threats, shutting down respectful dialogue.[20]

Men may also use their own silence as a means of domination. For example, if a woman's choice of topic is greeted with silence, she may bow to the male speaker's choice. As one variation, a woman might make a point at a public meeting and no one responds. When a male later makes the same point at greater length, even if he credits the woman with the idea, he gets credit for articulating the point more effectively.[21]

Male silence in response to female expressions of emotion or appeals to group solidarity can also serve to reinforce messages of female inferiority, encouraging further female silence:

> [O]ne reason little boys become inexpressive is not simply because our culture expects boys to be that way—but because our culture expects little boys to grow up to hold positions of power and prestige. What better way is there to exercise power than *to make it appear* that *all* one's behavior seems to be the result of unemotional rationality. Being impersonal and inexpressive lends to one's decisions and position an apparent autonomy and "rightness." Keeping cool, keeping distant as others challenge you or make demands upon you, is a strategy for keeping the upper hand. This same norm of political office—an image of strength and fitness to rule conveyed through inexpressiveness—is not limited to the public sphere; all men in this culture have recourse to this style by virtue of their gender.[22]

Finally, men may seek to silence women by interrupting them. Interruptions can serve many purposes but are usefully divided into two types: power-oriented and collaborative. A collaborative interruption is done to express support, agreement, interest, or solidarity. But in a "power-oriented" interruption, the listener cuts off the speaker to change the topic and shift attention from speaker to listener. In such a case, the "interrupter is seen as a malevolent aggressor, the interrupted an innocent victim. . . . [T]he interruption is an intrusion, a trampling on someone else's right to the floor, an attempt to dominate."[23]

Many theorists assert flatly that men consistently interrupt women more often than vice versa as a way to assert power. Other theorists believe that no sound generalizations can be made about gendered interruptions. Both these extreme positions are wrong. Properly read, the data show that men interrupt women more often than the opposite in short, task-oriented, or competitive laboratory settings. Moreover, men in these settings are more successful than women at using the interruptions to gain control of the floor.[24]

These data can be generalized from the laboratory to the boardroom. Studies show that in a wide range of settings and relationships, higher-status and more-powerful individuals engage in more power-oriented interruptions than do those of lower status, and men by definition are of higher status than women in our culture. Indeed, a variety of studies show, as predicted, that higher status reduces but does not erase gendered interruption differences. Male subordinates continue disproportionately to interrupt their female superiors.[25]

The combination of these sociolinguistic mechanisms serves literally to silence women relative to men, or at least to make it harder for men to hear women's voices. Such silence limits women's say in the agenda. Silence is also painful, limiting women's capacity to see themselves as rational and to use language to shape their own coherent, personal narrative. This silent pain we will see magnified manyfold in the rape trial.[26]

There is, however, cause for cautious optimism. Institutions can be redesigned to equalize female access to the floor. One modest example involves the distinction between "singly-developed" and "collaborative" floors. "Singly-developed floors" hold as an ideal that single speakers take turns in sequence. For example, a department chair at a university faculty meeting may call on one speaker at a time, as each potential speaker raises a hand. Because each speaker gets a chance to display intellectual competence, singly-developed floors confer individual status. Such floors invite male report talk, yet they predominate in activities designed to reach a decision or solve a problem in a public way. As we would expect, women's share of the floor is unequal relative to men's in the status-enhancing, singly-developed floor.[27]

The results are different for collaborative floors. With these floors, the ideal is that more than one person speak at a time in free-for-alls, in which speakers "jointly built one idea, operating on the same wavelength."[28] Because multiple persons are expected to speak simultaneously, making a contribution is not seen as a status-enhancing push to control the floor. Ideas are viewed as the product of the group rather than the individual. In such communal, non-status-enhancing circumstances, women's share of the floor is relatively equal to men's.

A creative university department chair might thus try to encourage more informal work, more brainstorming by small committees using collaborative floors. Additionally, where a singly-developed floor is necessary, the department chair might call on every individual, encouraging each to speak without first having to raise a hand. Such modest institutional reform should significantly enhance women's contribution to departmental deliberations. This lesson should be remembered as we move toward exploring institutional reform of the rape trial.[29]

Gendered Expectations and a Women's Language

Even when women do speak in public contexts, their words may not be well received. This resistance to women's words arises in part from the perception that they speak a "women's language."

Some feminist theorists have indeed posited a unique "women's language," a set of linguistic features characteristic of how women speak in most settings. Among the posited features are the use of "meaningless particles," like "my goodness"; "empty adjectives" expressing entirely emotional assessments, as in "It's adorable!"; and use of hedges like "I guess" or "I think," conveying uncertainty.[30] These features were viewed by some as learned behaviors, hallmarks of women's inferior social position:

> Women's language developed as a way of surviving and even flourishing without control over economic, physical, or social reality. Then it is necessary to listen more than speak, agree more than confront, be delicate, be indirect, say dangerous things in such a way that their impact will be felt after the speaker is out of range of the hearer's retaliation.[31]

Research has failed to confirm, or disconfirm, the existence of a women's speech constant across contexts. Nevertheless, research has revealed some linguistic forms that women are more likely to use than men in a wide variety of settings. These forms include more expressions of positive politeness, sympathy, and understanding; fewer commands and threats; more phrases like "you know," which show an effort to engage the addressee's attention; and more statements of self-reference, such as "It seems to me," which show respect. Moreover, when women use imperatives, they are more likely to do so in question form and with qualifiers, as in "Would you get me that report by Monday, if at all possible?" Many of these observed differences are, however, more likely due to setting, topic, role, and status. For example, those in lower-status positions (as are many women) use such politeness strategies toward those of higher status.[32]

Even when women do not use "women's language," however, they are perceived as doing so. This perception arises because our stereotypes or "folklinguistic" beliefs about how women speak closely track the descriptions of women's language. Stereotypes lead us to ignore contrary evidence while attending to confirming evidence. Furthermore, these biases are magnified by the "fundamental attribution error," our tendency to attribute behavior more to personality than context. Consequently, when we see many women in low-status roles speaking politely, we attribute that behavior to women's essential nature rather than to their role. The resulting linguistic stereotypes resist change, as they have in American culture for more than twenty years.[33]

One effect of perceiving women's language where it does not exist and of viewing it as typical female behavior is the self-fulfilling prophecy. Women learn that they will be ignored or disliked if they violate stereotypical norms, so they try not to deviate too much from those norms.[34]

Although other factors, such as age, race, and class, can reduce the effects of stereotypes, the effects are greatest where gender is most salient. But gender is most salient in initial encounters or where women are in the minority. Our gendered cognitive biases lessen as we get to know individuals better. Interestingly, female crime victims at trials face precisely those initial encounters (between victim and jurors) in which women are often in the minority. Moreover, the very nature of the crime of rape suggests that gender will be salient.[35]

The effect of the real or imagined use of women's language can be devastating to a woman's credibility. Anyone using women's-language is evaluated as more caring but less credible, competent, and intelligent. These evaluations are magnified when women, rather than men, are the speakers. Furthermore, the indirectness supposedly characteristic of women's language may be seen as insecurity, apology as weakness. Additionally, women's language speakers' use of shorter, less aggressive responses in public settings commands less attention. Similarly, their giving reasons for their suggestions and arguing from their personal experience rather than from abstract principle, two "feminine" strategies, are relatively unpersuasive to men. These effects are much larger in laboratory settings than in the few studies involving naturally occurring speech, but even modest effects can be decisive in criminal cases. There, defense victory requires only "reasonable doubt."[36]

Yet women face a double bind if they violate stereotypical speech norms. Most men simply do not like aggressive women. "There is a sense in which every woman is seen as a receptionist—available to give information and help, perennially interruptible."[37] Women who violate stereotypes may seem unlikable or unworthy to many men. Furthermore, men resist receiving information from those, like women, whom men perceive as of lower status because being lecturer rather than listener is the superior (i.e., men's) role.[38]

In sum, women may be perceived as using women's language when they are not, a perception marking them as stupid, incompetent, and incredible. Yet too masculine a style means they will be disliked or ignored. For a woman to be seen as credible, she must walk a fine line between opposed stereotypes.

Lexicon

Women also have trouble being heard by men because the sexes use the same key words to mean different things. Some words may not even exist to describe women's experience concisely. Linguist Suzette Elgin made this last point in her science fiction novel *Native Tongue*. In *Native Tongue,* women invented their own language, Laadan, to describe experiences that their patriarchal culture ignored. One of those experiences Laadan expresses as "doloredim":

> This word has no English equivalent whatsoever. Say you have an average woman. She has no control over her life. She has little or nothing in the way of a resource for being good to herself, even when it is necessary. She has family and animals and friends, and associates that depend on her for sustenance of all kinds. She rarely has adequate sleep or rest; she has no time for herself, no space of her own, little or no money to buy things for herself, no opportunity to consider her own emotional needs. She is at the beck and call of others, because she has these responsibilities, and obligations, and does not choose to (or cannot) abandon them. For such a woman, the one and only thing she is likely to have a little control over for indulging her own self is food. When such a woman overeats, the verb for that is "Doroledim." (And then she feels guilty, because there are

women whose children are starving and who do not have even THAT option for self-indulgence. . . .)[39]

The "doroledim" translation problem is real. The problem was understood by women who first named "sexual harassment," and before that, by Betty Friedan in her feminist classic, *The Feminine Mystique*. There, Friedan articulated the "problem that has no name."[40] Even when the English language has a word for a concept, the male understanding of that word may not reflect female experience. Thus, there is some evidence that men define "violent" conduct as the wrongful, "intense, deliberate and *avoidable*" use of force. Women define violence as the wrongful, "intense, deliberate and *harmful*" use of force.

Suzette Elgin's description of a woman named Paula viewing a science fiction movie with her family makes the point. The movie showed a man using force in his dream to express his lust for a woman. Paula viewed the scene as violent: "[I]t was force; it caused the woman pain. . . ." But Paula's husband and son saw no violence: "The man wooed the woman . . . ; in the course of the wooing she gave in and yielded to him, and what happened next was natural and unavoid-able. . . . [N]o 'harm' was done."[41]

Talmudic debates in the Bavli and Yerushalmi, two sacred Jewish texts, concerning the proper damages to be paid by a rapist for his crime offer further illustration. The rabbis tried to grasp a woman's experience in being raped. One rabbi saw the pain as that of being thrown "down on the ground." Another argued, "A rapist does not pay for pain because this is what awaits her in the future from her husband [i.e., upon marriage, she will have her hymen torn]."

Rape is like "one who cuts a wart off his friend's foot that his friend was anyway planning to remove," said one rabbi. But the majority of rabbis rejected this cynicism: "There is no comparison between engaging in sex on a dunghill and engaging in sex in the bridal chamber."[42]

The rabbinic majority fortunately came to recognize the psychological pain of degradation as part of rape. But the mere fact of the debate demonstrates male difficulty in understanding female experience. Although we live in a very different culture from these rabbis, the communication problem persists. Men have a very different view than do women about what constitutes "rape" and "forced" sex. The words "rape" and "force" simply mean different things to men and women.[43]

This discussion does not mean that men cannot come to understand women's experience or lexicon but that the task will be hard, especially in rape trials.

A related problem arises from the gendered nature of narrative. When men tell stories, they "celebrate the song of the self."[44] Male stories involve men in physical, verbal, and intellectual combat. There is more action than talk (at least relative to women's stories). Details focus on time and place rather than people. If men act together, it is largely as relatively independent "co-present buddies."[45]

When women tell stories, the stories are more often about community norms and actions, including how a community overcomes contest. Neighbors volunteer, families act together, people matter; stories often end in a "triumphant celebration of neighborly love." While there may be competition, even for status, it is status through group affiliation. The goal is to be part of the in, not the out, group. Furthermore, the *appearance* of equality matters even when women compete. These stories suggest that women's sense of power comes from their role in their community; men's sense of power from themselves.[46]

If this observation is correct,[47] women who are cast in roles as individuals, adrift from their communities, may feel particularly at sea. Yet a rape trial treats a woman as an isolated individual in contest with defense counsel. Although the prosecutor and the victim's family may be present, they can do little other than register the occasional objection to help the victim. The judge is a neutral umpire, the silent jury a communal judgmental gaze. Moreover, cross-examination stresses prior sexual conduct, "sexy" dressing, hair, mannerisms, and other breaches of community norms. The victim, isolated in the witness box, is physically separated from the community. In this hyperindividualistic, adversarial environment, it will be hard for a woman to tell stories her way and thus harder still for men to understand them. She may feel weaponless, alone in a war she cannot win.[48]

Race Chat, Class Chat

Is this rape-trial war, however, one in which only middle-class white women are disadvantaged? The question must be asked because such women were the subjects of most of the research on male-female linguistic differences. We arguably, therefore, do not know how other women speak. My response is that women of other races and classes may suffer even more. The experience of African American women, who are disproportionately represented among rape victims, shows why.[49]

African American culture supposedly values adversarial argument. Indeed, many black scholars have taken pride in this observation. They argue that high-spirited black debate is rooted in "soul." Here "soul" means being frank: judging people by what they are, exuding warmth, getting straight to the point. Black linguistic styles reflect soul in the African American verbal tradition (AVT). The customs of this tradition include "signifying," the verbal art of ceremonial put-down; indirection and humor; quick verbal repartee; personalization; and concreteness. Other AVT customs include "tonal semantics"—impassioned, loud, heated delivery, with emotionally charged rhythms and repetitions and sermonic tones.[50]

Because the AVT values greater assertiveness for all African Americans, black women are seen as more assertive than white women. This assertive style was magnified by a long history of working black women, in contrast to their passive white-homemaker counterpart.[51]

This image of black women as strong, assertive, and combative has unfortunately justified discrimination. The infamous "Moynihan Report" concluded, for example, that black social problems stemmed from aggressive black matriarchs. Those matriarchs stopped the black "male animal" from "strut[ting]." Similarly, today, black battered women who kill their assailants are viewed as too strong to suffer from battered woman's syndrome. That view makes it harder to prove that the women killed in self-defense. Black women are thus seen as too invulnerable to be raped or harassed:

> We speak in tongues, when the words are not part of the script, when we fail to remain solidly locked into our preassigned roles. You can be Eliza on the ice floe. Mammy in the kitchen. Tina Turner on the dance floor. You can call on Jesus, that's O.K. You can fall on your knees as if in prayer, unzip his pants and open your mouth. But whoever heard of a hot-blooded Negress being sexually harassed, much less offended?[52]

Despite the concerns about abusing the data, there is indeed some evidence in the few studies done that black females are more confrontational than white females. But the studies also show important similarities. For example, in the most comprehensive of those studies, black girls, ages four to fourteen, were generally found to prefer talk to play; smaller, more egalitarian groups; cooperation; and mitigated directives ("Let's try this") relative to black boys of the same age.

Furthermore, this study did not examine black-white interaction. African Americans most often communicate with whites to negotiate for status, get a position, obtain a favorable evaluation, or be seen as getting along. Yet African Americans routinely alter their speech to further these goals.[53] They switch styles to accommodate white culture and institutions. It is likely that African American rape victims will accommodate white expectations at trial by adopting the subordinate's role.

"Women's ways of speaking" are one way that lower-status speakers accommodate those of greater status. Black skin is still perceived as a marker of low status, as is being female. Thus black women who are victims of rape are likely to shift their trial speech patterns toward low-status behavior similar to that of the white women who were the subjects of most of the research. For this same reason, class, ethnicity, or other indicators of low status should not alter rape victims' linguistic behavior in a way that undermines my conclusions. At the very least, the burden should be on those who argue the contrary to prove their case.[54]

Black women finally face a race-based catch-22. If they speak "women's language," they will be less credible, as is true of white women adopting the same style. But if black women adopt a more assertive style, white jurors will perceive them as rude, hostile, out-of-control, and hence less credible. Black jurors, on the other hand, while comfortable with black speaking styles, are more likely than whites to give weight to cultural rape narratives that construct rape as consensual sex. Race and class complicate the analysis, making institutional reform all the more urgent.[55]

One related objection to relying on the gendered-differences research is that it describes only averages. Many women of various races and classes will use the male style; many men the female. Indeed, within-gender linguistic differences may exceed cross-gender differences. Further, we all are capable of displaying a wide range of linguistic behaviors, depending on context, so we cannot make gendered generalizations. But these observations do not justify avoiding institutional change.[56]

First, if our system unfairly disadvantages feminine-style speakers, that is a wrong that needs righting, even if many of those speakers are male.

Second, *institutional* context is central to eliciting linguistic behaviors. The argument in this chapter and the next is that the courtroom context elicits behaviors that help the powerful and hurt the powerless. Because gender is a strong marker of status, women are relatively powerless next to men in adversarial contexts like trials. Gender is especially salient in rape trials, so rape victims are more likely to choose "feminine" styles and to be perceived as doing so. Even small real or perceived linguistic differences can have great consequences, especially given the power of cultural rape narratives. There is a moral imperative to equalize the contest.[57]

Third, the notion of "complementarity": the idea that social, political, and economic health requires giving equal concern to perceived opposites in crafting a "total reality." We need competition *and* cooperation, hierarchy *and* equality, in a relatively balanced mix to make a just world.[58]

Fourth, a fair legal system must accommodate the tension between individual and group justice. This tension is part of what the affirmative action debate is all about. Consequently, rules that on average disadvantage one group more than another may, for that reason alone, be unjust.[59]

Male-female language differences work to women's disadvantage in public settings. One such public setting is the criminal trial. Evidence rules and customs, codes of ethics, and adversarial values create trials governed by male rules. The manipulators of those rules are lawyers. Justice or its denial lie in lawyers' language.

5

Lawyers' Language and the Rape Trial

The Adversary System

The "adversary system" is aptly named. The system assumes that trials achieve truth through the clash of equally matched adversaries. The adversaries are meant to be tough competitors. The American Bar Association says, "Advocacy is not for the timid, the meek, or the retiring. Our system of justice is inherently contentious in nature and it demands that lawyers have the urge for vigorous contest."[1]

Vigorous contest need not necessarily be uncivil. Moreover, lawyers may try to connect emotionally with witnesses or adversaries, but that effort has instrumental goals: to gain the witnesses' trust before "going for the kill." Ethics codes set broad limits on fair tactics, but within those limits trial lawyers are taught to be "[l]ike Rambo . . . tough, aggressive, and intimidating."[2] Metaphors of litigation as combat or sport dominate lawyers' professional magazines and conversation. Lawyers speak of "playing hardball," "taking no prisoners," "destroying," and even "raping" witnesses. They brag about "points scored" and "duels" won, and urge their colleagues to have an "instinct for the jugular."[3]

Franklyn Strier, a longtime critic of the adversary system, describes its culture as quintessentially male (although he uses more essentialist language than I would):

> The adversary system of trial justice mirrors the male model of dispute resolution. Whether innately or by socialization or both, women typically avoid conflict as means of dispute resolution. At the risk of oversimplification, women are more likely to be compassionate, nurturing, and sensitive to the feelings of others. These qualities lend themselves to dispute resolution by conciliatory methods. On the other hand, men are prone to aggression, confrontation, and verbal if not physical hostility—traits congruent with courtroom battle. . . . Of course, women can and do become skilled

litigators. But in so doing, they generally adopt male behavioral models and play by men's rules.[4]

Most women lawyers do play by male adversarial rules. Indeed, that is why a rape victim faces a harrowing cross-examination whether by male or female defense counsel. Yet, many female lawyers are uncomfortable with those rules, and a sizeable minority of those lawyers have experimented with effective relational alternatives to male adversarial combat. Nevertheless, male rules still prevail.[5] These rules track those seen in everyday male conversation and are better illustrated than described.[6]

Dominating Rape Victims Through Lawyers' Language

Cross-Examination

On Easter weekend, 1991, Patricia Bowman met William Kennedy Smith, Senator Edward Kennedy's nephew, at Au Bar, a nightclub in Palm Beach, Florida. The two danced and talked until around three o'clock in the morning, when Bowman gave Smith a ride home to the Kennedy estate. At Smith's invitation, Bowman entered the house, then accompanied Smith to the beach. There, alleges Bowman, Smith raped her.[7] Defense attorney Roy Black's cross-examination of Smith at trial included the following:

> *Defense Counsel (DC):* Now you said that after you left the—uh—
> Kennedy home that you felt dirty, is that correct?
> *Alleged Victim (AV):* I felt dirty before I left the home.
> *DC:* When you drove home you still had the same panties on.
> *AV:* Yes sir.
> *DC:* When you got to your house, you stayed there for several hours
> without removing those panties.
> *AV:* I-I'm not quite sure how long I was at my house, but I, but I—the
> underwear was still on me.
> *DC:* It was at least a couple of hours, wasn't it?
> *AV:* I, I'm not sure.
> *DC:* And when you went to your mother's house, when you left your
> house and went to your mother's house, you kept those same
> panties on, didn't you?

AV: Yes.

DC: And when you went from your mother's house to go to pick up Johnny Butler, you still wore the same panties.

AV: I was pretty terrorized, I - I - I'd never, I just, it's like you're—you're just functioning, and—and to be at the sheriff's office? And I was just, just . . .

DC: Even though you—you - felt dirty, you felt awful, and what have you, you kept those same panties—on is that what you said, Miss Bowman?

AV: I—I couldn't think to, t—I, I didn't know what to think.[8]

Defense counsel, by his power to raise and enforce topics, led Bowman to accept counsel's critical assumption: that how long Bowman kept her panties on was relevant to whether she consented. It is significant that counsel never said why feeling "dirty" should have required Bowman to remove only one particular article of clothing, her panties. But defense counsel did not need to do so. He implied that if Bowman were telling the truth, then the reason she felt symbolically dirty was because of the "polluting powers of male seminal fluids." Therefore, if Bowman were indeed raped, she would have quickly removed the source of her moral pollution, her panties.[9]

Defense counsel importantly stressed only Bowman's keeping her panties on. Counsel did *not* contest Bowman's claimed feeling of "dirtiness." If she felt dirty but did not remove her panties, counsel suggested, then the locus of the dirtiness could not have been the physical acts of penetration and ejaculation. The locus of filth lay elsewhere: in Bowman's guilt about having impersonal, consensual sex with a man she had just met.

Critically, Bowman tried to resist defense counsel's implications by insisting that terror explained her "irrational" behavior in not removing the panties. Yet this tactic tacitly accepted that it was indeed irrational for a rape victim to keep her panties on. Defense counsel had successfully defined what was relevant, making Bowman's protests sound like panicked rationalizations for being "caught" in an inconsistency.

Defense counsel's power to define relevance also includes the standard claim that the victim's promiscuous character made it more likely that she consented. Rape shield laws do purport to exclude or limit the promiscuous-character argument.[10] Still, defense counsel often seeks to circumvent such laws by using character traits other than promiscuity as proxies for "sluttishness." Examples of such proxies are being on welfare, drinking, using drugs, or being poor.

Moreover, defense counsel may repeatedly ask questions about sexual history, despite sustained objections. The hope is that the jury will infer loose character from the questions alone. References to "sexy clothing" (still permitted in most states) also serves as sluttishness proxies. Counsel will, therefore, emphasize that a victim wore a short dress, a plunging neckline, or a tight blouse as strong indicators of loose character and thus consent to intercourse.[11]

In the William Kennedy Smith case, defense counsel chose a particularly subtle series of questions to impugn Bowman's character. Defense counsel stressed that Bowman willingly entered Smith's house at 3:00 A.M. Bowman protested that she was interested "in the house," not in Smith. Defense counsel countered this impression by accusing Bowman of removing her pantyhose, surely an indicator of a sexual interest in Smith. That interest, defense counsel suggested, seemed especially strong, given that it was so early in the morning. Entering the house seemed particularly odd, counsel further implied, because Bowman knew that she would have to get up in a few hours to care for her child. Bowman indeed did not deny removing her pantyhose but asserted simply that she did not remember how they came off.

Defense counsel intimated, however, that Bowman's memory lapse was convenient, given her clear expression of sexual desire. Bowman and Smith had kissed in the parking lot, before the events on the beach. Bowman, the defense stressed with great drama, had originally described this action as a "short, sweet little kiss."[12] But only sexually experienced women distinguish among grades of kisses. Moreover, only a woman eager to repeat such an experience could use an affectionate term of that kind to describe a kiss with a man whom she had just met.

In sum, defense counsel implied, the absence of pantyhose, an item of clothing "guarding" the female genitalia, bespoke a woman of deep sexual craving, a craving so urgent that she entered a man's home late at night knowing that her child would be waiting in her own home. The key was counsel's effort not simply to paint Bowman as desirous of Smith but, rather, to do so by assailing her character, portraying her as a bad mother and a woman so sexually experienced that she can grade and critique with precision the quality of kisses.

A penchant for promiscuity can also be explored under another guise. In a gang rape case, for example, defense counsel picked up on the victim's direct examination testimony that her assailants had not ejaculated:

> *DC:* Would you explain to me why you now think they didn't?
> *V:* I just do.
> *DC:* Do you know what that feels like?
> *V:* Yes.
> *DC:* To have somebody climax inside of you?
> *Prosecutor:* Objection, your honor.
> *Judge:* Objection sustained.
> *DC:* Your Honor, I'm not delving into this woman's past sexual history.
> *Prosecutor:* Objection to this speech, your Honor.
> *Judge:* The Court understands your reason, Counsel, and objection sustained.[13]

Although the objection was sustained, defense counsel's questions sought to imply that the victim had an active sex life *without* directly so asking. By indirection, therefore, counsel sought a way around the rape shield laws. Questions about the sources of a woman's "vaginal infections" strive toward a similar goal.[14]

Cross-examining, counsel's control over what topics will be discussed and for how long, also allows counsel the power of categorization. Once a category is used, the victim, prosecutor, and judge are likely to adopt it, a phenomenon called "semantic contagion."[15] Although the prosecutor will strive to remove the victim from the category, its mere invocation has emotional power. Jurors will treat a witness fitting into a category as displaying all the traits and behaviors associated with the category.[16] Yet, despite prosecution objections, defense counsel can by indirection often lure a victim into accepting defense counsel's definition of the relevant category:

> *DC:* So one of the objectives, when you left . . . the parking lot was to go out and party, is that correct?
> *V:* Yes.
> *DC:* What's meant among youthful people, people your age, Brian's age, by partying?
> *V:* Some take it just to go and with some friends . . . have a few drinks and some do smoke, some do take the pills.

DC: Partying.

V: Drugs.

DC: Is it not true partying among people your age does not mean go to a party?

V: That's true.

DC: It implies to many people that implies sexual activity, doesn't it?

P: Objection, your Honor.

J: Overruled.

DC: To many people your age that means sexual activity, does it not?

V: To some, yes. I guess.

DC: And at the very least it means the use of intoxicants.

V: Yes.[17]

Defense counsel pressed the victim to define what young people meant by "partying." The victim conceded that partying included alcohol or drugs and, to some kids, sex. Once these concessions were made, however, the victim was placed into the category of a drinking, drug-using nymphomaniac. The syllogism became: (1) partyers engage in consensual sex, (2) the victim was a partyer, (3) therefore, she consented.

A more subtle example of categorization again comes from the William Kennedy Smith case:

DC: And you had a difficult time with your daughter's father?

V: I had a difficult time losing my daughter's twin.

DC: And one of the worst parts of it is that you didn't get support from the man involved, did you?

V: He tried, sir, to do his best. . . .[18]

Here, the key phrases were "your daughter's father" and "the man involved." These terms, unlike "husband" or even "partner," implied a brief, casual relationship, rooted largely in sex. Bowman now fit the category "unwed mother." The "man involved's" failure to contribute child support also suggested anger toward men who did not turn casual sex into more of a relationship. That picture of anger invoked the category "spurned woman." Indeed, defense counsel repeatedly returned to both these categories, portraying Bowman as a woman with a history of casual sexual relationships, followed by anger at the men involved. The defense sought to portray this anger as directed at Smith when, after intercourse, he showed no further interest in Bowman.

Categorization can also be accomplished not only by word choice but by the invocation of metaphor. When Black portrayed Bowman as a spurned woman, he sought to invoke the metaphor of the "war" between the sexes:

DC: [W]hat you're saying here is that you do have a lot of anger against men.
V: Not all men, no.
DC: You don't trust men.
V: There are . . .
DC: At least that's what you said here.
V: There are some men I don't trust.
DC: And there were, no, uh, contraceptives used that night, were there?
V: No.[19]

The words "war" or "battle" are never used, but they fit the picture. If sexual relationships are a war, warriors will do what they must to win. Bowman, the defense suggested, had been rejected before and saddled with a child by irresponsible men who ignored contraceptives. Bowman hated men; *she* viewed sex as a war. Consequently, when Smith rejected Bowman's entreaties for a more sustained relationship, Bowman staged a retaliatory strike: she claimed rape.

Defense counsel may also seek to recharacterize a victim's description to invoke categories involving consensual sex, as in this exchange, in which a rape victim testified to a forced walk in an unfamiliar neighborhood:

DC: Did he have you by the hand or—
V: He had his arm around me.
DC: In other words, a gesture of affection.[20]

The term "gesture of affection" invokes the category "romance," the most common male-female adult relationship involving affectionate behavior. But romance is a category implying consensual, not forced, sex.

Defense counsel's control over how long the victim may speak additionally means that the lawyer does most of the talking. The lawyer uses this domination of linguistic space to convey vivid, detailed images. Yet the lawyer can limit the victim to flat yes or no answers. These tactics aid defense credibility. Empirical research reveals that detailed, vivid answers are more persuasive than short, spare answers. Furthermore, jurors assume that there is a basis for the lawyer's questions or the lawyer would not ask them.[21]

Moreover, the lawyer can structure questions in a "poetic" fashion. "Poetic" talk in ordinary conversation parallels the use of poetic devices in literary discourse: repetition, parallelism, irony, alliteration, and rhythm. These devices are used to increase emotional impact and offer lawyerly commentary on the credibility and "true" meaning of the victim's testimony.[22] An extended excerpt from the William Kennedy Smith trial makes clear both how lawyers dominate linguistic space and how they achieve power by poetic talk. This excerpt is from Roy Black's cross-examination of Ann Mercer, a friend of Bowman's whom she called to pick her up at the Kennedy estate:

> *DC:* You say you went to the Kennedy home on the early morning hours of March thirtieth? Is that correct?
> *AM:* Yes.
> *DC:* Your friend says that she was raped, is that right?
> *AM:* Yes.
> *DC:* But what she tells us is that she wants her shoes, is that correct?
> *AM:* Yes.
> *DC:* Several times she was worried about her shoes.
> *AM:* Yes.
> *DC:* So you went into the house, is that correct?
> *AM:* Yes.
> *DC:* Into the house where the rapist is, right?
> *AM:* I guess you could say yes.
> *DC:* It's dark in there.
> *AM:* Yes.
> *DC:* You go through the kitchen, right?
> *AM:* Yes.
> *DC:* Into this little hallway.
> *AM:* Yes.
> *DC:* It's dark in this hallway, isn't it?
> *AM:* Right.
> *DC:* You meet up with this man who your friend says is a rapist, isn't that correct?

AM: I was not afraid of him, no, I was not afraid of him.

DC: That's not my question Miss Mercer, you understand my question? My question is did you meet this man who your friend says is the alleged rapist?

AM: Yes.

DC: And you ask him to help—help—you ask the rapist to help you find her shoes, is this correct?

AM: Yes.

DC: And he turns around and goes with you uh, out of the house, is that right?

AM: Yes.

DC: Through the dining room to begin with, is that correct?

AM: Yes.

DC: It's dark in that house, right?

AM: Yes.

DC: You're walking through the dining room with this man, is that correct?

AM: Yes.

DC: You go out the door of the dining room, don't you? Into a little patio area?

AM: Correct.

DC: With this man who's the alleged rapist is that right?

AM: Right.

DC: It's dark out, isn't it?

AM: Right.

DC: With this man who's the alleged rapist?

AM: Yes.

DC: You go across the lawn with him, is that right?

AM: Yes.

DC: Towards the beach?

AM: Yes.

DC: As you go across the lawn, you get to an area where there are hedges? And a concrete wall, isn't that right?

AM: Yes.

DC: And you're still with this man who's the alleged rapist, is that right?

AM: Yes.

DC: You get to a dark stairway, isn't that correct?

AM: Mm', Yes.

DC: There're no lights in that stairway, are there?

AM: No.

DC: You go down the stairway, right?

AM: Right.

DC: With this man?

AM: Right.

DC: There's a door down at the bottom of the stairway, is that right?

AM: Right.

DC: You and this man who's the alleged rapist go out the door, that correct?

AM: Right.

DC: And you spend, uh, several minutes looking for these shoes with this man who's the alleged rapist? Is that right?

AM: Right.[23]

The cross-examination continues in this fashion for a total of forty-four questions,[24] covered in three and one-half minutes, on the same subject: Ann Mercer's accompanying "the alleged rapist" alone, in the dark. The implication, of course, is that Mercer must not have believed that her friend had been raped. No woman would be so unafraid of being alone with a rapist as she was. Yet if even Ms. Bowman's friend disbelieves her, the defense suggests, then the whole scenario, including Bowman's demeanor, must have been "fishy." These points are driven home by endless repetition.[25]

Note how easy it is for the defense to achieve the effects of repetition. When Mercer briefly tries to elaborate on her answer, the defense insists that she simply answer the question asked. Thereafter, that is precisely what she does. Research indeed shows that "forced-choice" questions—those requiring a yes or no answer—are quite effective in limiting the witness's independent voice.[26] Moreover, note how the endless repetition of one or two narrow points slows down the action. It feels like Mercer was with Smith for a far longer time than was in fact the case. The sense of a long time spent looking for a trivial object—a shoe—also makes Bowman's claim seem ludicrous: "If you had just been raped, would you promptly return to the scene of your pain for a lengthy search for, of all things, a shoe?" is counsel's implied argument. The research shows, however, that this argument is effective precisely because it is merely implied. Jurors are often more persuaded when they, not the attorneys, initially draw the conclusions.[27]

The defense also magnifies the power of his oratory by careful word choice. The recurrent use of the phrase *"alleged* rapist"—rather than "rapist," "defendant," or "Mr. Smith"—seeks to mock Bowman's tale as unsupported allegations, not facts. Defense counsel also recounts the tale of past events in the present tense, heightening the drama of absurdly being alone at night with the alleged rapist. The focus is always on the word "alleged" so that the phrase "alleged rapist" is heard as "innocent man falsely accused."

Three further related poetic devices help create drama. One, the "sequential puzzle," portrays an inconsistency between a witness's story and her behavior as puzzling. The defense suggests an implied solution to the puzzle: the witness is lying or mistaken. The sequential puzzle is illustrated by an acquaintance rape case in which the victim and her assailant met in the parking lot outside a bar after closing time:

DC: When you left the parking lot that night, did you know this Mister Winwood's first name at that point?

V: Yes.

DC: Did you know his last name? When you left the parking lot that night?

V: No.

DC: Did you know Brian's last name? When you left the parking lot tha - that night?

V: No.

DC: Did you know where Brian was from? When you left the parking lot—that night?

V: From Illinois.

DC: Did you know where Winwood was from? When you left the parking lot that night?

V: No.

DC: Did you know where Winwood was work[ing]? When you left the parking lot that night?

V: No.

DC: How did you wind up in his automobile?

V: I got in.

DC: Why?

V: Because he said we were going to a party at a friend of his house.

DC: But you didn't know his last name, where he worked, or where he was from, correct?

V: Yes.
DC: You didn't know a thing about him, did you?[28]

A woman is expected to know certain basic personal facts about a man before she accompanies him to a social engagement. Certainly, she should know his full name, residence, and place of employment. That she does not know these things and yet accompanies him is puzzling. The victim senses this too, feebly answering that she knew that the alleged rapist was from Illinois. But that vague, general knowledge is not what we expect. We want to hear that she knew that he grew up in Chicago, near the Loop, but later moved to the suburbs. Her vague answer underscores her ignorance about her "escort's" background. Defense counsel makes the puzzle more overt by asking shocked questions: "How did you wind up in his automobile?" "I just got in," she replies. In with a man you "didn't know a thing about . . . ?" the lawyer asks, amazed. The jurors will search for a solution to this puzzle, and defense counsel hopes that that solution will be simple: the "victim" is a tramp. That solution is indeed a likely one for the jury to find because the victim breached patriarchal rules of silence. By the drama of a sequential puzzle, defense counsel renders the woman nonrapable.

A second poetic device, the "contrast set," underscores irony by demonstrating an incongruity between our society's expectations and the witness's behavior.[29] The irony is shown by using terms like "but" that highlight a contrast[30] and by lists using repetition to increase a question's power: "But you didn't know his last name, where he worked, or where he was from, correct?" is an example. Another example is taken from a defense counsel's questioning a victim about a friend who accompanied her one night to a bar:

DC: Did she only have two drinks?
V: Yes—I think—if she did drink, it was a few.
DC: Not many?
V: No.
DC: But she drove right across some strange people's lawn, didn't she?
DC: She was in a partying mood, wasn't she?"
V: Yes.
DC: So were you, weren't you?
V: Yes.[31]

Here, the "But she drove right across some strange people's lawn" question creates an inconsistency, a contrast with the behavior expected of someone who has had only a few drinks. The "but" announces the contrast, and the contrast's implications are completed in the next question: "She was in a partying mood, wasn't she?" Defense counsel made use of a very clear summary list too, elsewhere in his cross:

DC: Isn't it true that Brian told you that:
—he had a girlfriend and a child
—and that he was very concerned about them
—and that's why he could not perform that night?
V: No.[32]

Lists, contrasts, and sequential puzzles, either alone or in combination, amplify persuasive power. But that amplification is due to the device's structure, not merely the message's content. Puzzles create suspense. Contrasts create emphasis and irony. And lists emphasize items, convey blame through rhythm, and persuade through repetition.[33] When the persuasive effect of these devices is amplified by content appealing to patriarchal tales, the effect is tremendous.

Other poetic devices too numerous to illustrate here include "detailing to death" (probing minor details to demonstrate flawed memory or lies by means of many small inconsistencies); pursuing an answer aggressively to suggest witness evasiveness; and demonstrating large inconsistencies among witness statements (saying one thing to the police, another on the stand). Additional effective tactics include rapid-fire questioning that halts witness care and reflection in answering; needling (prods and jibes, making fun of the witness as an absurdly obvious liar); and "preemptive interruption" (cutting off a witness who is about to offer a satisfactory explanation for her behavior).[34] These tactics might be used in the hope of angering the witness, for an angry, aggressive woman, because she thereby violates patriarchal norms, is disbelieved.[35] Direct challenges to credibility—such as accusations, displays of doubt, skepticism, disbelief, or surprise—can also be quite effective.[36] Unfortunately, "much like the physical act of rape, where the . . . [victim] is relatively powerless in the face of male aggression and brute strength, so she is similarly passive and limited in response to the . . . [defense counsels'] influence during questioning. . . ."[37]

One final tactic is the manipulation of silence. Notably, the woman's failure to report her rape promptly—her silence while nursing her wounds—is used to suggest that she lies. Under the heat of rapid-fire questioning, a victim might also hesitate before answering. That hesitation feels endless, a virtual perceived canyon of silence between question and answer. Yet, such silence is viewed as a marker of blame. The implied explanation for delay is the victim's shame because she has been caught in a lie or in a behavior contrary to social norms. Alternatively, the silence suggests that the victim is stalling as she seeks to craft a suitable lie.[38]

Defense counsel may also use his own silence—the "pin-drop" effect—as a way to attribute blame to a victim. When a witness completes her answer, the lawyer is expected to follow up with a question. When he violates this expectation, greeting the answer with stunned silence, the message is clear: he condemns the victim's answer as damning. And he condemns more effectively by his speechlessness than by words. In this brief example, the numbers in parentheses are seconds of silence:

> DC: It is your testimony? (1.0) under sworn—sworn oath—that in
> *four hours* at the Grainary you only had two drinks?
> V: Yes.
> DC: Linda (45.0).[39]

The forty-five-second delay after the victim's answer speaks volumes. The victim has flatly denied having more than two drinks. Yet, the lawyer wants jurors to find this claim of only two drinks over four full hours in a bar to be incredible. But he does not make his argument overtly. He waits close to one full minute in utter silence, thereby implicitly making his point. He ends the silence by reciting her name—her first name—in a tone of disbelief. His message: she has shown herself to be such a blatant liar that she no longer deserves the respect of courtroom formalities. She is not "Ms. X" but simply "Linda."

To say that most victims are relatively passive in the face of lawyerly linguistic power does not mean, however, that victims have no means to fight back. They do.

Victim Resistance

Victims struggle against defense counsel's control of cross-examination. Notably, a victim may repeatedly respond to requests for details by saying, "I don't remember."[40] To confirm a detail's accuracy might be to acknowledge the truth of a piece of the defendant's case. But to deny a detail's accuracy ("No, I did not smile at him") is to concede that the detail was important enough to remember. To instead respond, "I don't remember," avoids both these traps. Not remembering sends the metamessage, "I had no reason to think he was sexually interested in me, nor did I have any such interest in him, so I just wasn't paying attention to him and didn't notice what he was doing." If believed, therefore, a witness's answer that she does not remember can support nonconsensual intercourse:

> DC: Didn't he ask you if . . . he wanted you to be his girl? Didn't he ask you that?
> V: I don't remember what he said to me that night.
> DC: Does it [the defendant's car] have a spoiler on it?
> V: I don't remember.
> DC: About how far away was the defendant from you when you had this conversation? In feet, if you can estimate it?
> V: I don't know how many feet.
> DC: How many phone calls would you say that you had received from the defendant between February and June twenty-ninth?
> V: I don't know. I didn't answer all of them.
> DC: Excuse me?
> V: I don't remember. I didn't answer all of them.[41]

The device works less well if it is obvious to the jury that the victim is saying that she did not remember precisely in the hope of getting a tactical advantage:

> DC: And at that time he asked you to go out with him, isn't that correct?
> V: Yeah.
> DC: With him. Isn't that so?
> V: I don't remember.[42]

The victim at first admitted being asked out by the defendant. When defense counsel nevertheless repeated the question for emphasis, challenging the victim to admit again that the defendant had indeed asked her out, she changed her answer to "I don't remember." The impression created was that she inadvertently let the truth slip out. But she did not want to admit her error, so she lied, asserting that she simply did not remember. Claiming a memory lapse will also fail as a tactic for details that anyone would remember or where the lapses are so frequent as to seem implausible.

A victim might also resist by offering an alternative description of events. The victim does not explicitly deny the defense version. Rather, the victim's answer offers the alternative:

> DC: Well you had some, uh, fairly lengthy conversation with the defendant, uh, didn't you?
> V: On that evening of February fourteenth? Well, we were all talking.
> DC: Well you knew, at that time, that the defendant was interested in you, didn't you?
> V: He asked me how I'd been en j—just stuff like that.[43]

Here, defense counsel suggested long, intimate conversations between the victim and the defendant. The victim did not deny this allegation directly but changed the description: "We were *all* talking." The alternative description might be consistent with a long conversation, but it was a conversation among members of a group, not a private chat between two intimates. When defense counsel then suggested that the victim knew that the defendant had a sexual interest in her, she replied, "He asked me how I'd been." That description suggests that little happened (something, but not much) that constituted a display of sexual interest. The victim then volunteered "just stuff like that." This last phrase suggests that the rest of the conversation between the victim and the defendant was, *at most*, as intimate as asking her, "How have you been?"[44]

Alternative description in response to a question can also broadly characterize a scene:

> DC: An' during that evening, uh, didn't Mister [name] come over to sit with you?
> V: Sat at *our* table.[45]

By rejecting the suggestion that the defendant specifically came over to *sit with the victim*, replacing it with the defendant's saying simply sitting at "our" table, the victim recharacterizes her entire relationship with the defendant. The victim was simply part of a group that the defendant joined. But the victim was never "with" the defendant.

Victims also, of course, have the option of a more confrontational response: a direct denial, followed by an alternative description:

> *DC:* Now, Miss [name], when you were interviewed by the police, some time, some time later that evening, didn't you tell the police that the defendant had been drinking?
> *V:* No.
> *DC:* Didn't you tell them that . . .
> *V:* I told them there was a cooler in the car, and I never opened it.[46]

The problem with this tactic is that the more confrontational a woman is, in general, the less credible she will be perceived to be.[47]

Despite these modest ways of resisting, however, defense counsel continues to dominate cross-examination. As we have seen, most witnesses are easily bullied away from longer answers, back to yes/no responses. More important, because the lawyer asks the questions, the lawyer can use the various poetic and other devices discussed above to manage impressions. One well-known scholar of language studies put it this way:

> What we find . . . is that the person who is asking the questions seems to have first rights to perform an operation on the set of answers. You can call it "draw a conclusion." Socrates used the phrase "add them up." It was very basic to his way of doing dialectic. He would go along and then say at some point, "Well, let's see where we are. Let's add up the answers and draw some conclusions." And it's that right that provides for a lot of what look like struggling in some conversations, where the attempt to move into the position of questioner seems to be quite a thing that persons try to do. . . . As long as one is in the position of doing the questions, then in part one has control of the conversation.[48]

The "struggling" in ordinary conversation over who asks the questions does not, however, happen in trials. In trials, it is only the lawyer who asks the questions. Consequently, it is the lawyer who "control[s] . . . the conversation."

Direct Examination

On direct examination, of course, it is the prosecutor who does the questioning. His goal, unlike defense counsel's, will be to maximize how much the victim speaks, encouraging her to give long, narrative answers. The result indeed will usually be that the witness, not the lawyer, does most of the talking. But this talking will not always be in the form of un-interrupted narrative. "It calls for a narrative, Your Honor" is a short-hand objection for saying, "If the witness gives a long answer to a broad question, she may say something inadmissible before I can object. You can't unring a bell. Once the jury hears the answer, an instruction to ig-nore it will be useless. Therefore, Your Honor, please ask prosecuting counsel to use shorter, less open-ended questions." Where this objection is sustained, the victim's testimony will be fragmented into shorter pieces. Such testimony is less persuasive than a more natural, open-ended narra-tive.[49]

Indeed, objections generally serve as a way for defense counsel to wrest control from the victim and the prosecutor. There is an enormous num-ber of possible objections. Some objections exclude evidence entirely on grounds of "hearsay," "lay opinion," "lack of personal knowledge," or "inadmissible character," among many other options. Other objections require questions to be rephrased because they are ambiguous, assume facts not in evidence, inaccurately restate testimony, and so on. Objec-tions, therefore, force the witness to delete large portions of her story, fragmenting it, while rattling her with interruptions. Objections increase the adversarial heat, intimidating the witness. It is true that defense coun-sel will also face objections from the prosecutor when the defense cross-examines the victim. But this does not equalize the effect of objections. Objections always shift speaking time and attention away from the vic-tim to the lawyers. Leading questions have the same "lawyercentric" ef-fect, and they are generally permitted only on cross. Yet attention on the lawyers, not the victim, is precisely what defense counsel wants. For the defense, objections to a victim's direct examination thus complement leading questions on cross as a way of dominating the conversation.[50]

Too many objections will, of course, annoy the jury. Yet a few carefully placed objections, followed by justifying minispeeches within the jury's hearing, can be quite effective.[51] Even without objections, however, the victim faces a difficult task. The trial is a "ritualized art form." The ritual is necessary to obtain public legitimacy. "Formality, ceremony, and the inculcation of awe and intimidation . . . [are] aspects of the trial specta-cle . . . [as] artful creations. . . ."[52]

> The judge's role is especially revealing in these respects. In the courtroom
> the trial judge enjoys virtually absolute authority and an exalted status that
> traditional rituals underline: the audience rises when the judge enters the

room; she is addressed as "Your Honor"; her seat is elevated; lawyers must ask permission to "approach the bench"; the judge can punish lawyers, witnesses, or spectators for misbehavior, including insufficient respect for the court; and the judge exercises the most dramatic individual authority known in a democracy: to determine the severity of punishment of people convicted of violating a law.[53]

Awe, intimidation, and adversariness; reliving rape trauma; and lawyer domination of language are a combination well designed to silence victim voices.

Yet, the logic of our justice system itself further promotes such silencing:

> Trial judges are severely constrained in yet another way that is rarely apparent to the public and probably not usually apparent even to the judges. Their mandate to apply statutory, constitutional, and common law to particular cases means that there is a strong bias toward ignoring or minimizing the social and economic conditions that explain a great deal of the behavior that is found in violation of those laws. To put the point another way, the rules and the conduct of trials artfully place the blame for illegal conduct on individuals who act rather than on the social conditions that often make it inevitable that they will violate the law. As Anatole France put it, the law in its majesty penalizes both the rich and the poor for stealing a loaf of bread or sleeping under bridges. In this way the law helps judges to rationalize classist, racist, and sexist actions with a clear conscience.[54]

Judges therefore fail to consider the "social and economic conditions" of patriarchy in making their trial rulings. They fail to see that the fundamental assumption of the adversary system—that opponents are equally matched—does not hold in rape trials. Victims are usually not practiced in the adversarial machismo of our system. Business as usual in the courtroom aids patriarchy, not justice.[55]

PART III

Feminist Evidence Law

Until now, I have been concerned with explaining why the adversary system reflects male assumptions about justice and gender. Those assumptions distort jury reasoning in rape cases. I here suggest a feminist alternative, explaining how to re-vision the adversary system to promote fairer rape trials. I also argue that this feminist revisioning is mandated by certain basic constitutional values, if not necessarily by current understandings of the constitutional text.

Chapter 6 examines the flaws in the market metaphor on which the adversary system is modeled. Market mechanisms fail at rape trials because the market reinforces gender bias and ignores "externalities"—costs that the trial imposes on society but not on the trial participants. Chapter 6 suggests reforms to the trial market to reflect more feminist notions of justice that reduce gender bias and account for externalities. Those reforms include permitting uninterrupted victim narratives on direct examination, using empathic experts, and using "intermediaries," neutral professionals who "translate" defense counsel's questions into less abusive forms. Chapter 6 concludes by defending the intermediary procedure against assertions that it violates the defendant's constitutional right to confront the witnesses against him.

Chapter 7 argues that today's procedures at rape trials effectively silence women as a group for political purposes. Because rape trials currently mute women's voices, today's procedures threaten both First Amendment free speech and equal protection values. Chapter 7 appeals to legislatures to enact the reforms recommended in Chapter 6 to give women a more equal voice at rape trials. Chapter 7 also argues that the reforms suggested here are necessary to enable the jury better to fulfill its constitutional function of checking abuses of public and private power, including patriarchal power.

The final chapter offers a brief historical commentary on how the reforms suggested here fit into the history of rape law reform. Having reviewed where rape law reform has gone in the past, it concludes with a call for legislative action.

6

Market Failure

The adversary system is based on a market metaphor. In the market for justice, lawyers sell persuasive discourse to jurors in exchange for a verdict. The free clash of opposing ideas achieves truth as each side competitively seeks to prove its case while pointing out the weaknesses of the opponent's case. The battle of equally matched adversaries is the way to justice, so the judge must largely stay out of the way.[1]

Supplementary markets help to improve the working of the trial market. Thus, lawyers are expected to turn information exchange and settlement offers into a game. The goal is to give the other side as little information and as little money as possible. But the competitive struggle by lawyers over these matters will perversely maximize high-quality information needed for trial. This information in turn leads either to fair settlements or well-informed verdicts.[2]

The competition between the lawyers is, moreover, not a competition goading each to be the best that he or she can be. It is thus not a race in which all can hope to cross the finish line simultaneously. Instead, the game is zero-sum: one lawyer wins only by another's losing. Besides, winning is all, and devotion to the client is alone what matters. Despite rhetoric about the lawyer's being an "officer of the court," the lawyer has little real obligation to anyone other than the client. The profession imposes few limits on the means to meeting that obligation.[3] Little has changed in this regard in the almost two centuries since Lord Brougham, in defending Queen Caroline, said of the lawyer-advocate:

> [I]n the discharge of his duty he knows but one person in all the world, and that person is his client. To save that client by all means and expedients, and at all hazards and costs to other persons, and, amongst them, to himself, is his first and only duty; and in performing this duty he must not regard the alarm, the torments, and the destruction which he may bring upon others.[4]

Some professional groups have recently made token efforts to tidy up the image of lawyer brutality with civility codes, and some courts have done so by civil discovery reform that requires one side's lawyer, even if not asked, to hand over important information to the other side. But even these small changes have largely not reached criminal litigators.[5]

The breadth of the "ethically" available means in the lawyer's arsenal is shocking to laypersons. Lawyers may discredit witnesses whom the lawyers know to be telling the truth. They can exploit an adversary's mistakes, stay willfully ignorant of facts that might limit their strategic options, and coach witnesses in ways that at times may encourage particular answers that the lawyers need. Lawyers may often use dilatory tactics so long as there is also some other weak but "nonfrivolous" purpose for them. They may sometimes lie in negotiations, rely on investigators who use false identities, and take advantage of another lawyer's ignorance. All this is justified in the name of adversarial combat.[6]

Not every lawyer uses these tactics. Sometimes civility and honesty are more effective than rudeness and lies. Other lawyers' own personal sense of ethics moderates their behavior. But the lawyers' culture promotes winning at almost any cost, and few lawyers remain immune to victory's pull.

Evidence law, which, along with ethics codes, provides the few available limits on lawyers' means, warmly embraces the competitive ideal. In one recent case, *United States v. Mezzanato*,[7] a prosecutor agreed to negotiate a guilty plea with the defendant on one condition: that if no plea agreement was reached, the prosecutor could use the defendant's statements during the negotiations against him at trial. That condition required the defendant to waive the protection of an evidence rule that prohibited any trial use of plea-negotiation statements. Congress passed that rule to promote the candor needed to achieve guilty plea agreements, reducing the need for expensive trials. The defendant, probably because of his weak bargaining power, agreed to the condition. But the defendant and prosecutor ultimately did not reach a plea bargain. The defendant was convicted when his plea-negotiation statements were then used against him at trial. In upholding the conviction, the United States Supreme Court approved the transaction as a fair market exchange: "[I]f the prosecutor is interested in 'buying' the reliability assurance that accompanies a waiver agreement, then precluding waiver can only stifle the market for plea bargains. A defendant can 'maximize' what he has to 'sell' only if he is permitted to offer what the prosecutor is most interested in buying."[8]

The market metaphor similarly governs the law of spousal immunity. In most jurisdictions, a prosecutor cannot compel a reluctant spouse to testify against a defendant spouse. Although many of these states make an exception to this rule for certain crimes committed by one spouse against the other, that exception is frequently interpreted narrowly so that it does not apply to significant numbers of spousal assaults. Furthermore, some jurisdictions recognize no exception whatsoever for interspousal crimes. Whether a battered wife will testify against her husband is often thus her choice. The courts deem it irrelevant that she may fear her husband or worry about her children's safety. The rationale is a market-based one: she can decide whether the costs of testifying outweigh the benefits. But the result of the woman's "free" choice often is that the batterer goes free, only to batter again.[9]

That the masculine market competition of the adversary system is unpleasant is not necessarily a reason to reject it completely. What, after all, would be the alternative in a criminal trial: an inquisitorial investigation by free-roving judges in the European style? That is neither wise nor practical for the American culture. Similarly, evidence law's frequent adoption of the market metaphor does not alone prove that it is unwise. But the present conception of the metaphor fails to achieve truth or justice in many criminal trials, especially ones for rape. Understanding why this is so, and what kinds of reforms are necessary, has broad implications for the law of evidence generally and helps us fix what is broken in rape law reform.

The Adversary System's Flaws

There are two major relevant flaws in the adversary system: first, it reinforces gender bias; and, second, it ignores externalities.

How Adversarialism Reinforces Gender Bias

Markets, many economists argue, do not like bias.[10] Suppose a racist eyeglass manufacturer refuses to hire African Americans. A competitor hires only the best workers of all races. With a better workforce, the nonracist makes lower-cost, higher-quality eyeglasses than the racist. Eyeglass buyers flock to buy the cheaper, better glasses, driving the racially biased manufacturer into bankruptcy.

A similar theory ostensibly governs the courtroom. An adversary appealing to racial bias faces an opponent who explains the nature and illogic of the racist appeal. Jurors recognize the illogic, rejecting racism and choosing the better product, that is, the side with the soundest arguments. The court intervenes, but only to prevent overt emotional appeals, such as to race hatred. In the free marketplace of ideas, emotionally detached jurors choose reason over bias.

The theory is wrong. The adversary system reinforces rather than cures bias. To see how this is so, return to our eyeglass manufacturer. In an openly racist society, like the American South of the 1950s, buyers might flee (boycott) a manufacturer who hires blacks into skilled, high-paying jobs. The psychic benefit of whites keeping blacks "in their place" exceeds the financial cost of buying more expensive, lower-quality eyeglasses. To survive, the nonracist manufacturer must fire his black workers, even if he thinks doing so is morally wrong and economically inefficient.

The same principle operates in the courtroom. A lawyer who fails to appeal to race or gender bias will start losing cases if biased appeals work with juries. The psychic benefit to whites of their (often unconscious) racism may exceed the psychic cost of buying into an otherwise flawed argument. To survive, the lawyer will have to incorporate bias into trial strategies and arguments. Indeed, one strident objection by members of the American Bar Association to recent efforts to prohibit race- or gender-biased appeals is that they work. To bar them would thereby undermine the lawyers' duty of zealous representation.[11]

Even many well-meaning jurors are swayed by the biases fed by the justice market. The problem stems from the nature of cultural narratives.[12] The narratives, as we have seen in the context of rape, construct how we see, select, reject, and interpret reality. They do their work through largely unconscious cognitive processes. A committed feminist juror may simply not believe a rape victim who fails to fit "good woman" cultural narratives, despite the juror's progressive political commitments. Lawyers' efforts to change a juror's perceptions may fail too because the juror unconsciously interprets new stories in light of old ones, rejecting tales deviating too far from dominant narratives. The juror simply will not see his or her own bias at work.

Other, less progressive jurors may, on the other hand, view bias as part of the prefeminist past or may even openly embrace patriarchal values.

But such jurors face no market punishment, no loss of job or diminution of income because of their biased or uninformed vote.

The lawyers' combat compounds the problem. The adversaries present jurors with a dichotomous choice: either the prosecution theory or the defense theory is right. Moreover, competitive pressures often push each side toward extreme positions. Jurors are thus denied the multiplicity of views needed for fair judgment. Moderate theories or ones completely outside the box constructed by the lawyers are not heard. But lawyers' immoderate appeals based on inadequate information and options tempt jurors to fill in the gaps by drawing on their own biased preconceptions.

The assumption of equally matched adversaries is also often wrong. One lawyer may have more money to conduct more thorough investigations and hire better experts than the other. Or one lawyer may simply be more talented than the other. In such cases, an adversary loses because of poor performance, not better arguments. The assumption of truth's emerging from a fair fight between opposed positions in a "free market of ideas" fails.

The adversarial model's binary thinking further tends to promote debate over whether a thing exists at all rather than what is its true nature. Hence, both sides may buy into dominant notions of "consent": the defense showing its presence, the prosecutor showing its absence. But a more productive exchange would seek to press jurors to deliberate about the very nature of consent itself, for the term is not and cannot be fully defined by the law.

The judge's understanding of evidence rules further obscures a rape victim's ability to tell her story to the jury. Most judges are committed to race- and gender-neutral application of evidence law. All witnesses, male or female, are examined in the same fashion. But current neutrality masks past wrongs. The relevant past wrong here is gender-role socialization. Partly because of that socialization, many female rape victims will use "women's ways of speaking" in court. Yet that manner of speaking may do much to undermine a woman's credibility, especially when male rules for witness examination silence, mute, or distort the woman's testimony. The application of neutral rules fails to recognize difference and promotes injustice.

The very nature of adversarial tit-for-tat debate also requires one side provisionally to accept aspects of the other's position, for you cannot debate if you disagree about everything. Lawyers tend, therefore, to attack one argument at a time. Judges, indeed, insist on such a sequential focus, generally ruling on objections individually, in isolation, as they arise. Unfortunately, although each isolated ruling may seem perfectly fair and reasonable, the judge is thereby distracted from its holistic and systemic effects. Each small ruling may imperceptibly hurt the rape victim's position, and the accumulation of these small disadvantages works to mark the rape victim as not credible. Similar effects on women's advancement have been documented in other settings. For example, the adversarial style of law school teaching leads female students to have just slightly lower grades than their equally qualified male counterparts. But those slight differences give men more honors, like being allowed to serve on law review, that lead to more prestigious jobs and from there to positions of power. In similar fashion, rulings that insist on male rules of interruption, timing, and topic control cumulate to minimize the rape victim's persuasive power.[13]

Judges are also acculturated to view their role as resolving the narrow dispute before them. The substantive criminal law, itself molded by ideological considerations, similarly tends to focus on the criminal act itself and the immediately preceding circumstances. Contributing factors rooted in the defendant's or victim's life stories or in broader social injustices are usually ignored. Judicial notions of relevancy are thereby cramped, and efforts to educate the jury about such pervasive social ills as patriarchy may fail. But without such education a jury has little chance to resist dominant rape narratives.[14]

Similarly, judges view appeals to emotion as irrelevant. This view is based on a false reason/emotion dichotomy. Cognitive scientists widely recognize that emotion often plays a role in our reasoning. Emotions identify what matters to us and permit us to assign values to what we perceive and do. The key is to distinguish between "rational" emotions, which are properly part of public judgment, and irrational ones. One rational emotion, empathy, is central to all criminal trials. We cannot know a defendant's or victim's mental state if we do not know what she thought and felt at the time. Yet, limits on psychological experts, an insistence on a witness's calm demeanor, and a refusal to let her tell her narrative in a natural fashion may make empathy hard for jurors to feel. Note that empathy is both reason and emotion, permitting fair assessment. To seek a jury's empathy is not to seek to sway its passions but to inform its judgment.[15]

Narrow relevancy notions and lawyers' control over questioning pace and style reinforce as well lawyers' tendency to craft their own tales rather than facilitate the telling of the client's or victim's. In any trial, lawyers try to fit client narratives into preexisting legal categories. By omitting or reordering facts to achieve this fit, they may distort the client's tale. These tendencies are buttressed in rape trials by the various mechanisms discussed in this book for excluding or muting the client or rape victim's tale. Once again, dominant narratives, and thus gender biases, are re-created.[16]

How Adversarialism Ignores Externalities

DEFINING TERMS

The ill effects of the adversary system also extend beyond the courtroom because the justice market generates negative externalities: costs of a market transaction imposed on persons who are not parties to the exchange. A classic example is an auto manufacturer whose plant pollutes the skies and land of the plant's neighbors. Absent government regulation, it is the neighbors who bear the costs of the pollution, not the manufacturers, distributors, or purchasers of the cars. Consequently, the manufacturer has no incentive to reduce the pollution.[17]

Justice systems, like auto manufacturers, impose costs on others not fully borne by the parties to a lawsuit. The United States Supreme Court recognized this in *J.E.B. v. Alabama*.[18] The Court held that the equal protection clause of the Fourteenth Amendment to the Constitution prohibits the state's dismissal of persons from a jury based on their gender. Central to the holding were the Court's concerns about group-subordinating, antirepublican externalities. Although the Court recognized that litigants and individual jurors were hurt by gender discrimination, it worried more about the ill effects on the broader community that would come about through the law's expressive function:

> Striking individual jurors on the assumption that they hold particular views simply because of their gender is "practically a brand upon them, affixed by law, an assertion of their inferiority." [Citations omitted.] It denigrates the dignity of the excluded juror, and, for a woman, reinvokes a history of exclusion from political participation. The message it sends to all those in the courtroom, and *all those who later may learn of the discriminatory act*, is that certain individuals, for no reason other than gender, are presumed unqualified by state actors to decide important questions upon which reasonable persons could disagree.[19]

The Court here recognized that the exclusionary message itself constituted subordination. But elsewhere in its opinion, the Court also decried other ill effects. First, the message threatened to promote current exclusion of women from civic life; this result could come about because the message "ratif[ied] and reinforce[d]" the very stereotypes that had historically been used to justify devaluing women's potential civic contributions.[20]

Second, appeal to those stereotypes created cynicism about the jury's neutrality and the judicial system's stacking the deck in one side's favor. Such cynicism was especially likely, said the Court, in cases where "gender-related issues are prominent," such as rape, sexual harassment, or paternity.[21]

The Court also worried about the impact of gender discrimination on the jury's deliberative, political function. The jury's political role, the Court suggested, enhances respect for, and the proper functioning of, a republican democratic society. The equal protection right to nondiscrimination thus extended to the individual jurors themselves. That right to equal opportunity to participate reaffirmed that "all citizens, regardless of race, ethnicity, or gender, have the chance to take part directly in our democracy."[22] Indeed, noted the Court, with the exception of voting, the honor and privilege of jury duty is most citizens' most significant opportunity to participate in the democratic process.

The Court hinted, as well, that women had a special role in that process. It agreed that women do not by virtue of their shared sex alone act as a class. Nor does women's presence on a jury necessarily alter a case's ultimate verdict. Nevertheless, the Court cited with approval an earlier case that emphasized that women often bring new voices to debate in a way that enriches the democratic process: "The truth is that the two sexes are *not* fungible; a community made up exclusively of one is different from a community composed of both; the subtle interplay of influence one on the other is among the imponderables."[23]

J.E.B. involved the state as a party in a civil suit to compel J.E.B. to pay child support. The *J.E.B.* principle also applies in criminal cases. Well-respected commentators have argued, however, that criminal cases should be different. Their reasoning: in criminal cases so much is at stake and the state has so many resources that unbridled adversarialism is necessary to check abused state power.[24] Therefore, externalities akin to those discussed in *J.E.B* by the Court pale in comparison to the need to counterbalance state power.

But the assumption that the defendant is no match for the state is sometimes wrong. Indeed, this entire book has in part been an attempt to demonstrate that in rape cases involving a consent defense, it is the defendant who has more power. In rape cases, *reducing* adversarialism may in fact be necessary to check state power, for the state otherwise becomes complicit in gender bias.

More important, the greater need for some kinds of adversarialism in criminal cases does not justify all current tactics. We have seen that unbridled adversarialism can reinforce dominant narratives, leading to ill-informed juries engaging in stilted deliberations. A properly functioning jury is one of our best checks on abuses of both state and private power.[25] In any event, the excessive state power argument for unbridled adversarialism in criminal cases simply gives too little weight to countervailing externalities.

The current version of the adversary system is not the only one that can be conceived. Leading criminal practitioners have begun to concede that some change is needed. Three such practitioners recently put this well:

> An individual cannot be un-raped or un-robbed. But the criminal justice system should at least prevent any additional victimization that may otherwise arise from the adversarial nature of the trial process. For example, while vigorous cross-examination is an essential part of any trial, it should be used to clarify, not to intimidate, browbeat, trick, or embarrass a witness merely to gain a tactical advantage.[26]

THE PUBLIC COSTS OF A RAPE TRIAL

Current rape-trial evidence practices generate negative externalities much like those in *J.E.B.* In particular, it is the everyday acts of discrimination and abuse that constitute patriarchy. Every time that a boss pats a woman employee's hip, or a woman employee's contributions at a meeting are ignored, patriarchy is re-created. Correspondingly, every time we treat a rape victim as neither competent nor credible *because* she speaks "like a woman," we re-create women's subordination.[27]

Trials, unlike pats on a hip and stifled comments at business meetings, are *public* events. Widespread dissemination of trial practices, such as the "second rape" of rape victims by defense counsel, occurs in news reports, movies, radio, popular books, and television programs. The gendered messages at rape trials are thus heard powerfully both inside and outside the courtroom.[28] Those messages themselves constitute the subordination of women as a group. Relationships of subordination exist partly because we agree at some level, as expressed in our language practices, that one group is superior, one subordinate. It is this type of argument on which some feminists rely in contending that "pornography is not expression depicting subordination, but is the *practice of subordination* itself."[29]

Rape trial language practices also constitute the "practice of subordination itself." The implicit agreement at rape trials is that the victim, because she is a woman, is subordinate to male offenders, lawyers, and justice institutions. The male rules for trial discourse send precisely the message that women are of lower status than men.

Social groups value high status as a good in its own right. High status may also bring a group more access to money, jobs, and political power. Governmental expressions of group ranking are among the most powerful indicators of status; the age of Jim Crow is an obvious example. Groups accordingly vie for control of government expression, and various modern debates over abortion laws, homosexual marriage, and pornography can be understood as efforts to control group status through such expression. Remember that rape victims use "women's language" at trial partly because they and other trial participants' have been conditioned to perceive women as of low social status. It is male speech that our culture sees as the speech of Reason, female speech as that of Unreason.[30]

A group's status is also affected by its access to public speech. When a group's voice is silenced, it cannot present counterimages of its competence and worth. The group might be labeled lazy, dependent, or stupid, categories that lead to skepticism toward any speech the group does have. The muting of women's voices at rape trials thus worsens the status of women as a whole. As in *J.E.B.*, their exclusion from equal participation in the trial process is "practically a brand upon them, affixed by law, an assertion of their inferiority."[31]

As in *J.E.B.*, that exclusion also denies women as a group the benefits of participating in the jury trial as an institution central to republican self-government. Society too is denied the benefits of women's special voices. When our rape trial practices bar the jury from hearing the victim's full story in the context of patriarchy, we stifle serious public deliberation.[32]

One of our methods for stifling that deliberation—adversarial warfare—reflects an individualistic, one-up, one-down notion of social life. Human relationships are portrayed as entirely competitive. Alternative types of human relationships, such as care and empathy, are ignored.

Conditions necessary for the flourishing of caring relations, for example, protecting privacy about our sexual selves (as serious rape shield laws would do), are devalued. Furthermore, by instantiating dominant cultural stories, we treat the rape victim and others as categories, not individuals. In this way the rape trial teaches poor lessons about civic life and human meaning.[33]

Rape trial practices also reinforce oppressive social norms. Among the gendered norms are that a woman should not go out at night without a male protector, should dress modestly in public, and should not openly express sexual interest in a man. Women are taught that violating these norms risks rape. Correspondingly, to violate these norms risks being labeled a "slut," for whom any assault is nonrape. When the rape victim is treated as a slut at trial and her assailant found not guilty, the citizenry publicly expresses approval of these norms. Yet, these norms limit women's freedom of movement and expression. They contribute to a gendered caste system.[34]

Rape trial practices thus reenact women's subordination, lower their status as a group, exclude them from public deliberations, denigrate their concerns with empathy and connectedness, and limit their autonomy— external costs entirely ignored by dominant views of the benefits of trial adversarialism.

Toward Reduction of the Cost of Externalities

Separate versus Connected Knowing

Feminist researchers have explored ways of knowing the world. Two contrasting ways are "separate knowing" and "connected knowing."[35]

The "separate knower" is the model for our adversary system. The separate knower plays the doubting game, looking for flaws in reasoning: he or she questions whether a proponent of an idea has misinterpreted the evidence, ignored competing interpretations, or omitted contradicting data. The separate knower relies on objective and impersonal standards agreed upon and codified by logicians and scientists.

The connected knower, by contrast, reads with an empathic, receptive eye. Instead of the doubting game, the connected knower plays the believing game. Another's initially absurd-seeming ideas are not immediately rejected. Instead the connected knower asks, "What do you see?

Help me to share the vision in your head." The concern is not with a position's soundness but its meaning for the proponent.

Separate knowing takes an adversarial stance toward ideas. The typical mode of discourse is argument. Images of war are used in describing separate knowing: "I never take anything for granted. I just tend to see the contrary. I like playing the devil's advocate, arguing the opposite of what somebody's thinking, thinking of exceptions, or thinking of a different train of thought."[36] Separate knowing is associated with Tannen's report talk.

Connected knowers instead try to find what is right in an idea, even if it initially seems wrong. "Why do you think that?" is the first question on the connected knower's lips when facing an initially worrisome argument: "When I have an idea about something, and it differs from the way another person is thinking about it, I'll usually try to look at it from that person's point of view, see how he could say that, why they think they're right, why it makes sense."[37] Connected knowing is reminiscent of Tannen's "rapport talk," for such knowing involves a relationship between knower and known, a "bold swinging into the life of the other."[38]

Separate knowers, finally, regard each person as an object, an instance of a category to be measured against universal objective standards. Connected knowers, however, focus on the uniqueness of the person or object in all its particularity of detail. Firsthand experiences and anecdote therefore become for the connected knower, unlike the separate knower, relevant sources of data.

Neither way of knowing is easy. Separate knowing requires emotional distance, skepticism, and endless challenging. Connected knowing involves imagining the other, a process that requires drawing on personal experiences, metaphorical connections, analogies, and associations. Furthermore, both ways of knowing involve judgment. But connected knowers, unlike separate ones, postpone judgment as long as possible, for only then can one have the open-mindedness to perceive another's views accurately.

Each type of knowing has its strengths and weaknesses, but connected knowing is a superior first step when we must judge another person: "No matter how mean or hideous a man's life is, the first thing is to understand him."[39] Moral judgment, which is involved in every criminal trial, first requires taking a perspective, imagining the other's perceptions, thoughts, and emotions. Only when we have stepped into another's shoes can we then step back for external assessment.[40]

Yet, external assessment also requires separate knowing. The separate knower's skeptical stance may help us to identify lies or confusion. Moreover, the separate knower's emotional and intellectual distance may ultimately be needed for the external assessment involved in fair judging. Even so, without the connected knower's openness, search for uniqueness, and capacity for empathy, our public judgments may be based on distorted or incomplete knowledge.[41]

The ideal model for the courtroom, therefore, is "constructed knowing," a type of knowing that makes flexible and complementary use of both separate and connected procedures. It modifies the separate knowing of our current adversary system without rejecting it entirely.[42]

The male model of adversarialism would be replaced by a more empathic alternative, one that better enables juries truly to hear the victim's tale. Fully informed, empathic judgment, less encumbered by patriarchal bias, in turn reduces negative externalities. The market for justice begins to reflect more accurately the social costs and benefits of decision.

Empathic Adversarialism

What would a more empathic adversarialism, one modeled after constructed knowing, look like in rape cases? It would have at least three features: (1) rape victims would be permitted to tell uninterrupted narratives on direct examination; (2) they would be cross-examined through an "intermediary" who would translate defense counsel's questions into less abusive forms; and (3) their testimony would be supplemented by expert testimony about rapes' social context, men's and women's differing communication styles, and the subconscious cognitive processes blocking rape jurors' empathy for victims.

UNINTERRUPTED NARRATIVES

Part of a rape victim's problem on direct examination is her inability to tell an uninterrupted narrative of her abuse. The prosecutor asks a series of questions that preclude the victim's simple telling of her tale.

Prosecutors do this to ensure that only information helpful to the state is revealed while inadmissible evidence is avoided. Moreover, prosecutors fear the defense objection, "Calls for a narrative, Your Honor!" The objection argues that broad, open-ended questions such as "What happened?" lead to objectionable answers. Consequently, the defense presses the point that the prosecutor must use shorter, focused questions that make clear what information is requested. In that way the defense may object to the question itself before any harmful answer.[43]

Prosecutors understand, of course, that uninterrupted narratives are more persuasive[44] and proceed by aiming for a middle ground between an open and a controlled narrative. But sharp defense counsel find grounds to object. They object precisely to create the "staccato effect" of a choppy, question-by-question presentation. Objections also give defense counsel the chance to make miniarguments mocking the victim's testimony. Thus do defense counsel draw the jury's attention away from the victim. Side bar conferences to resolve these objections outside the jury's hearing only lengthen the interruption. The result is a confusing, often technical-sounding recitation. What is more, the victim is unsettled by the adversarial warfare. She is also frustrated by, and less convincing because of, her inability to speak in her own way.[45]

The solution is to permit the victim to speak in an uninterrupted narrative. She should be free to tell her tale in a way closer to what is natural for her and relatively free of defense counsel intimidation. Several procedural changes are needed to make this work.

The prosecution in particular must treat rape victims as equals. That means extended preparation sessions in which the prosecutor educates the victim about the law of evidence. I routinely held such victim preparation sessions when I was a prosecutor. When, for example, a victim recounted hearsay, I would explain in simple terms what hearsay was and why it was inadmissible. I would suggest natural ways for her to avoid the objectionable part of her answer. At the same time, I took care to help her search for her own words, not mine. Explanation and practice enabled most victims to testify naturally within the confines of the rules of evidence.

Trial judges already have the power to permit uninterrupted narratives,[46] but they often avoid them for fear of evidence-code breaches. I found it effective to be able to represent to the court, "Your Honor, I have carefully explained to the witness what she may not say and why. I am confident that she can testify in an unobjectionable fashion." Judges who then let the witness testify largely on her own soon learned they could trust my representation. I was amazed, however, at how few prosecutors followed my approach. Many simply thought victims incapable of understanding or had a need to take charge. I found even victims with little formal education up to the task. They also appreciated the respect I showed them by assuming their intelligence and letting them find their own voice.

Nor did I fear that defense counsel would impeach the victim by inquiring about our preparation sessions. Witness preparation sessions are both common and ethical.[47] Defense attorneys who asked heard victims say things like "Mr. Taslitz told me to tell the truth, to explain things in my own words, and to obey the evidence law." Such answers brought a smile to my face.

Even such preparation sessions do not avoid all need for focused questions, however. Witnesses sometimes leave out important details. Reminding witnesses of those details in preparation sessions can help minimize the need for focused questions on the stand. When a prosecutor asks such questions, it should done infrequently, concisely, and unobtrusively, prodding the victim back to her tale.

Still, even the best preparation sessions cannot stop defense counsel from objecting on some arguable ground. To the prosecutor, these objections seem designed purely to break up the victim's narrative. But defense counsel will argue that the objections must be made in a timely fashion so as not to waive the client's rights on appeal. To avoid these objections, therefore, evidence codes must be amended to permit defense counsel to raise objections in rape cases *after* the victim's testimony without waiving appellate rights.[48] Defense counsel will challenge the efficacy of this solution because the "cat is out of the bag." The jury will have heard the objectionable matter, and no instruction to ignore what they heard will work. My response is to allow trial judges to retain the authority to return to ordinary modes of examination if the victim proves egregiously incapable of playing by the rules. But prosecutors, wanting to avoid appeals, will have a strong incentive to prepare witnesses well. Judges certainly also might cut off victims as soon as they start to mouth objectionable matters. "He told me . . ." is, for example, a flag that the witness may be about to recount hearsay. There are risks in an uninterrupted narrative, but the risks are worth it.

THE INTERMEDIARY

The incentives of the adversary system are such that it is hard to expect defense counsel to cross-examine rape victims in ways that clarify rather than obfuscate. Defense counsel will continue to use metaphoric word choice, rapid-fire questioning, unsupportable innuendo, known objectionable matter, insult, and confusion. No matter what the change in evidence codes or the high-minded calls for civility, defense counsel will zealously do whatever works.

The trial judge is ill-equipped to curb defense counsel's tactics. The need to appear impartial renders the trial judge reluctant to intervene on cross-examination. Indeed, the judge's own socialization in adversarial culture makes distinguishing aggressive from abusive and distorting cross hard. Furthermore, if the judge joins too actively in questioning, the distance necessary to the role of objective umpire may be lost. Additionally, the judge is not trained in the skills needed for noncombative communication and the building of empathic human relationships.[49]

The solution is to create a buffer—an"intermediary"—between victim and defense counsel in consent defense cases. This intermediary is modeled after a similar program that has shown promise in child-sexual-assault cases in South Africa, another common law, adversarial regime.[50]

The intermediary would be a nonlawyer, preferably a social worker or psychologist trained in the workings of the adversary system, the dynamics of rape, and the complexities of male-female communications styles and jury reasoning processes. He or she would be certified as having adequate theoretical knowledge and clinical experience. But the intermediary would be a neutral participant, never meeting or discussing the case with any witness or attorney. The intermediary's role would be that of an aide to the court in administering justice.

The intermediary's primary function would be to "translate" defense counsel's questions into a less abusive, more productive form. The procedure would work as follows. After properly instructing the jury on the point of the procedure and the need for decorum, the judge, attorneys, and defendant leave the courtroom, perhaps going to the judge's chambers. They leave so that jurors do not hear defense counsel's questions directly or hear legal argument about those questions. The victim and intermediary remain in the courtroom, however. The judge, attorneys, and lawyers see and hear all that happens in the courtroom by means of closed circuit television. The intermediary can hear defense questions and judicial instructions through a headset. In the rare and unlikely event that the judge needs, for reasons of decorum, to address the jury directly during the victim's testimony, the judge can either reenter the courtroom or speak on an intercom.

Defense counsel then begins his examination, but the intermediary, who is the only person in the courtroom hearing defense counsel's questions, is free to alter them. Generally, the intermediary would be required to convey a question's gist, if not its precise form, and not to weaken or erode intelligent, meaningful, and penetrating cross-examination. The intermediary seeks instead to limit aggression, intimidation, and unfair, insensitive, misleading, or confusing questions. The point of the procedure is to encourage clarifying rather than abusive or confusing questioning.

The judge would retain ultimate control over the proceedings, intervening if necessary, to counteract any intermediary bias (which should result in barring the intermediary from future proceedings), to improve clarity, to respond to sound defense objections, or to protect the witness. A concern for efficiency might require asking defense counsel to provide judge, prosecutor, and intermediary—but not the victim—with a written statement of the most important cross-examination questions immediately before the testimony. That would enable rephrasing of major questions before the victim testifies, although defense counsel must remain free to be flexible as cross proceeds.

To avoid the appearance of special distrust by the court of defense counsel, the intermediary procedure should also be used during direct examination of the victim by the prosecutor. The uninterrupted narrative procedures for direct examination would still be used, just as I have described them. But the actual questions in court would come from the mouth of the intermediary. The intermediary would be expected to rephrase any unfair prosecutor questions, but the intermediary's goal would, unlike on cross, still be to achieve an uninterrupted narrative.

These procedures help to educate the rape trial judiciary in new forms of witness examination while permitting the sitting trial judge the distance to serve as a relatively objective umpire, managing the rules of fairness. The victim is shielded from a "second rape" by cross-examination.[51] Defense counsel retains appellate rights and significant control over what will be asked and when. At the same time, truthfinding is promoted by minimizing misleading adversarial linguistic abuses. Ultimately, however, the success of such a program depends on trial judge education in, and acceptance of, the procedure.

Because the double jeopardy clause prohibits retrying an acquitted defendant, a prosecutor has no right to appeal when a judge's manifestation of bias at trial leads to a not guilty verdict.[52] If the trial judiciary resists the intermediary procedure, it will not work. But the judiciary as a whole has sometimes taken responsibility for resocializing its members. Most recently, the federal courts have undertaken a substantial campaign to educate judges to be more informed and effective screens against baseless scientific testimony.[53] The problem of sexual assault deserves a similar commitment of resources.

The intermediary program also must tolerate some mistakes. Implementation and error will doubtless reveal flaws that require correction. Certainly, time will be needed to train all relevant parties, but especially the intermediaries. Mock use of the technique to train intermediaries and improve the procedure would be advisable before it is implemented. Additionally, the procedure should be viewed as experimental but worth trying. The similar program in South Africa for child sexual abuse victims has drawn praise from some local observers. That is cause for hope.

The policy objection to the program will be precisely that it is inappropriate to extend to adults a procedure created for children. The feminist movement has in part struggled to have women viewed as fully competent adults able to handle the same responsibilities as men.[54] But the intermediary program is not justified by any purported female incapacity for rational thought. It is instead justified by the intense linguistic trauma wrought by the present system and the immense failure of adversarial "truth-finding" assumptions in rape cases.

A second objection, then, will be that "handicapping" defense counsel undermines truth. American lawyers are particularly fond of glorifying cross-examination as "the greatest legal engine ever invented for the discovery of the truth."[55] This entire book has sought to give the lie to this statement in rape cases.

To say that traditional cross-examination fails in rape cases does not necessarily mean that the intermediary procedure will do better. Still, there are good grounds for optimism.

"Truth" Discovery and Rape Trials

The primary justification for traditional cross-examination is its centrality to adversarial dialectics. The competitive clash of equally matched opponents ensures that all relevant evidence is produced, all evidentiary weaknesses revealed.[56]

Continental European systems are nonadversarial; the judiciary conducts most of the investigation. There is a greater reliance on documentary evidence and reduced trust in the importance of demeanor. Judges do most of the questioning of witnesses at trials, and witnesses testify in largely uninterrupted narratives with few objections from counsel. Although judges ask clarifying questions, there is generally nothing like the aggressive cross-examination customary in the United States.[57]

There are good reasons not to adopt Continental procedures wholesale here. In particular, the political role of the jury, our distrust of state authority, and our hyperindividualism make that course of action impractical and unwise.[58] But that does not mean we cannot learn from the Europeans.

One can for the most part rightly believe that Continental systems are better than adversarial ones at discovering realist truths such as who hit whom first in a fight. Any sound fact-finding activity, even a dialectical one, aspires to neutrality: "[I]ts protagonists are expected to be disinterested actors rather than zealous champions of someone's self-interest."[59] Yet the adversary system works on precisely the opposite premise. The result of this partisan advocacy is that information not clearly beneficial to one side or the other is often not produced. Common ground in testimony is ignored, differences magnified.

Rational fact-finding systems also do not rely on a passive fact-finder: a jury that quietly listens while the parties decide what information to present, when, and how. Even in Continental systems moving closer to adversarialism, the fact-finders retain the power to ask questions and conduct investigations on their own. It is viewed as wrong to be responsible for a decision but not for ensuring the adequacy of the data on which the decision is based.

Sound fact-finding systems also aim for lucidity. Our party-controlled system has each side present its case on a point at different times rather than producing all evidence relevant to the point at once. Focused questions and objections further fragment testimony in a confusing fashion.

Continental systems reduce this fragmentation. Further, the right to contest evidence is thought best served by the opportunity for rebuttal evidence and clarifying questioning. Continental courts thus limit "in your face" challenges to evidence. They rely on narratives that are, by adversarial standards, "the testimonial yield of relatively mild, unpenetrating interrogations—sometimes even crediting testimony obtained by a judge in the absence of the parties."[60] This more gentle inquiry into the weaknesses *and* strengths of multiple perspectives (not just the two parties' versions) is consistent with much feminist and Continental theory on how to gain true knowledge.[61]

Even taken on its own terms, the adversary system often fails in its search for truth. Improper evidence worms its way into court by innuendo: "A query may improperly seek to reveal, for example, that a witness has invoked a privilege in a situation where that invocation creates a basis for a reasonable inference adverse to the witness. Or a question that is 'withdrawn' can improperly insinuate something about a person's past life—say, prior sexual conduct. . . ."[62] Judges are reluctant to intervene by questioning witnesses themselves or significantly limiting cross for fear of becoming a "blind and blundering intruder"[63] in a case about which they know little. Moreover, the assumption of equally matched adversaries is often wrong, as is true in rape cases:

> Absent this condition, the resultant forces of the two partisan vectors, so to speak, [are] likely to deviate from the correct view of reality. A weak case brought by a resourceful litigant can appear unduly strong. And even in relatively simple cases, adversary clashes become a source of confusion, obliterating clear outlines as quickly as snow.[64]

Accordingly, "the Anglo-American method of collecting and presenting evidence not only deviates from ordinary decision making but . . . also strikes discordant notes with arrangements recommended by a model of inquiry aimed at obtaining only accurate, trustworthy knowledge."[65]

The intermediary procedure, by involving a third party in witness examination and reducing the "heat" of cross, takes a small step in the direction of Continental procedure. But our comparative excursus shows that this step is likely to enhance, not undermine, truth discovery. The step is also required by the high likelihood that adversarial procedures obscure rather than reveal a rape victim's reality. The modesty of this step notwithstanding, it will be perceived by common law lawyers as radical. Yet, defense counsel, not the court or the intermediary, remains the primary initiator of cross-examination questions. Defense counsel continues to select in the first instance the topics for examination and the details of importance. Defense counsel will *not* be barred from any relevant inquiry, only limited in ability to confuse, mislead, or intimidate. In its essence, the intermediary procedure is fully consistent with a party-controlled adversarialism.

The intermediary procedure also furthers the political goals of the adversary jury system. Some facts, such as the existence of "consent" in a rape case, are socially constructed. For these facts, a "fact-finding" includes value judgments. Values reflect, and are informed by, different worldviews, and worldviews are embodied in plausible stories. We assign laypeople, the jurors, the task of deciding which values win, which stories make sense. By better enabling jurors to get past their own cognitive biases, the intermediary procedure improves the chances that the jury will hear and fairly consider the victim's tale. In this way, the procedure enhances the community's voice as well as the victim's.[66]

Confrontation Clause Concerns

Unfortunately, the procedure may be subject to constitutional challenge. The Sixth Amendment to the United States Constitution says in part that "the accused shall enjoy the right . . . to be confronted with the witnesses against him. . . ."[67] The Supreme Court has held that the right to confrontation presumptively includes the rights to (1) face-to-face confrontation between accuser and accused, and (2) meaningful cross-examination. The use of closed-circuit television arguably violates the first right; intermediary "translation" violates the second. A sensible understanding of the confrontation clause would reject both challenges.[68]

Closed-Circuit Television. In child sexual assault cases, the Supreme Court has been unwilling to compromise the right to face-to-face confrontation simply because of the child's tender age and the sensitive nature of the crime.[69] But the Court has been willing to limit face-to-face confrontation, given a judicial finding that a particular child would otherwise suffer such serious emotional distress that he or she would not be able reasonably to communicate. The Court in *Maryland v. Craig* approved taking a child's testimony through closed circuit television, outside the courtroom and the immediate presence of the defendant and the jury, where such a finding was first made.[70] Defense counsel, who, along with the prosecutor, accompanied the child during the out-of-court questioning, was in constant electronic communication with the defendant. The Court approved the procedure despite the child's being unable to see the defendant during the examination:

> We find it significant, however, that Maryland's procedure preserves all of the other elements of the confrontation right: The child witness must be competent to testify and must testify under oath; the defendant retains full opportunity for contemporaneous cross-examination; and the judge, jury, and defendant are able to view (albeit by video monitor) the demeanor (and body) of the witness as he or she testifies. Although we are mindful of the many subtle effects face-to-face confrontation may have on an adversary criminal proceeding, the presence of these other elements of confrontation—oath, cross-examination, and observation of the witness' de-

meanor—adequately ensures that the testimony is both reliable and subject to rigorous adversarial testing in a manner functionally equivalent to that accorded live, in-person testimony. These safeguards of reliability and adversariness render the use of such a procedure a far cry from the undisputed prohibition of the Confrontation Clause: trial by an ex parte affidavit or inquisition.[71]

The intermediary procedure proposed here has every one of these "safeguards of reliability and adversariness." Nevertheless, there are some differences.

Notably, there still must be a good reason for overriding the law's "preference" for face-to-face confrontation. In *Craig*, the Court's justification was that the child would suffer "trauma" from seeing her assailant. The Court was unclear about *why* the trauma mattered. There is language in the *Craig* opinion suggesting that the trauma showing permitted the Court to engage in interest balancing: preventing psychological harm to the child was simply more important than the defendant's right to eyeball-to-eyeball contact with his accuser. Thus the Court found that the "important public policy" in protecting the "physical and psychological well-being of child abuse victims" was sufficiently important to "outweigh," in the case before it, the defendant's right to face his accuser in court, given that reliability was otherwise being assured.[72]

In other constitutional evidence doctrine cases, the Court has recognized the need for interest balancing.[73] If interest balancing was indeed what justified doing away with face-to-face contact in *Craig*, similar balancing supports the same result here.

The intermediary procedure is not justified, however, by *internal* costs, such as the rape victim's psychological trauma from seeing the accused. Rather, part of the justification lies in the external costs generated by traditional cross-examination of rape victims: heightened subordination of women as a group, their lowered status and reduced autonomy, and their exclusion from real participation in trials as institutions of self-government. These costs are imposed on the rape victim individually but are also systemic costs imposed on society as a whole.

Indeed, although the Court worried in *Craig* about proof of trauma to the individual child, it understood that the procedure followed in *Craig* was created by the legislature to address a portion of the broader social problems created by child abuse. Thirty-seven state legislatures, the Court noted, had created special trial procedures for abused children. The Court saw these procedures as stemming from "the State's traditional and 'transcendent interest in protecting the welfare of children'" and from the "growing body of academic literature documenting the psychological trauma suffered by child abuse victims who must testify in court."[74]

The intermediary procedure similarly seeks to address some of the social problems created by rape, including the increased oppression of women resulting from abusive rape trials. The state's strong interest in those problems is embodied in the decades-long efforts of feminists and state legislatures at rape law reform[75] and is supported by the growing body of social science literature reviewed in Part II of this book. These are ample reasons for compromising the accused's right to face-to-face confrontation. Chapter 7 will show that these reasons, unlike those in *Craig*, have constitutional status: fundamental concerns of free speech and equality weigh heavily in favor of the intermediary procedure.

An alternative way to read *Craig*'s trauma requirement however is that trauma mattered because it undermined testimonial reliability. Under this reading, the state must show that trauma would render the child's testimony unreliable. For example, a minor victim might distort his or her testimony because of having been threatened by the defendant or being overwhelmed by guilt. Alternatively, the child might feel intimidated or be easily confused. If reliability is the touchstone, then *Craig* did not "balance away" the right to face-to-face contact. Rather, the right never existed in the first place because its exercise under the circumstances would have defeated the confrontation clause's function in enhancing testimonial reliability.[76]

Craig did indeed require trauma caused by the child's *seeing the accused*, not simply the ordinary trauma from testifying. Moreover, the Court at one point noted:

> [T]he use of Maryland's special procedure . . . *adequately ensures the accuracy of the testimony* and preserves the adversary nature of the trial. [Citations omitted.] Indeed, where face-to-face confrontation causes significant emotional distress in a child witness, there is evidence that such confrontation would *in fact disserve the Confrontation Clause's truth-seeking goal.* See, e.g., [Justice Blackmun's dissenting opinion *in Coy*]: (face-to-face confrontation "may so overwhelm the child as to prevent the possibility of effective testimony, *thereby undermining the truth-finding function* of the trial itself"). . . .[77]

The intermediary procedure, like the closed-circuit television setup in *Craig*, compromises the face-to-face aspect of confrontation to serve the

"Confrontation Clause's truth-seeking goal." Traditional cross-examination in rape trials makes it extraordinarily difficult for a rape victim fully and accurately to communicate to the jury the victim's circumstances, thoughts, and feelings. This difficulty is caused by the linguistic "trauma" inflicted by defense counsel. The victim must be shielded from direct contact with defense counsel's unmediated questions, not from contact with the defendant. However, under the intermediary procedure, defense counsel remains the initiator of cross-examination. When he leaves the courtroom, he will need to consult with his client in formulating appropriate cross-examination questions. To permit the defendant to remain in the courtroom, apart from his counsel, would be to compromise counsel's opportunity to pose effective cross-examination questions. Yet that opportunity is at the heart of the confrontation right. Nor can a microphone connection between the defendant and his lawyer cure the problem, for there is too great a danger that the jury will overhear the discussion. Furthermore, personal lawyer-client contact is an important aspect of effective communication. In any event, if the defendant is permitted to be in the courtroom with the victim "unprotected" by the prosecutor or the judge, that could be extraordinarily intimidating. Trauma in the sense of emotional harm to the victim is not the primary justification for the intermediary procedure, but such trauma may significantly impair the reliability of the victim's testimony if she feels that she is left "alone" with her rapist.

Craig's requirement of a case-specific need for proof of the necessity of a special examination procedure should nonetheless not apply to the intermediary. Under such a requirement, the victim's testimony about her fear of abusive defense cross would probably not be needed because the Court rejected a similar argument concerning the children in *Craig*.[78]

But linguists and psychologists might need to testify about women's ways of speaking generally and this victim's linguistic style specifically. These would be time-consuming efforts. Challenges to the experts' abilities might make for especially lengthy hearings. Moreover, it is not clear that linguists or psychologists can tell a specific person's linguistic style simply by observation.[79] Even if they can, making that judgment would probably require experiments and observations that could not be completed at a reasonable cost before the trial's end. More important, linguistic style varies with context, so the victim would need to be observed in a wide variety of contexts, especially those where she is placed in an overtly subordinate position to men. Such observations may not be practicable. Defense counsel might also argue that the victim needs to be observed for some significant time in the precise circumstances of the trial. Although the Court has rejected similar arguments in the child abuse context, trial courts might view an adult rape victim differently. But if the victim has to endure significant defense examination before the judge and to repeat her testimony before the jury, the trauma of a rape trial is dramatically heightened, further discouraging victims from coming forward.

A far better procedure is simply to use an intermediary in every case. Cultural rape narratives always have great power. Similarly, male-female linguistic differences are magnified where women are placed in subordinate positions and gender is salient, as in a rape trial. Further, the duty of zealous representation ensures that defense counsel will use every tactic that works, truth be damned. The chances of a need for the intermediary are so high in every case that individualized inquiries should not be required. The Court should recognize these realities and reject the relevance of narrow interpretations of its child sexual abuse precedents to the contrary.

The Court has recognized the need for categorical rules elsewhere in its confrontation clause jurisprudence. Thus it has declared that evidence admitted under hearsay exceptions that are "firmly rooted" in Anglo-American history and jurisprudence carry adequate indicia of reliability to survive confrontation clause challenge.[80] It has distinguished the hearsay context, however, from that in which a live-witness is on the stand. In the live witness situation, the Court has rejected any use of categorical rules without clearly explaining why it was doing so. Rather, it has simply insisted on a case-specific finding of the necessity for modifying traditional procedures.[81]

In *Coy v. Iowa*,[82] the Court held that use of a screen to block two thirteen-year-old girls from seeing their accused abuser violated the confrontation clause. The Court left "for another day" (that day came in *Craig*) whether it would make exceptions to the right to face-to-face contact. Its majority opinion noted, however, that any exceptions would require more than a generalized finding or legislative presumption of the exception's need.

Justices Blackmun and Rehnquist dissented from this insistence on a case-specific inquiry. "[L]egislative exceptions to the Confrontation Clause of general applicability are commonplace,"[83] they concluded. Moreover, the dissenters found confrontation clause hearsay jurisprudence relevant. That jurisprudence required case-specific showings of trustworthiness for hearsay not fitting within "firmly rooted" exceptions. But those case-specific inquiries were required precisely because hearsay lacks traditional confrontation clause guarantees of trustworthiness. Where those core guarantees—an oath, testimony in full view of the jury, and cross-examination—are present, "there can be no argument that . . . testimony lacked sufficient indicia of reliability."[84] The dissenters implicitly saw little chance that eye contact would promote reliability and therefore disparaged as "narrow" the defendant's right to be within the witness's sight while he testified. Additionally, the dissenters surveyed the empirical data documenting the widespread nature of child abuse and the long-term emotional scars facing abused children who testify. In their view, both truth and interest-balancing supported the constitutionality of the categorical, legislatively adopted no-eye-contact rule in all child sexual abuse cases.

The intermediary procedure retains the same core confrontation clause reliability guarantees—oath, jury observation of the witness' demeanor, and cross-examination—of which the dissenters wrote. Moreover, there is ample empirical proof of the reliability-distorting effects of traditional rape victim cross-examination. The dissenters' concerns about efficiency, accuracy, and need are even stronger here than in *Coy*. Only a categorical use of the intermediary procedure in every consent defense rape case makes sense.

"Translating" Cross-Examination. The purpose of cross-examination is to "augment accuracy in the fact-finding process by ensuring the defendant an effective means to test adverse evidence."[85] This is not a guarantee of actual effectiveness. Rather, all that is guaranteed is a realistic and fair chance of calling a witness's credibility into question. Cross-examination functions to promote accuracy by "affording the trier of fact a satisfactory basis for evaluating the truth. . . ."[86]

The Court has found that a wide range of obstacles to defense questioning still results in adequate cross-examination. Thus it did not matter under the confrontation clause that the state failed to produce medical records that a defense attorney deemed essential to his adequately examining a child sexual assault victim.[87] Nor did it matter that a prosecution expert forgot the basis of his opinion.[88] In yet another case, an assault victim identified the defendant from a photospread. At trial, however, the victim simply could not remember whether police or others had suggested to the victim that he should choose the accused's photograph. The Court found the examination adequate.[89] Indeed, the Court has upheld the complete absence of cross-examination where there were particularized guarantees of a hearsay statement's trustworthiness.[90]

None of the Court's cases has, however, addressed anything like the intermediary procedure. Furthermore, the procedure unquestionably departs from traditional notions of cross-examination. But the Court has been willing to accept novel procedures under other Sixth Amendment provisions where needed to promote fairness and accuracy.[91] The intermediary procedure alters the form but not the essential content of relevant, admissible questions. Additionally, the procedure takes place under a trial judge's watchful eye to ensure adequate, fair challenges to witness credibility. The intermediary serves as a buffer against confusion and prejudice, and enhances, not diminishes, the adequacy of the jury's basis for evaluating truth.

The adversary system is not meant to be a system of abuse and intimidation. The hallmark of the system, which the intermediary procedure retains, is that parties, not judges, have the primary responsibility for investigating facts and questioning witnesses. The reliability justification for the system is that truth comes from the clash of ideas, not personalities or linguistic styles. That clash is thought to motivate parties to produce complete evidence and to test the weaknesses in one another's cases.[92]

The confrontation clause promotes these ideals by "ensuring that evidence admitted against an accused is reliable and subject to the rigorous adversarial testing that is the norm of Anglo-American criminal proceedings."[93] "Rigorous testing" means a "clashing of forces *or ideas.*"[94] The rigorous testing required by the confrontation clause is "'generally satisfied when the defense is given a full and fair opportunity to probe and expose [testimonial] infirmities [such as forgetfulness, confusion, or evasion] through cross-examination, thereby calling to the attention of the factfinder the *reasons* for giving scant weight to the witness' testimony.'"[95] Adversarial lawyering is hence intended to promote testing the strength and wisdom of positions but not the obfuscation of their premises.

Accordingly, the confrontation clause does not countenance trials as "sporting contests" or survival of the most brutal, though that may well describe the system in practice. Rather, the system's ideal is to promote sound decision making based upon reliable evidence. The intermediary procedure seeks to help the system live up to this ideal, replacing trial by fire with trial by reasoned debate.

Professor Lucy McGough, one of the leading scholars on child sexual abuse prosecutions, has proposed an instructive alternative to traditional cross-examination in juvenile sex abuse cases.[96] The empirical evidence, says McGough, shows that children's testimony is distorted when children are examined by partisan or unskilled questioners. These partisans include cross-examining defense lawyers. Besides, the combined effects of memory fade, repeated questioning, and suggestibility render children's trial testimony, often taken long after the incident, unreliable. On the other hand, research shows that children's reliability is enhanced if they are questioned near the time of the incident by "a skilled neutral professional unaligned with either the prosecution or the defense who is . . . a specialist with expertise and training in interviewing children."[97]

McGough therefore recommends the routine videotaping of child sex abuse victims as they are being questioned by properly court-certified neutral expert interviewers. The interview would be done subject to a laundry list of reliability safeguards required by the empirical evidence. The only persons present would be the interviewee and the court-certified questioner. However, both the prosecution and defense would be entitled to submit proposed questions to the neutral interviewer.

At trial, the prosecution would elicit only the child's assertion that the statement she or he gave was accurate when made. But the substance of the child's direct trial testimony would usually be the playing of the videotaped interview. Defense counsel would then cross-examine the child about her or his bias or other motives for giving false or shaded videotaped testimony. The defense could also question the victim about her or his ability personally to observe and accurately to report the events or transactions described on videotape. But the child could not ordinarily be cross-examined at trial about current recollections of the events described. Exceptions to this limited cross rule could be made if the child declared the earlier statement inaccurate. But the presumption would be against much trial questioning because of the danger that the child's current memories would then be unreliable.[98]

McGough, taking the Supreme Court at its word in saying that reliability guarantees are the essence of confrontation, concludes:

> The recollection-recorded videotaping proposal should survive constitutional attack because it provides an adequate substitute for contemporane-

ous cross-examination by requiring a skillful interview by a neutral professional. As Wigmore explained, cross-examination during the taking of a statement is but one means of assuring accuracy of recollection. "There are many situations in which it can be easily seen that such a required test [of cross-examination] would add little as security, because its purposes had been already substantially accomplished. If a statement has been made under circumstances that even a skeptical caution would look upon it as trustworthy . . . it would be pedantic to insist on a test whose chief object is already secured."[99]

Some commentators would reject, however, McGough and the Supreme Court's stated position that reliability is the confrontation clause's sole concern. The clause was also designed to restrain state power. Some commentators see this restraint as stemming from the exposure of governmental abuses. Others view empowering defense counsel as a counterweight to state authority. These critics would likely agree that at its core the confrontation clause was meant to prohibit ex parte affidavits and depositions by the government—ones created without significant defense opportunity then to contest the testimony. McGough's videotape procedure would be challenged as just such an ex parte governmental abuse.[100]

But the intermediary procedure proposed here has no such flaw. The intermediary operates *at trial*, in the presence of defense counsel, the prosecutor, and the court. And, the intermediary does not initiate any questioning. All questioning is at first posed by the prosecutor and defense counsel. Like the specially trained interrogator in McGough's proposal, the intermediary uses his or her expertise to ask questions in a way that empirical data suggest should improve the reliability of the trial process. But unlike McGough's proposal, the intermediary actively involves defense counsel as the primary initiating force in the contemporaneous examination of the strengths and weaknesses of the victim's statement. The intermediary proposal is far less radical than McGough's proposal and therefore even more likely than hers to survive constitutional scrutiny.

EMPATHIC EXPERTS

The primary experts now testifying in rape cases opine about rape trauma syndrome (RTS), a set of physical, behavioral, and psychological reactions sometimes resulting from rape. Courts are most likely to admit RTS testimony in rebuttal to claims that the woman did not behave in the way a real survivor would. Courts shy away from using RTS to prove that a woman is telling the truth or was in fact raped.[101]

Cultural rape narratives are, however, omnipresent. There should be no need to await rebuttal. The prosecution must have a chance in its initial case to unsettle restrictive cultural paradigms. A less objectionable and more effective way to do this would be to use experts who educate the jury about the demographics and sociology of rape. The information would not be used to prove propensity—to show that a suspect behaves like a rapist, therefore raped—but to unsettle cultural narratives. The goal would be to open jurors' minds to plausible alternative tales to the dominant ones.

The experts would discuss rape survivor demographics, explaining that women of all ages and backgrounds are raped. The experts would point out empirical flaws in cultural narratives, explaining why a "true" victim might delay reporting the crime or that acquaintance rape is common.[102] Most controversially, the experts would debunk the myth that only deviants commit rape. Some courts have already permitted this last type of testimony. In a Texas case, an expert testified in the prosecution's case-in-chief about how rapists choose their victims. He explained that it was not uncommon for a rapist to establish a brief relationship with the victim, "'i.e. to be seen in public with the victim before raping her so that she would be unsuspecting of any potential danger and so that her credibility would be diminished.'"[103] The appellate court upheld the conviction because the testimony gave the average person new information with which to understand "the victim's passive conduct." It concluded that probative value outweighed any unfair prejudice:

> James [the expert] drew no conclusions as to the truthfulness of the victim or the believability of her story. She only provided a context within which the jury might understand certain behavior. The testimony complained of did not directly concern this victim, this defendant or this sexual assault. Rather, the witness testified as to particular classifications and behavior patterns.[104]

Finally, these experts would testify about the rapist-victim relationship. Why might a woman engage in "alluring" conduct yet have no interest in sexual intercourse? How does a date rapist isolate a victim and overcome her resistance without the need for bruising physical force? Understanding these dynamics provides a framework for jurors' understanding the case before them.[105]

Available empirical data suggest that such education can have an impact on attitudes toward rape yet will not overawe the jury. Indeed, the impact of such general background testimony, while significant, is quite limited next to testimony that links general principles to the case before the court. Such case-specific testimony has a better chance than background testimony alone of overcoming juror biases. For an expert overtly to offer an opinion about the specific case before him, however, often raises difficult evidentiary bars to admissibility. Traditional RTS testimony, which does link general principles to the specific case, should therefore still have a role, where admissible.[106]

A second new general type of expert testimony would go beyond educating jurors about rape. It would educate jurors about why they resist giving fair consideration to rape victim's tales. Specifically, the expert would explain juror cognitive processes, including the impact of cultural rape narratives and why jurors disbelieve witnesses with "feminine" linguistic styles. Cognitive research demonstrates that well-learned stereotypes persist "long after a person has sincerely renounced prejudice."[107] Someone who concludes that rape myths are wrong may thus nevertheless continue to render decisions based on those myths. The myths continue to operate subconsciously. Discrimination is a habit that is hard to break. But if subjects who view a prejudiced belief as wrong are told how it may nevertheless affect their judgments, they are better able to monitor and thereby reduce the belief's impact. Making unconscious biases conscious biases does seem to help jurors to evaluate victim testimony more fairly.

7

Group Voices

The argument made thus far has depended upon an important assumption: that the fate of the individual and her group are linked. In other words, silencing individual rape victims harms women as a group, and silencing women as a group harms individual rape victims. This assumption needs further defense, one that clarifies the nature of the harm at issue: the "silencing" of women for political purposes. When the government silences groups, both First Amendment free speech and equal protection values are implicated.

The Group-Individual Justice Connection

The link between the individual and the group is rooted in the idea articulated in chapter 6: a group's status is power. The United States Supreme Court acknowledged decades ago, in *Beauharnais v. Illinois,* that harm to a group's status harms its individual members.[1] Beauharnais, president of the White Circle League, was convicted for violating a criminal statute prohibiting defaming groups. He was alleged to have been responsible for the distribution of a leaflet urging whites to unite against blacks: "[I]f persuasion and the need to prevent the white race from becoming mongrelized by the Negro will not unite us, then the aggressions . . . rapes, robberies, knives, guns, and marijuana of the Negro surely will," said the leaflet.[2]

Beauharnais argued that convicting him for arranging distribution of the leaflet violated his First Amendment right to free speech. The Court disagreed:

> Long ago this Court recognized that the economic rights of an individual may depend for the effectiveness of their enforcement on rights in the group, even though not formally corporate, to which he belongs. . . . It is not within our competence to confirm or deny the claims of social scientists

as to the dependence of the individual on the position of his racial or religious group in the community. It would, however, be arrant dogmatism, quite outside the scope of our authority in passing on the powers of a State, for us to deny that the Illinois legislature may warrantably believe that a man's job and his educational opportunities and the dignity accorded him may depend as much on the reputation of the racial and religious group to which he willy-nilly belongs as on his own merits. This being so, we are precluded from saying that speech concededly punishable when immediately directed at individuals cannot be outlawed if directed at groups with whose position and esteem in society the affiliated individual may be inextricably involved.[3]

The "claims of social scientists" to which the Court acceded are beyond serious dispute: if a group's status is devalued, the individual members suffer.[4] Indeed, Part I of this book established precisely one instance of this phenomenon: group-based narratives about women harm individual rape victims' status at their attackers' trials.

But the chain of causation works the other way too: harm to the individual harms the group. We partly define ourselves by our group affiliations. Are we black or white? Jewish or Christian? Republican or Democrat? Our attitudes, beliefs, and assumptions are in part shaped by the groups with which we identify. Gender (a salient group identity at rape trials) is certainly at the core of self-identity. Our sense of being "male" or "female" and what we believe that means are central to who we are. Although all individuals are unique, some part of how we express ourselves draws on group self-concepts as "man" or "woman."[5]

But groups are defined not only by their members' self-concepts but also by how others define the group. In particular, a group's identity can inhere in the eyes of an oppressor group.[6] The oppressive Others' vision of the oppressed ties the group's fate to the individual's: the awareness of the Other creates a common interest for each member of the group. It is an interest in the sense that each person comes to care about how each member is treated, for because each person is treated as indistinguishable from each other person, how your neighbor is treated counts as a strong indication of how you will be treated, or would have been treated had you been there instead of your neighbor. This interest is common because it is true for each person who thinks about it because it is not based on subjective but objective conditions—namely, how the Other is reacting toward each member of the group as a group member, not as an individual.[7]

Women constitute a coherent oppressed group for whom the fate of each affects the fate of all. Women have a shared set of expected cultural behaviors and experiences. Those expectations mean that their status *as women* shapes how they must behave to succeed at their jobs, where they may safely go at night, and what kinds of behavior they may engage in while in public. Culturally pervasive stereotypes of women as dependent, weak, and overly emotional limit their life options: "The empirical case is overwhelming that women have suffered, and continue to suffer, group-based harms."[8]

When any individual woman succeeds at a job requiring independence, strength, and intellect, that unsettles images of women as incompetent weaklings. When many women so succeed, preconceptions about women as a group start to change. Individual women find it easier to break into "male" professions, to participate in previously male-dominated organizations, and to be heard when voicing political concerns.

Correspondingly, each time that a woman fails at a "male" job, reacts to stress "emotionally," or is treated in a subordinate fashion, that feeds negative stereotypes about women. Individual women find it harder to get particular jobs, to obtain favorable reviews from superiors, and to be heard at public meetings.[9]

These observations are part of what is meant by the slogan "The personal is political,"[10] which recognizes that what happens to individual women affects the group. Even how individual women are treated in their "private" lives—as wives and mothers—affects the ability of women as a group to participate equally in the "public" lives of work and electoral politics. Political power is thus seen as pervasive. Male control of public institutions shapes ideologies that in turn shape private female behavior, and private female behavior reinforces that control. The effect of the circularity is to exclude or mute the female voice in the public arena.

Subordination of women at rape trials furthers this muting of female voices. One way this happens is by the many not-guilty verdicts that result from courtroom abuse of rape victims. Every time a woman who breaches patriarchal rules—say, by openly expressing sexual desire—charges rape, she seeks to assert her right to behave as she has. The not guilty verdict tells her and other women that she has no such right. If she is insubordinate and is punished for it by violence, society will not defend her. The message the law sends to women is this: be passive, sensitive to male needs, fearful of venturing out at night in public spaces, and dependent on the protection and presence of a man.[11] But these subordinate behaviors both limit women's involvement in the political sphere and lower their social status.

Rape trials harm women as a group in another way. Because much of our identity is a function of group affiliations, silencing that part of us rooted in group experience silences the group. Groups speak largely through individuals. If every individual is silenced, there is no group voice. If many individuals are silenced, the group voice is small. A rape victim has been hurt based on her status as a woman. She turns to the courts for redress. When she is effectively silenced by discriminatory evidentiary practices, all women lose a voice in the immediate political process—the jury's assignment of blame—and in the broader political contest over women's status and options in both "public" and "private" life."

Feminist Free Speech

Rape victims are not literally silenced at rape trials. They do speak, but they are not heard. They often are dissenters, protesting, for example, against prevailing ideas that a woman who drinks and wears short skirts cannot be raped. But their protests are stifled and ignored. Their avenue for redress—the rape trial—is a sham.

The need for meaningful voice is central to the American concept of self-government. The Declaration of Independence itself expresses this concept:

> In every stage of these Oppressions We have Petitioned for Redress in the most humble terms: Our repeated Petitions have been answered only by repeated injury. A Prince, whose character is thus marked by every act which may define a Tyrant, is unfit to be the ruler of a free people.[12]

Well-known law professor Stephen Carter explains the point of this clause:

> But what, in the end, makes . . . [the King] tyrannical? It is not merely, perhaps not mostly, that he, in alliance with Parliament, has done oppressive things to the Colonists, although that is true and the list is quite an extensive one. The nub of the matter, however, seems to be that he has ignored their complaints. . . . It seems to be the rejection of the petitions for redress—the fact that the Crown is ignoring the particular concerns of the Colonists—that provides the justification for revolution.[13]

Carter tells us that the lack of meaningful hearing for dissenters can lead to disallegiance, a severing of a commitment to the legitimacy of the sovereign. This disallegiance stems from the sense of a "stacked deck," a hearing as but a formality. One father relates a story that explains in a concrete way the sense of frustration that such empty formalities breed:

> The other night I told my ten-year-old son, who is an erratic sleeper, that his bedtime would be fixed at 9:30. His response: "That's not fair." So I convened a meeting. My wife, my son, and I sat down to discuss the issue. He argued for a later bedtime, and we listened patiently as he presented his case. We then took a vote. Surprise! The vote was two to one in favor of 9:30, with Alex dissenting.
>
> • • •
>
> After sixteen years of marriage, and some past discussions about the issue, I had little doubt as to where . . . [my wife] stood. And given both our common interests and our desire for marital harmony, the odds that I would be defeated were practically nonexistent.
>
> We had a vote. Each of us had the opportunity to be heard. Nobody could dispute the formal fairness of the process. But it is hard to say that the outcome was fair. The deck, as it were, was stacked. Formal fairness was not enough to offer any meaningful protection for Alex's interests. Nor is it enough in America.[14]

A rape victim's testimony being truly heard at a trial can promote catharsis and empowerment. The catharsis of being heard makes hierarchy less oppressive, as does the sense that the oppressor's worst abuses will be exposed and therefore chilled.[15] But rape victims must not have the sense that the deck is stacked, that their "petitions for redress" will be met "by repeated injury." Evidentiary practices must be designed to promote not merely the voicing but the "effective voicing" of the rape victims' dissenting views. Yet we have seen that a rape victim's views both consist of and reflect shared female attitudes and experience. Effective voice therefore requires voice for the circumstances and experiences of rape victims and of the many women who fear being raped but have not been raped. To prevent a dominant group (men) from drowning out a subordinate one (women), special efforts must be made to ensure that dissenting individual and group voices are heard. But dissenters can be heard only if they have some real measure of power. Both the rape victim and female observers must feel they can articulate their interests with a real chance of those interests' being realized. Both must help to set the framework for debate and to define the participants' roles. They must be free to give new meaning to old concepts (like "consent") before an attentive tribunal. They must feel that they have a real opportunity to create pressure to change prevailing practices and ideas about gender roles and rape. In short, their participation must be meaningful.[16]

The changes proposed in this book help to promote women's meaningful participation in the rape trial process. Revised jury selection procedures foster a tribunal (the jury) more willing truly to listen. Use of uninterrupted narratives and victim intermediaries reduces subconscious blocks to women's telling, and juries hearing, rape victims' complete tales. Special experts and revised character-evidence rules add to the stock of quality information needed to understand those tales.

A meaningful hearing of rape victims' grievances also promotes another free speech value: collective self-rule. "Self-rule" does not mean majoritarianism. When a majority imposes its will on a minority, the minority has been excluded from self-rule. Self-rule happens when the laws are made by the people to whom they apply. In practice, this means that self-rule requires participation by all citizens, minority and majority, male and female, in making the laws. Trials involve law creation as much as law application. When a jury decides that a man committed (or did not commit) rape, it applies its own notion of "consent." But that definition of consent is the law—the rule for deciding the case before the jury. Meaningful, open participation by interested parties in this process of law creation by the jury is thus an act of self-rule. In the Supreme Court's words, "[M]aintenance of the opportunity for political discussion to the end that government may be responsive to the will of the people . . . [is] an opportunity essential to the security of the Republic."[17]

Self-rule is often misconceived as an individualistic project: if all citizens can express their views in a free marketplace of ideas, we have self-rule. But mere individual expression to those who will not listen is not a "discussion . . . responsive to the will of the people." Self-rule is at heart an effort to reconcile individual wills with a general will. But a "general will" requires deliberation about our identity *as a people*, "who we shall be, for what we shall stand."[18] Our sense of being a people or a "public" in a culturally diverse society requires confrontation of divergent attitudes. Only when we learn to speak across our differences in search for a common ground can our decisions be said to reflect a "general will."

Hearing the rape victim as dissenter promotes collective self-rule. Dissent is chilled when women know that if they have by words or deeds voiced dissenting views on gender roles (ignoring the theme of "silenced voices" in Part I), they can be raped with impunity. Some women will fall into line. Others will not even reflect on whether there is good reason to step out of line. Still others, if raped, will not come forward. If they do come forward, police will ignore their cases or prosecutors will dismiss them as "unwinnable." For the rare victim/dissenter who makes it to trial, her story will be ignored or altered, her dignity abused. Her "voice" will be a sham, an ineffective ritual. This silencing is not the meaningful, engaged participation necessary to self-rule. The silencing works at the group level: silencing individual rape victims mutes women's voices generally in the dialogue about consent, rape, and proper gendered behavior.

It is not simply collective self-rule but also individual self-rule or autonomy that is undermined by the lack of a meaningful hearing for rape victims. Individual autonomy requires one's choices truly to be one's own rather than choices coerced by force, ignorance, or social habit. Critical reflection about a wide array of options is necessary to ensuring that the choices are informed of what one deems wise rather than what society's will requires. When the jury is exposed to new ways of seeing gender relations and rape, critical reflection and jury autonomy are promoted.[19]

But the jury's choices are not made in isolation. The trial is a public event, and the jury's verdict reaches a wide audience, verdict and trial being especially intensely scrutinized by the media. When media coverage includes dissenting views on gender relations, debate on that subject and citizen autonomy are enhanced.

Such debate aids the victim's autonomy too. Our sense of who we are is closely tied to the sentiments of the communities and groups with which we affiliate. Women—an especially salient group for rape victims—begin to imagine new ways of understanding rape, consent, and violence, and rape victims find it easier to see themselves in a new light. They come forward more often and more clearly. In this way, toleration of their dissenting views contributes to everyone's critical reflection, illustrating the more general principle that true autonomy requires that

> voices that challenge the status quo must be allowed or even encouraged to exist and to be heard in social discourse on important issues. This discourse must be available to the average person, and society must be set up in a way that citizens are able to effect political change based on this discourse.[20]

Excluding rape victims from meaningful trial participation undermines a final free speech value: promoting the search for truth. Truth does sometimes exist "out there." For example, whether the alleged rapist hit his victim or not has an objectively true answer. But "truth" is sometimes a social notion. When a jury judges an act "consensual," it does not discover some independent, objectively verifiable truth. Rather, it creates an interpretive truth based on its notions of worthy, coherent narratives and its moral judgment about the gendered meaning to be ascribed to the man's and woman's social behavior.[21]

If a rape jury creates truth, then rape trial verdicts deserve allegiance only to the extent that all affected parties and groups have had their say. "Having your say" for women requires an equal chance for the victim to initiate and continue conversations, make assertions, and offer explanations. Furthermore, women, through the rape victim, must have an equal chance to express their feelings, to order and resist orders, and to demand the accountability of others. If male-centered rules for who speaks when and how, and male-centered cultural narratives dominate the trial debate, rape victims are robbed of their equal chances to assert, explain, and emote. A "truth" born of such dissenting women's exclusion is not a "truth" worthy of being so recognized.

Moreover, any "truth" will be bought at the price of ignoring the "free marketplace of linguistic styles."[22] The free-speech market metaphor posits an exchange of idea content, not linguistic style. But linguistic style differences are exchanged too. The exchanges of difference communicate relations of power, hierarchy, solidarity, and intimacy; they partly account for how rape victims are treated at trials.

Thus, a woman may adopt a subordinate style when speaking to men, especially in the public, largely male, and potentially status-enhancing atmosphere of the rape trial. Yet, style differences themselves stem from group status and experience, such as women's often being socialized to defer to men. But linguistic style domination by men also distorts perceptions of witness credibility, for many women's more connected, less competitive style is seen by juries as markers that they are not credible. The trial verdict comes to result more from a marketplace of styles than of ideas. Power is substituted for reason. The verdict reflects women's subordination as the only "truth" to be found.

Feminist Equal Protection

Equal protection and free speech principles converge toward the same result: rape victims are entitled to *meaningful* participation in their assailants' trials. At the heart of the Fourteenth Amendment is the concept of equal citizenship. The right to equal citizenship is historically grounded in the right to belong and participate, to be a full member of society.[23] One of the evils of slavery was that it denied blacks the right to participate as equal citizens.[24] Congress adopted the Civil Rights Act of 1866 precisely to guarantee former slaves and others the same civil rights as were "enjoyed by white citizens."[25] Those rights included the right to participate in government judicial processes as parties and witnesses.[26] The Fourteenth Amendment indeed begins by declaring, "All persons born or naturalized in the United States, and subject to the jurisdiction thereof are . . . *citizens* of the United States and of the State wherein they reside."[27] The amendment as a whole was clearly partially intended to constitutionalize the 1866 act.[28] But it was also intended to reject *Dred Scott*,[29] the Court's decision holding that blacks were not "fellow-citizens and members of the sovereignty."[30] As noncitizens, blacks could not bring cases before federal courts on the ground of invoking the Court's jurisdiction over matters involving diversity of "citizenship."[31] *Brown v. Board of Education* can also be understood as recognizing that one of educational segregation's evils was that it denied blacks the right to participate as equal citizens.[32] Indeed, the modern civil rights movement and allied movements were efforts to extend equal participation in critical institutions to all groups, including women, racial minorities, and the disabled.[33] A long line of constitutional scholars, historians, and philosophers have recognized that participation is central to equal citizenship.[34] One renowned philosopher explains that the primary good that a society has to distribute is not liberty or substantive equality but membership. Membership and the concomitant right to participation lead to the production of all social goods and give them meaning.[35] The basic premise of our post–Civil War constitutional democracy is that all citizens should have an equal right to participate in the critical institutions of political and cultural life.[36]

The means of excluding groups from equal participation work most often by daily ceremonies of degradation at the individual level. One leading constitutional scholar expressed it in this way:

> The harms of exclusion unquestionably happen to people one by one, but those individual harms result from the subordination of groups. When the instrument for excluding a group is the law, the hurt is magnified, for the law is seen to embody the community's values. For a "degradation ceremony" to succeed, the denouncer "must make the dignity of the supra-per-

sonal views of the tribe salient and accessible to view, and his denunciation must arrange to be invested with the right to speak in the name of these ultimate values." When a city segregates the races on a public beach, the chief harm to the segregated minority is not that those people are denied access to a few hundred yards of "surf." Jim Crow was not just a collection of legal disabilities; it was an officially organized degradation ceremony, repeated day after day in a hundred ways in the life of every black person within the system's reach.[37]

Equal protection therefore demands dismantling the daily rituals of degradation that work to exclude groups from participation in critical institutions—those where autonomy, societal values, and social norms are constituted. The courts, because of their expressive value, universal authority over all citizens, and fusion (in the jury) of the community's judgment with the state's power to use violence, are unquestionably critical institutions in which autonomy and social values and norms are formed.[38]

Dismantling courtroom rituals of degradation and exclusion runs into a conceptual problem. Modern political life embraces the idea of "universal" citizenship. But "universality" has generally been understood to embrace two notions. First, the universal is defined in opposition to the particular. What citizens have in common rather than how they differ is seen to be what matters. Second, laws and rules are meant to be applied universally, the same rules for all citizens, regardless of group and individual differences. The effect of these two notions, however, is to exclude those who are different or to mute their voices, prodding them toward homogeneity.[39]

The first notion (the universal opposes the particular) is unrealistic and wrong. People are necessarily influenced by their experiences and group social relations. There will be differences in both individual and group perceptions. To listen to these differences does not mean assuming that each group seeks to serve only its own selfish interest. People can and do offer their views everyday and then, in exchange with others, take a critical distance from their own immediate desires and gut reactions to reach public-regarding understandings. Our faith in the jury's ability to reach a public-regarding outcome from among diverse and partial views is one key example. "[H]aving the voices of particular group perspectives other than one's own explicitly represented in public discourse best fosters the maintenance of such critical distance without the pretense of impartiality."[40]

The second notion—application of the laws despite individual and group differences—perpetuates disadvantage. If, for example, a pregnant woman is denied accommodations at work, or if her pregnancy is viewed as a "disability," she is denied full participation in work life and viewed as a less worthy employee.[41]

These two aspects of "universal" citizenship can operate together to promote exclusion by silencing. White middle-class men assume authority more often than others and are more practiced at speaking persuasively than are many others. Rules of "equal participation" may thus operate to amplify the white male voice, drowning out others. In one study, community control of public schools led to increased segregation, because the more privileged whites were better able to promote their perceived interests against blacks. No special efforts had been made to ensure that black perspectives were adequately aired.[42] In another study, all present at a town meeting were given an "equal" right to participate. But women, blacks, and working-class and poor people tended to participate far less than whites, middle-class professionals, and men.[43] This results in the "paradox of democracy": "social power makes some citizens more equal than others, and equality of citizenship makes some people more powerful citizens."[44]

An oppressed group can indeed be identified by its exclusion from full participation in major social and political activities or by its being stereotyped in ways that contribute to its having little opportunity for the expression of its experience and its perspective on social events. A democratic republic committed to *equal* protection must, therefore, have a mechanism for the effective representation and recognition of its constituent groups' distinct voices and perspectives. Voicing a group's perspectives is especially important regarding policies that affect group members.[45]

Evidence rules that take a male, adversarial perspective on justice as the consistent, acontextual, universal norm function like the "equal participation" rules at a town meeting. Women speak less, their voices are less effective. By treating all alike, the court perpetuates inequality. That rape victims are abused one at a time should not mask the reality that the consequence is silencing women as a group. To treat women as equal citizens, their differences in perspective and ways of expression must be taken into account. Our evidence rules, ethics codes, and courtroom customs and practices must be sensitive to context, ready at times to treat women differently so that they may be treated the same. But the "sameness" that matters is that they receive the same chance for effective voice as do men. The "equal" appears in "equal protection" for rape victims only when they can participate fully in their self-rule. Free speech and equality are not in conflict but are one and the same.[46]

The Jury's "Checking Function"

The Framers of the Constitution saw "the 'big idea' behind the jury . . . not so much [as] protecting discrete individuals (though that is certainly important) as preserving a democratic culture."[47] One of the ways the jury preserves democracy is by enabling ordinary citizens to act as a check on governmental oppression. Just as the legislature has a less populist house (the Senate) and a more populist house (the House of Representatives), so the courts have "two parts—judges and juries—with the latter far closer to the people."[48]

The jury's "checking" role included, in the Framers' scheme, ensuring voice for group expression and individual dissent. Juries prevent repression by preventing punishment of the opposition press or opposition speakers and pamphleteers.[49]

The Framers recognized too that jury verdicts in individual cases sometimes have far-reaching political implications.[50] As Tocqueville observed: "To regard the jury simply as a judicial institution would be taking a very narrow view of the matter, for great though its influence on the outcome of lawsuits is, its influence on the fate of society is much greater still. The jury is therefore above all a political institution."[51]

The jury's political role extended to another task as well: to be a breeding ground for good citizenship. It is as jurors that citizens learn their rights, but it is also where they practice the deliberative public judgment so necessary to effective citizenship.[52] For most people, it is only in the jury box that we meet "citizen to citizen, face to face, not just to exchange greetings or currency, but to listen to, learn from, and work with one another in the solemn task of self-government."[53] That task, moreover, requires jurors to debate normative standards, for cultural values are inseparable from factual and legal questions such as the "reasonableness" of a defendant's acts.[54] The citizen-training function of the jury should be seen as part of a broader theme in the Framers' philosophy and American history: the need for an informed citizenry as the cornerstone of a republican democratic culture. The freedoms of the press, religion, speech, and assembly, and the institutions of political parties, public schools, and the media join with the jury to educate our populace about the issues of the day.[55] An educated populace is in turn far better able to restrain governmental abuses and promote wise policies.

Today, however, unlike in the Framers' day, we need not fear only governmental oppression. Private oppression, private power, wounds many of us in ways the government does not reach us. Private power is often diffuse. It works through social structures like racism and sexism, which may involve government action as well. But the government sometimes must act to protect its citizens from private abuses of power. That governmental obligation comes from the Reconstruction amendments, especially the Fourteenth Amendment, which radically altered the Framers' vision.[56]

A progressive understanding of the Fourteenth Amendment begins by understanding its abolitionist roots. The Thirteenth Amendment abolished slavery but did not abolish slavery's essence: subjecting another to at least two sovereigns: the state and the master. The post–Civil War wave of Ku Klux Klan violence against whites, blacks, and abolitionists; the refusal of southern and sometimes northern states to check that violence; and the states' refusal to give slaves the contract and property law protections necessary to economic life created precisely the relationship of private sovereign (master) to subordinate (slave) that abolitionists sought to end. The Fourteenth Amendment can be viewed as a necessary next step to ensuring that newly freed slaves faced only one sovereign: the state. "Equal protection" of the law thus meant at least that no state may deny to any citizen the protection of its criminal and civil laws against private violence or private threats to the economic opportunity necessary for survival. Robin West explained the point this way:

> Indeed, in the post–Thirteenth Amendment and pre–Fourteenth Amendment world, the pattern of subservience, acquiescence, and obedience of the freed slaves to the commands, will, desires, or values of whites, all grounded in a fully justified fear of unchecked violence and unchecked violations of trust, was the clearest evidence one could possibly require that the states had denied to one class of citizens the equal protection of the law.[57]

The Fourteenth Amendment in its narrowest progressive reading, therefore, guards against private acts of violence and economic terrorism that render a citizen subject to a private sovereign. But this narrow reading would also be inconsistent with the amendment's design. The amendment enacted a grand principle to guide future debate: "The Framers and Ratifiers understood their task to be the moral one of proclaiming vague principles of civic reformation, not the academic or bureaucratic one of engaging in precise conceptual definition. . . ."[58] What is more, applying a legal formulation from one generation to another always requires an act of translation: How do we translate the message of post–Civil War America to address the problems of today? The amendment's design and sound jurisprudence thus require us to give life to the amendment's central philosophical goal of protecting against two sovereigns, a goal that may extend beyond limiting force and economic terrorism as means of subordination.[59]

This broad principle may have a potentially enormous scope. Difficult philosophical and practical issues must be resolved for each unique social problem to define the limits of that scope. One boundary can be stated with some certainty, however: the principle should extend centrally to protecting certain identifiable subordinated groups. Traditional equal protection analysis has long recognized women as such a protected group, applying "middle scrutiny" (the second-highest level of constitutional protection) to state action discriminating against women.[60]

The non-dual-sovereign principle's boundary determination requires at its core asking, "What is so central to our human essence that only if it is protected, nurtured, or furthered, can we be called free?"[61] Again, whatever difficulties this question raises in some instances, there is little difficulty in identifying gender as at the core of human identity.[62] Yet, patriarchy is by definition a social system in which one group (women) are rendered subject to another group (men) as sovereign based on gender.[63] Robin West has recognized that even the narrow formulation of the progressive equal protection principle reaches some aspects of patriarchy. Hence, West argues, the many women who perform vast amounts of unpaid domestic labor are "like slaves, rendered subject to the whim of a separate sovereign, the check-bearing spouse on whom they depend for material survival."[64] The state has failed to ensure that no group of citizens, here women, lives under two sovereigns.

One need not accept West's precise argument about unpaid domestic labor or worry much further about the precise scope of the equal protection principle for it to help here. The argument I am advancing is procedural, not substantive. The central claim is this: post–Fourteenth Amendment, the jury's "checking function" must include monitoring both state and certain private abuses of power. Certain forms of power are diffuse, all-pervasive, and complex, implicating both state and private action. This observation is particularly true of racial subordination and patriarchy. Where either social system may be involved, the jury has a checking function to play.

This equal protection analysis brings us back to storytelling. We have seen how the muting and distortion of women's and minorities' stories at trials work to support group subordination. The framing of narrative, therefore, carries profoundly political implications. Put differently, the terms of narrative are prizes in a pitched conflict among groups to describe their social identity and vindicate their social existence. "Narrative can [also] be subversive. What is taken for granted in a dominant narrative—truth, common sense, unreasonableness—may be fiercely contested in the outsider version."[65]

When the state by its evidentiary policies silences outsider group narratives in a way that buttresses group subordination, the state has denied the group the equal protection of the laws. Simultaneously, denying the jury access to tales reflecting a critical view of social reality also undermines the jury's role as citizen-educator. Citizens learning only the dominant narrative are seriously misinformed.

The progressive understanding of the equal protection clause articulated here could create difficult institutional and practical problems involved in the Court's embarking on massive social change. Picture what would be required, for instance, if the Court accepted Robin West's argument that the state must not permit unpaid domestic labor to continue. But no such widespread social change is required here. Rather, policy makers need only make relatively small changes in the day-to-day operation of the courts: permitting rape victims to give uninterrupted narratives, introducing intermediaries in rape trials, prohibiting appeals to gender bias, and being more receptive to certain kinds of empathy-enhancing expert testimony. Although these changes are manageable, however, even changes of this size require legislative, not judicial, action.

The Legislative Constitution

The constitutional arguments made in this chapter are meant to enter into a court's balancing of interests under the confrontation clause. Other than that, my arguments are directed to legislatures, not courts. Legislatures may have a constitutional obligation to act even where courts do not. Constitutional obligations vary among the branches because institutional competence varies: "As the Supreme Court has always been quick to point out, the federal judiciary is ill equipped to remedy the structural, institutional, and social inequalities, practices, and attitudes that [often] result in constitutionally problematic states of affairs. . . ."[66]

This institutional competence principle is illustrated by the late-nineteenth century and early-twentieth-century Supreme Court's invalidation of legislative efforts to regulate economic activity. Most infamously, in *Lochner v. New York*,[67] the Court invalidated a New York statute that prohibited employing bakers for more than sixty hours in any one week. The Court saw the "liberty" protected by the Fourteenth Amendment as embracing a right to contract over terms of employment. In the Court's view, state officials generally lacked authority to interfere with the exercise of that liberty, at least absent very good reasons, which the Court found missing. Yet the Court presumed that it had authority to secure economic liberties by exercising the power of judicial review. The Court similarly exercised its purported authority to secure economic liberties in a wide array of cases in the late nineteenth and early twentieth centuries based on narrow readings of congressional authority under the commerce clause and relying on the Fifth and Fourteenth Amendment due process clauses or the Tenth Amendment. These decisions blocked many early attempted New Deal reforms.[68]

But the Court changed direction in the middle of the New Deal stream, the famous "switch in time that saved nine." The justices retreated from economic laissez-faire, thereafter consistently affirming the validity of New Deal legislation. The justices did so by expanding their interpretation of Congress's commerce clause authority, deferring to legislative judgments as to the importance of various economic ends and the reasonableness of the chosen means, and restricting the scope of substantive due process liberties under the Fourteenth Amendment. The Court's switch can be understood, contrary to traditional interpretations, as reflecting changed views as to institutional competence: "Through legislation, Congress and state legislatures could pursue objectives that courts were ill-equipped to promote through more disjointed judicial decision-making. Even as they preempted some persons' separate choices, federal and state laws empowered other persons whose rights had been hollow shells under a regime of judicially supervised markets."[69] The Court's switch did more than simply bow to legislative authority; it implicitly recognized the legislature's *constitutional obligation to act*:

It is not necessary to conclude that rights and powers of economic autonomy lost constitutional status as federal judges withdrew from enforcing them as limits on legislative and executive authority. On the contrary, it would be reasonable to conclude that legislative and executive officials provided security for *constitutional* prerogatives (characterized as "liberties," "privileges," or "immunities") in ways that judges alone could not: by making and enforcing laws of general applicability. Judges in effect conceded, moreover, that legislatures had *authority,* based on *the Constitution,* that the judges lacked.[70]

Recognition of a right as *constitutionally obligating* the legislature to act commands moral authority in a way that a bare argument that legislation is good policy does not. Indeed, Antifederalists, in opposing adoption of the Constitution, viewed constitutions as statements of the "principles 'upon which the social compact is founded.'"[71] They argued against adoption of a constitution that lacked a bill of rights setting forth the "purposes for which the compact is made."[72] They relied for their arguments on state constitutions' bills of rights, which were "often of an exhortatory kind" that "served to promote republican virtue among citizens as well as provide standards for evaluating government actions."[73] Bills of rights served to shape a republican culture.

James Madison, in moving from opposition to a federal bill of rights to support, adopted variants of many of the Antifederalist arguments. In particular, he agreed that enumerated rights could serve educative functions:[74] "the political truths declared in that solemn manner acquire by degrees the character of fundamental maxims of Free government, and as they become incorporated with the national sentiment, counteract the impulses of interest and passion."[75] Moreover, at least where evils spring from the usurped acts of government, a bill of rights will be a ground for "an appeal to the sense of the community."[76]

This exhortatory function of constitutional rights as urging legislators and the people to action is consistent with the abolitionist-based vision of equal protection as a guarantee against bowing to dual sovereigns:

[T]he general concept of equal protection advanced by the abolitionists (as well as modern antisubordinationists) requires the exercise not of . . . adjudicative virtue but of citizen and legislative virtues. To know what the equal protection clause requires us to protect, and what it requires us to protect against, requires a view, articulated or not, widely accepted or not, debated and debatable or not, of the content of liberty, of human nature, of natural rights, and given our commitment to democracy, of human and citizen obligation. We need to know who we are and how we should distribute our collective resources: what we owe to whom. . . . These distributive and re-distributive questions may not be questions that judges can or should answer. They are precisely the questions we need to ask of ourselves and of our representatives, however.[77]

The obligation of legislatures to act extends to state legislatures as well as to Congress. Section 1 of the Fourteenth Amendment identifies persons born or naturalized in the United States as citizens of both the United States and "of the State wherein they reside."[78] This language supports the idea that "the people" are constituted both as a nation *and* as members of states, who may act through state institutions of government.[79] "The constitutional design continues to allow state officials and the people of the respective states to play important roles not only in ratifying formal amendments but also in exercising other rights and powers in ways that shape political discourse."[80] Section 1 goes on to declare, "No *State* shall make or enforce any law which shall abridge the privileges or immunities of citizens of the United States; nor shall any *State* deprive any person of life, liberty, or property, without due process of law; nor deny to any person within its jurisdiction the equal protection of the laws."[81] Although section 5 empowers Congress, by appropriate legislation, to enforce the amendment, the amendment's proscriptions are directed *to the states*. If state governments are denying persons equal protection, those governments, including their state legislatures, are obligated to correct the problem in the first instance.

Even were this not so, however, arguments analogous to those made here as to the federal constitution can be made concerning each of the state constitutions. This observation matters because most rape cases are tried in state courts under state criminal law. States are obligated to ensure equal protection for rape victims at those trials, whether we root that obligation in the federal or state constitutions or the dictates of sound policy.[82]

The constitutional arguments made here hence all seek to promote systemic reform of rape trials by means of legislative action. Free speech and equal protection principles obligate state legislatures to ensure rape victims' meaningful voice at rape trials. Equal protection principles also obligate legislatures to act in a way that improves the jury's function in checking abuses of governmental or private patriarchal power.

Conclusion

A rape law reform movement swept the nation in the 1970s and 1980s. That movement urged courts and legislatures to treat rape the same as other crimes. Before that movement, rape was treated uniquely. Rape, unlike burglary, robbery, or even murder, required corroboration. The corroboration requirement reflected Sir Matthew Hale's fear that rape is a charge "easily to be made and hard to be proved, and harder to be defended by the party accused, tho[ugh] never so innocent."[1]

This same fear of female lies led judges to caution jurors about Hale's concerns. Again, for no other crime were jurors told to distrust the victim. "Hell hath no fury like a woman scorned," the "sense of shame after consenting to illicit intercourse," and similar motives to lie were said to explain why rape had to be treated differently. Notably, to avoid false cries of rape by women feeling guilty about their consensual sexual exploits, the law required women to resist to the utmost. That requirement also embodied a belief in the normalcy of male sexual aggression and of female feigned resistance.[2] The original Kinsey research team explained that men were "expected to overcome maidenly modesty or even mild disinclination, but not to overpower an active aversion." Furthermore, the team said, because "society expects the male to be the aggressor in heterosexual relationships, a certain amount of physical force and duress is consequently acceptable and perhaps even socially necessary."[3] Finally, rape differed from other crimes because the law "focus[ed] on the character and behavior of the victim rather than on the behavior of the offender."[4] The victim's prior sexual conduct was relevant, both to impeach her credibility (tramps lie) and to make her consent more likely. The courts distinguished between a woman "who has already submitted herself to the lewd embraces of another, and the coy and modest female severely chaste and instinctively shuddering at the thought of impurity."[5]

One early feminist writer highlighted these differences by asking her readers to imagine a robbery victim being questioned as rape victims were:

Mr. Smith, you were held up at gun-point at the corner of First and Main?
Yes.
Did you struggle with the robber?
No.
Why not?
He was armed.
Then you made a conscious decision to comply with his demands rather than resist?
Yes.
Did you scream? Cry out?
No, I was afraid.
I see. Have you ever been held up before?
No.
Have you ever *given* money away?
Yes, of course.
And you did so willingly?
What are you getting at?
Well, let's put it like this, Mr. Smith. You've given money away in the past. In fact you've quite a reputation for philanthropy. How can we be sure that you weren't *contriving* to have your money taken from you by force?[6]

The fictive defense attorney continues questioning Mr. Smith about what he wore, where he walked, and when. The attorney finally asks: "In other words, Mr. Smith, you were walking around the streets late at night in a suit that practically advertised the fact that you might be a good target for easy money, isn't that so? I mean, if we didn't know better, Mr. Smith, we might even think you were *asking* for this to happen, mightn't we?"[7]

The law reformers accordingly sought equal treatment between rape and other crimes. Equal treatment meant eliminating the corroboration and utmost-resistance requirements, barring cautionary instructions, and prohibiting inquiry into the victim's prior sexual conduct.[8]

Yet, the instrumental goals that the reformers sought to achieve by such equal treatment have eluded us. There has been, at best, modest success in encouraging more victims to prosecute, in increasing conviction rates for the guilty, and in promoting more humane treatment of rape victims. The reformers' symbolic victories were small too. The new laws did not foster a widespread rejection of patriarchal views. We still continue to live in a "rape culture" whose views on gender promote sexual violence. Indeed, there has been a cultural backlash in which icons like Camille Paglia glory in male sexual aggression and female passivity.[9]

The blindness of the law-reform arm of the antirape movement to rape's uniqueness is curious because the broader movement's theorists were not so blind. These theorists saw that rape, unlike robbery, is a crucial support for patriarchy. The fear of rape among women not yet raped leads them to rely on male protectors, avoid nocturnal public spaces, dress modestly, and repress their sexuality.[10] Moreover, rape itself serves as an assertion of male power, degrading all women while empowering the rapist's manliness. Susan Brownmiller, a leader in the antirape movement and author of the pathbreaking *Against Our Will: Men, Women, and Rape,* explained rape's unique role as a prop for male power:

> A world without rapists would be a world in which women moved freely without fear of men. That *some* men rape provides a sufficient threat to keep all women in a constant state of intimidation, forever conscious of the knowledge that the biological tool must be held in awe, for it may turn to weapon with sudden swiftness born of harmful intent. Myrmidons to the cause of male dominance, police-blotter rapists have performed their duty well, so well in fact that the true meaning of their act has largely gone unnoticed. Rather than society's aberrants or "spoilers of purity," men who commit rape have served in effect as front-line masculine shock troops, terrorist guerillas in the longest sustained battle the world has ever known.[11]

The fear by which this battle is waged is not easily unlearned. The messages underlying the fear are embodied in cultural narratives that invade rape trial courtrooms. Treating rape like other crimes fails to contend with the unique power of these narratives.

While failing to contend with rape's uniqueness, the reformers also failed to contend with one crucial way in which rape and other crimes *are* alike: all crimes are judged at adversarial criminal trials.[12] Our current adversarialism, however, is modeled after male "ways of speaking" in everyday life. Just as those ways of speaking mute the female voice in business, education, and politics, so do they mute that voice at trials.

The inability to engage with cultural narratives and macho adversarialism explains rape-law reform's failure. These primary mechanisms by which rape jurors determine credibility are unchanged. Consequently, unjustified acquittals mount.[13]

But the messages sent by those acquittals and by lawyers' treatment of rape victims at trials imposes heavy social costs. The voices of women as a group are muted, patriarchy's hold on all our lives is enhanced, and our justice system is deprived of the insights of female experience.

These costs are political ones. To view them as costs is to conclude that evidence law must embrace political values of voice, participation, and equality. To acknowledge that political values matter at trial is to unmask the myth that "facts" and "values" are entirely distinct. By embracing the narrative/linguistic critique of the rape trial as rooted in a false apoliticism and a flawed machismo inherent in the adversary system itself, we challenge current orthodoxies at work in our justice system everyday. The implications of the analysis offered here thus extend far beyond the rape trial. Fear of those implications may thus bolster opposition to the proposals made here.

Yet without the candor of challenging fundamentals, real change will continue to be a chimera. Moreover, although the method set forth here may have radical implications, the specific proposals made here relate to rape trials alone. The proposals also seek to tinker only around the edges of adversarialism. The political reality is that more far-reaching progressive changes in our justice system have little hope of surviving legislative debate. I have sought, therefore, to reconcile radical insight with political pragmatism. The modest changes advanced—revised prosecutorial tactics, new jury selection procedures, altered character evidence rules, a single addition to lawyers' ethics codes, enhanced expert testimony, uninterrupted narratives, and testimonial intermediaries—are meant to provide a workable agenda for legislative change. But both the method of justifying that change and the positive messages sent by its implementation are part of the broader, feminist project of building a more caring, just society.

Notes

NOTES TO THE INTRODUCTION

1. My apologies to the trial lawyers among my readers. I have deleted some objections and streamlined others to promote readability. I have also reconstructed this scene based on my memory of the events, unlike in later chapters, where I rely on actual trial transcripts.

2. *See* NATIONAL VICTIM CENTER AND THE CRIME VICTIMS RESEARCH AND TREATMENT CENTER, RAPE IN AMERICA: A REPORT TO THE NATION 1–16 (April 23, 1992) (survey and interview data on repeated rapes of the same victims, concluding that "39%, or an estimated 4.7 million women were raped more than once. . . ."); Mary P. Koss, *Hidden Rape: Sexual Aggression and Victimization in a National Sample of Students in Higher Education, in* RAPE AND SOCIETY: READINGS ON THE PROBLEM OF SEXUAL ASSAULT 44 (Patricia Searles & Ronald J. Berger eds. 1995) (41 percent of rape victims in college-student survey expected a *similar* assault to happen again); DIANA E. H. RUSSELL, THE POLITICS OF RAPE: THE VICTIM'S PERSPECTIVE 44–51 (1974) (recounting similar repetitive rapes of a single particularly vulnerable victim over a two-week period).

3. *See* Andrew E. Taslitz, *Myself Alone: Individualizing Justice Through Psychological Character Evidence*, 52 MD. L. REV. 1, 76–83 (1993) (recounting the qualifications and procedures required for reliable clinical psychological judgment).

4. *See* PAUL C. GIANNELLI & EDWARD J. IMWINKELREID, SCIENTIFIC EVIDENCE 242–56 (1986) (most courts exclude polygraph ("lie-detector") test results absent stipulation); PAUL EKMAN, TELLING LIES: CLUES TO DECEIT IN THE MARKETPLACE, POLITICS, AND MARRIAGE 279–98 (1992) ("Professional lie catchers—police, . . . judges, and government" often do no better than chance). Four members of the United States Supreme Court have also recently expressed concern about the polygraph's reliability. *See United States v. Scheffer,* 118 S. Ct. 1261, 1263–66 (1998) (per se rule against admission of polygraph evidence in court martial proceedings did not violate accused's constitutional right to present a defense).

5. For a recounting of the justice system's brutal denial of rape victim autonomy and dignity, *see* LEE MADIGAN & NANCY C. GAMBLE, THE SECOND RAPE: SOCIETY'S CONTINUED BETRAYAL OF THE VICTIM (1989).

6. *See generally* L. CUTLER & STEVEN R. PENROD, MISTAKEN IDENTIFICATION: THE EYEWITNESS, PSYCHOLOGY, AND THE LAW (1995). My experience as a prosecutor also revealed ready jury reliance on what I now realize were questionable eyewitness identifications.

7. For a summary of the literature on the justice system's courtroom treatment of rape victims and the failure of ever-changing law reform in this area, *see* Andrew E. Taslitz, *Patriarchal Stories I: Cultural Rape Narratives in the Courtroom*, 5 S. CAL. REV. L. & WOM.'S ST. 387 (1996) [hereafter *Patriarchal Stories*]. *But see* David Bryden and Sonja Lengnick, *Criminal Law: Rape in the Criminal Justice System*, 87 J. CRIM. L. & CRIMINOLOGY 1194, 1377–81 (1997) (arguing that rape report rates have improved and jury bias somewhat declined, but probably because of some changes in attitudes rather than because of rape law reform, while conceding that "there is a great deal of anecdotal and social-scientific evidence of public (and jury) bias against norm-violating victims of acquaintance rape."). For a discussion of the postincident behavior of rape victims, *see* JUDITH ROWLAND, THE ULTIMATE VIOLATION (1985). For an analysis of the degree of physical injury involved in rape, *see* NATIONAL RESEARCH COUNCIL, UNDERSTANDING VIOLENCE AGAINST WOMEN 75 (1996) ("[T]he data show that between one-half and two-thirds of rape victims sustain no physical injury . . . .").

8. *See* COLLEEN A. WARD, ATTITUDES TOWARD RAPE: FEMINIST AND SOCIAL PSYCHOLOGICAL PERSPECTIVES 101–7 (1995) (surveying rape jury research).

9. Regarding feminist conceptions of the social function of rape and that function's reflection in our treatment of victims, the pathbreaking work is SUSAN BROWNMILLER, AGAINST OUR WILL: MEN, WOMEN AND RAPE (1975). More recent works include STEPHEN J. SCHULHOFER, UNWANTED SEX: THE CULTURE OF INTIMIDATION AND THE FAILURE OF LAW 1–46 (1998); PEGGY REEVES SANDAY, A WOMAN SCORNED: ACQUAINTANCE RAPE ON TRIAL (1996); RUS ERVIN FUNK, STOPPING RAPE: A CHALLENGE FOR MEN (1993); and MARGARET T. GORDON & STEPHANIE RIGER, THE FEMALE FEAR (1989). On the status of early rape law and the failure of law reform efforts, *see* NANCY A. MATTHEWS, CONFRONTING RAPE: THE FEMINIST ANTI-RAPE MOVEMENT AND THE STATE (1994); CASSIA SPOHN & JULIE HORNEY, RAPE LAW REFORM: A GRASSROOTS REVOLUTION AND ITS IMPACT (1992); SUE BESSMER, THE LAWS OF RAPE (1984); and Taslitz, *supra* note 7, at 389–93.

10. *See* Taslitz, *supra* note 7, at 387–439 (reviewing ways in which criminal justice actors evade rape law reform).

11. *See e.g.,* Julie A. Wright, *Using the Female Perspective in Prosecuting Rape Cases,* 29 FED. PROSECUTOR 19 (1995) (noting many women "tend not to believe rape victims as a method of psychological self-protection. If women accept that such an intimate violation could happen to this woman, then they must in turn implicitly accept the fact that it could also happen to them."); WARD, *supra* note 8, at 78–82 (noting that men are nevertheless more likely than women to hold reactionary attitudes toward rape).

12. ROGER C. SCHANK, TELL ME A STORY: A NEW LOOK AT REAL AND ARTIFICIAL MEMORY 8–16 (1990).

13. *See, e.g.,* Nancy Pennington and Reid Hastie, *The Story Model for Juror Decision Making, in* INSIDE THE JUROR: THE PSYCHOLOGY OF JUROR DECISION-MAKING 195 (Reid Hastie ed. 1993); W. LANCE BENNETT & MARTHA S. FELDMAN, RECONSTRUCTING REALITY IN THE COURT-ROOM: JUSTICE AND JUDGMENT IN AMERICAN CULTURE (1981).

14. *See* SUSAN J. DOUGLAS, WHERE THE GIRLS ARE: GROWING UP FEMALE WITH THE MASS MEDIA 79–80, 202, 210–11, 236, 244, 294, 302–3 (1994).

15. *See* HELEN BENEDICT, VIRGIN OR VAMP: HOW THE PRESS COVERS SEX CRIMES 7–8 (1992).

16. GENESIS 39.

17. J. M. BARRIE, PETER PAN 30, 38, 66, 83 (1911); DOUGLAS, *supra* note 14, at 30 (defining "embonpoint").

18. *See, e.g.,* Wahneema Lubiano, *Black Ladies, Welfare Queens, and State Minstrels: Ideological War by Narrative Means, in* RACE-ING JUSTICE, EN-GENDERING POWER: ESSAYS ON ANITA HILL, CLARENCE THOMAS, AND THE CONSTRUCTION OF SOCIAL REALITY 323–30 (Toni Morrison ed. 1992); Taslitz, *supra* note 7, at 459 n. 479 (reviewing empirical data on juror reactions to black rape complainants).

19. *See* DAVID LUBAN, LAWYERS AND JUSTICE: AN ETHICAL STUDY 56–78 (1988).

20. *See* DEBORAH TANNEN, YOU JUST DON'T UNDERSTAND: WOMEN AND MEN IN CONVERSATION 24–48 (1990) (discussing differing linguistic worlds of men and women).

21. MARY CRAWFORD, TALKING DIFFERENCE: ON GENDER AND LANGUAGE (1995) (reviewing data on male-female language differences and articulating a "social constructionist" alternative to essentialist explanations of these differences).

22. *See* W. KIP VISCUSI ET AL., ECONOMICS, REGULATION, AND AN-TITRUST 324 (2d ed. 1995) (defining "externalities").

NOTES TO CHAPTER 1

1. DAN P. MCADAMS, THE STORIES WE LIVE BY: PERSONAL MYTHS AND THE MAKING OF THE SELF 17 (1993) (quoting Elie Wiesel).

2. For an interesting explanation of how storytelling shapes our memories and is intricately tied up with how we reason, *see generally* ROGER C. SCHANK, TELL ME A STORY: A NEW LOOK AT REAL AND ARTIFICIAL MEMORY (1990); WALTER R. FISHER, HUMAN COMMUNICATION AS NARRATION: TOWARD A PHILOSOPHY OF REASON, VALUE, AND ACTION 105–10 (1987). For analysis of the application of storytelling theory to jury trials, *see* RICHARD D. RIEKE & RANDALL K. STUTMAN, COMMUNICATION IN LEGAL ADVOCACY 94–102 (1990); SPECIAL COMMITTEE ON JURY COMPREHENSION, ABA SECTION OF LITIGATION, JURY COMPREHENSION IN COMPLEX CASES, App. 10, at 18–19 (Dec. 1989). Rieke and Stutman's text includes a thorough explanation of the concepts of "narrative coherence" and "narrative fidelity" developed here. For an analysis of the psychological reasons that cultural tales grip our evidentiary imaginations so powerfully, *see* Andrew E. Taslitz, *Patriarchal Stories I: Cultural Rape Narratives in the Courtroom*, 5 S. CAL. REV. L. & WOM.'S ST. 387, 404–33 (1996).

3. The Ms. B example is a modification of one presented at Richard J. Bonnie and Christopher Slobogin, *The Role of Mental Health Professionals in the Criminal Process: The Case for Informed Speculation*, 66 VA. L. REV. 427, 477–79 (1980). I have used the Ms. B example before to illustrate storytelling's power in another context. *See* Andrew E. Taslitz, *Myself Alone: Individualizing Justice Through Psychological Character Evidence*, 52 MD. L. REV. 1, 95–97 (1993).

4. *See* SCHANK, *supra* note 2, at 8–26, 57–60, 148–50, 201 (explaining how standard story "skeletons" affect our reasoning).

5. *See* idem at 83.

6. *See* Mark Cammack, *In Search of the Post-Positivist Jury*, 70 IND. L. J. 405, 463–66 (1995) (discussing implications of language categories and labels for the constitutional law of jury selection). *See generally* MICHEL FOUCAULT, THE ORDER OF THINGS (1972) (emphasizing contingent nature of linguistic classificatory schemes).

7. Valerie Fridland, *Language and Power in Male-on-Male Rape Trials*, in CULTURAL PERFORMANCES: PROCEEDINGS OF THE THIRD BERKELEY WOMEN AND LANGUAGE CONFERENCE 205–19 (Emily Bucholtz et al. eds. 1996).

8. MCADAMS, *supra* note 1, at 67.

9. *See* Stevi Jackson, *The Social Context of Rape: Sexual Scripts and Motivation*, in RAPE AND SOCIETY: READINGS ON THE PROBLEM OF SEXUAL ASSAULT 16, 21, 24 (Patricia Searles & Ronald J. Berger eds. 1995) (on cultural scripts concerning women who voice their own sexual needs or protest male sex-

ual aggression); RICHARD LEMPERT & JOSEPH SANDERS, AN INVITATION TO LAW AND SOCIAL SCIENCE 129 (1986) (noting role of foreseeability in moral judgments).

10. *See* SUSAN ESTRICH, REAL RAPE 1–26 (1987) (defining the concept of "real rape" and its consequences).

11. *See* AVERY CORMAN, PRIZED POSSESSIONS 58–62, 127 (1991) (novel in which rape literally silences the victim, a music major who can no longer sing until the tale's end, and who was raped to stop her "constant talking").

12. *See* ROGER HODGE & GUNTHER KRESS, SOCIAL SEMIOTICS 45, 83 (1988) (silence indicates lack of power); Peggy Reeves Sanday, *Rape and the Silencing of the Feminine*, in RAPE 84, 85 (Sylvann Tomaselli & Roy Porter eds. 1986) (women in rape-prone societies generally do not participate in public decision making, and those who do are treated with contempt).

13. The version of the tale told here comes from my own viewing of the rental video *The Little Mermaid* (Disney 1990), whose story contrasts sharply with the Hans Christian Andersen original. *See* Gwyneth Cravens, *Past Present*, THE NATION, May 11, 1992, at 638, 638–40 (making this comparison).

14. *See* SUSAN J. DOUGLAS, WHERE THE GIRLS ARE: GROWING UP FEMALE WITH THE MASS MEDIA 78–80 (1994) (summarizing film's plot but reaching some more hopeful conclusions than I do here).

15. Idem at 78–79.

16. *See* idem at 209–11.

17. Idem at 210–11.

18. The summary of the plot offered here is drawn from Ann Althouse, *Thelma and Louise and the Law: Do Rape Shield Rules Matter?* 25 LOY. L. A. L. REV. 757 (1992), and my own recent viewing of the film.

19. *See, e.g.,* Susan Wloszczyna, *"Thelma and Louise" Shoots Hole in Stereotypical Roles*, USA TODAY, June 6, 1991, at D4 (quoting one moviegoer, "It's nice to see women making decisions. And I must admit it would be nice to blow out the tires of some obnoxious trucker."); MOLLY HASKELL, FROM REVERENCE TO RAPE: THE TREATMENT OF WOMEN IN THE MOVIES (1987) (describing the movie as a "breakthrough . . . very radical in the way it threatens men.").

20. *See* MARGARET T. GORDON & STEPHANIE RIGER, THE FEMALE FEAR 68–69 (1989) (press primarily reports lurid rapes); HELEN BENEDICT, VIRGIN OR VAMP: HOW THE PRESS COVERS SEX CRIMES 193–95, 200–202 (1992) (defining and illustrating "vamp" stories). One author, relying on a flawed methodology that focused on only three selected high-profile cases, has challenged this claim of media bias. *See* LISA M. CUKLANZ, RAPE ON TRIAL: HOW THE MASS MEDIA CONSTRUCT LEGAL REFORM AND SOCIAL CHANGE (1996). *But see* Claudia Bayliff, *Changing the Climate*, 14 THE WOMEN'S REVIEW OF BOOKS 23 (March 1997) (cataloguing errors in Cuklanz's reasoning).

21. BENEDICT, *supra* note 20, at 19.

22. *See* Leonora Tanenbaum, *Good Victims and Bad, in* THE NATION, Oct. 11, 1993, at 397, 398 (on the whirlpool assault and Big Dan case); BENEDICT, *supra* note 20, at 255–59 (on William Kennedy Smith).

23. *See* Jennifer Temkin, *Women, Rape, and Law Reform, in* RAPE, *supra* note 12, at 19; LYNDA LYTLE HOLMSTROM & ANN WOLBERT BURGESS, THE VICTIM OF RAPE 157–213 (1978).

24. *See* Kim Lane Scheppele, *Just the Facts, Ma'am: Sexualized Violence, Evidentiary Habits, and the Revision of Truth*, 37 N.Y.L. SCH. L. REV. 123 (1992) (explaining why rape victims are initially silent and later face skepticism when they speak).

25. Idem.

26. See ROSALIND MILES, LOVE, SEX, DEATH, AND THE MAKING OF THE MALE 24 (1991).

27. *See generally* JUNE STEPHENSON, MEN ARE NOT COST EFFECTIVE: MALE CRIME IN AMERICA (1995) (summarizing data on percentages and types of violent crime committed by males). But *see* PATRICIA PEARSON, WHEN SHE WAS BAD: VIOLENT WOMEN AND THE MYTH OF INNOCENCE (1997) (documenting instances of female violence).

28. *See* ANNE CAMPBELL, MEN, WOMEN AND AGGRESSION 1–8, 10–11, 15–16, 60–62, 72 (1993) (differing meanings given aggression by men and women); Anne Campbell and Steven Muncer, *Men and the Meaning of Violence, in* MALE VIOLENCE 332–36 (John Archer ed. 1994).

29. *See, e.g.,* Elizabeth Powell, *I Thought You Didn't Mind, in* TRANSFORMING A RAPE CULTURE 108–10 (Emilie Buchwald et al. eds. 1993) (70 percent of students polled who had seen the movie *Pretty Woman* could not remember that it included a rape scene, apparently because throwing a woman on a couch and tearing her clothes off is not that unusual a behavior in our culture for a male who knows the victim of his aggressions); CAMPBELL, *supra* note 28, at 159 ("Among men, aggression is mundane and frequent. It demands a non-pathological account, for if every man who aggressed was deemed insane, there would be few sane men left.").

30. *See* CAMPBELL, *supra* note 28, at 7, 47–50, 55–57, 74–75 (on male aggression as a game).

31. *See* Chris O'Sullivan, *Fraternities and the Rape Culture, in* TRANSFORMING A RAPE CULTURE 26–27 (Emilie Buchwald et al. eds. 1993); PEGGY REEVES SANDAY, FRATERNITY GANG RAPE: SEX, BROTHERHOOD, AND PRIVILEGE ON CAMPUS 11–12 (1990).

32. *See* ROBERT T. MICHAEL ET AL., SEX IN AMERICA: A DEFINITIVE SURVEY 170 (1995) (far fewer men believe that they have used force to have sex than women believe that they have been forced to have sex).

33. *See* SANDAY, *supra* note 31, at 4, 13, 56, 74–75 (on females' assuming the risk of rape); Patricia Y. Martin and Robert A. Hummer, *Fraternities and Gang Rape on Campus*, in RAPE AND SOCIETY: READINGS ON THE PROBLEM OF SEXUAL ASSAULT 151 (Patricia Searles & Ronald J. Berger eds. 1995) (fraternity members often view the sexual coercion of women as a game); CAMPBELL, *supra* note 28, at 58–59 (for many men, "the 'ideal' fight is one in which, by dint of sheer will, the challenger simply withdraws before any blows land.").

34. *See* SUSAN JEFFORDS, HARD BODIES: HOLLYWOOD MASCULINITY IN THE REAGAN ERA 17–25, 30–78, 80–118 (1994) (summarizing *Rambo, Terminator*, and *Back to the Future* plots).

35. *See* RUS ERVIN FUNK, STOPPING RAPE: A CHALLENGE FOR MEN 26–56 (1993); CAMPBELL, *supra* note 28, at 18.

36. SANDAY, *supra* note 31, at 11–13, 29–35, 46, 57, 66 (on "riffing," "beaching," and related fraternity sexual practices).

37. *See* LYNN SEGAL, SLOW MOTION: CHANGING MASCULINITIES, CHANGING MEN 205–71 (1990) (noting most men's fantasy aspirations to hypermasculinity).

38. *See* bell hooks, *Seduced by Violence No More, in* TRANSFORMING A RAPE CULTURE 353–56 (Emilie Buchwald et al. eds. 1993)(many women are successfully trained to be eroticized by stereotypical male behavior); SEGAL, *supra* note 37, at 231.

39. *See* RICHARD NISBETT & LEE ROSS, HUMAN INFERENCE: STRATEGIES AND SHORTCOMINGS OF SOCIAL JUDGMENT 18–22 (1980) (common attitudes toward character); Taslitz, *Myself Alone, supra* note 3, at 65–72, 110–11 (similar).

40. Jackson, *supra* note 9, at 16.

41. DOUGLAS, *supra* note 14, at 209–11 (television movies); BENEDICT, *supra* note 20, at 7–8 (news media).

42. BENEDICT, *supra* note 20, at 35.

43. *"Wilding"—The Newest Term for Terror in a City That Lives in Fear,* N.Y. POST, Apr. 22, 1989, at 2–3.

44. *See* BENEDICT, *supra* note 20, at 201–2 (racial themes in wilding story); FUNK, *supra* note 35, at 57–63 (most rapists are not beasts). *See generally* JANE CAPUTI, THE AGE OF SEX CRIME (1987).

45. JOSEPH CONRAD, HEART OF DARKNESS 105–6 (1902).

46. James Baldwin, *The Black Boy Looks at the White Boy, in* SMILING THROUGH THE APOCALYPSE, ESQUIRE'S HISTORY OF THE SIXTIES 850–51 (1969).

47. *See* ROSE L. H. FINKENSTAEDT, FACE TO FACE, BLACKS IN AMERICA: WHITE PERCEPTIONS AND BLACK REALITIES 158 (1994) (white images of blacks are a sublimation of what the white suppresses); CALVIN C.

HERNTON, SEX AND RACISM IN AMERICA (1965) (tracing in detail the white American obsession with black sexuality, primarily in the South, but in the North as well).

48. HERNTON, *supra* note 47, at 119.

49. *See* SEGAL, *supra* note 37, at 177–78 (on lynching); Jennifer Wriggins, *Rape, Racism, and the Law, in* RAPE AND SOCIETY, *supra* note 9, at 217 (on jury instructions in black-white rape cases and source of quote). *See generally* LAURENCE ALAN BAUGHMAN, SOUTHERN RAPE COMPLEX: A HUNDRED YEAR PSYCHOSIS (1966).

50. *See* JAMES GOODMAN, STORIES OF SCOTTSBORO at xi, 21, 394 (1994); Wriggins, *supra* note 49, at 217; SEGAL, *supra* note 37, at 176.

51. *See* SEGAL, *supra* note 37, at 176 (source of quotes summarizing Fanon's work); PAUL N. SNIDERMAN & THOMAS PIAZZA, THE SCAR OF RACE (1993) (reporting the results of a recent survey about racial attitudes and myths).

52. FINKENSTAEDT, *supra* note 47, at 165 (quoting WILLIAM STYRON, THE CONFESSIONS OF NAT TURNER). On racist images from OTHELLO on, see SEGAL, *supra* note 37, at 176.

53. FINKENSTAEDT, *supra* note 47, at 167.

54. Norman Mailer, *The White Negro, in* PROTEST 304 (1960). *See also* SEGAL, *supra* note 37, at 178–80 (on Kerouac).

55. BENEDICT, *supra* note 20, at 202 (quoting Pete Hamill, *A Savage Disease Called New York*, N.Y. POST (April 23, 1989)); MICHAEL ERIC DYSON, REFLECTING BLACK: AFRICAN-AMERICAN CULTURAL CRITICISM 173–78 (1993) (on racial composition of Central Park jogger suspects).

56. BENEDICT, *supra* note 20, at 202–15; DYSON, *supra* note 55, at 173–78.

57. FINKENSTAEDT, *supra* note 47, at 159.

58. Wriggins, *supra* note 49, at 219.

59. *See* Comments of Professor Elizabeth Iglesias, MID-ATLANTIC SCHOLARS OF COLOR CONFERENCE, Howard University School of Law, April 1995.

60. *See generally* Wahneema Lubiano, *Black Ladies, Welfare Queens, and State Minstrels: Ideological War by Narrative Means, in* RACE-ING JUSTICE, EN-GENDERING POWER: ESSAYS ON ANITA HILL, CLARENCE THOMAS, AND THE CONSTRUCTION OF SOCIAL REALITY 323–30 (Toni Morrison ed. 1992); Nell Irvin Painter, *Hill, Thomas, and the Use of Racial Stereotype, in* RACE-ING JUSTICE, *supra*, at 210.

61. Nell Irvin Painter, *supra* note 60, at 210.

62. HERNTON, *supra* note 47, at 95–96, 124–33.

63. Idem at 96.

64. DIANA E. H. RUSSELL, THE POLITICS OF RAPE: THE VICTIM'S PERSPECTIVE 134 (1984).

65. *See* Taslitz, *Patriarchal Stories, supra* note 2, at 458–59 n. 476 (summarizing relevant empirical data); CATHARINE A. MACKINNON, TOWARD A FEMINIST THEORY OF THE STATE 175 (1989) ("rapable/non-rapable" distinction, but as to all women, regardless of race). For a more detailed analysis of the empirical data, *see* Andrew E. Taslitz, *Race and Two Concepts of the Emotions in Date Rape* (draft manuscript).

66. DYSON, *supra* note 55, at 175–76.

67. Painter, *supra* note 60, at 210.

68. NANCY M. TISCHLER, BLACK MASKS: NEGRO CHARACTERS IN MODERN SOUTHERN FICTION 65 (1969).

69. CHESTER HIMES, BLACK ON BLACK 129 (1973).

70. Jennifer Kabat, *Entrapment, in* THE SUBJECT OF RAPE 65, 66 (Whitney Museum of Art, 3d ed. 1993).

71. Idem at 65.

72. Ellen Rooney, *"A Little More Than Persuading": Tess and the Subject of Sexual Violence, in* RAPE AND REPRESENTATION 87, 93 (Lynn A. Higgins & Brenda R. Silver eds. 1991). *See also* PEGGY REEVES SANDAY, A WOMAN SCORNED: ACQUAINTANCE RAPE ON TRIAL 180–264 (1996) (history of American idea that "no" means either "yes" or "maybe").

73. SIGMUND FREUD, THE PSYCHOPATHOLOGY OF EVERYDAY LIFE 202 & n. 1 (A. A. Brill trans. 1914); *accord* John Forrester, *Rape, Seduction, and Psychoanalysis, in* RAPE, *supra* note 12, at 57, 58–60; SUSAN BROWNMILLER, AGAINST OUR WILL: MEN, WOMEN AND RAPE 315–17 (1975).

74. Forrester, *supra* note 73, at 61–63.

75. GLANVILLE WILLIAMS, TEXTBOOK OF CRIMINAL LAW 197 (1978) (quotation); GLANVILLE WILLIAMS, CRIMINAL LAW 34–36 (1961) (conscious desires matter).

76. Rooney, *supra* note 72, at 93.

77. Idem at 97.

78. The movie is *Tess* (Columbia Tri-Star, 1979). The plot and quotations here, unless otherwise noted, are from THOMAS HARDY, TESS OF THE D'URBERVILLES 15, 35, 45–46, 62–80, 74–79, 79–80 (Heritage Press 1956), with plot summaries and analyses drawn in part from PETER CASAGRANDE, TESS OF THE D'URBERVILLES: UNORTHODOX BEAUTY 11 (1992); Rooney, *supra* note 72, at 53.

79. IAN GREGOR, THE GREAT WEB 182 (1974).

80. HARDY, *supra* note 78, at 93 (emphasis added). On women as dangerous, irrational animals, *see* HELEN HASTE, THE SEXUAL METAPHOR 37 (1993); JAMAKE HIGHWATER, MYTH AND SEXUALITY 8–9, 22–23 (1990); WILLIAM IRWIN THOMPSON, THE TIME FALLING BODIES TAKE TO LIGHT: MYTHOLOGY, SEXUALITY, AND THE ORIGINS OF CULTURE 16, 250 (1981).

81. HARDY, *supra* note 78, at 101–3 (emphasis added).

82. Rooney, *supra* note 72, at 99–100. *Cf.* Kathleen Cairney, *Recognizing Acquaintance Rape in Potentially Consensual Situations: A Re-examination of Thomas Hardy's Tess of the D'Urbervilles*, 3 AM. U. J. GENDER & L. 301 (1995) (arguing Tess was a victim of "date rape," a point slightly different from my argument that Hardy intended ambiguity, a blurring of the rape/seduction line).

83. Robert Garcia, *Rape, Lies, and Videotape*, 25 LOY. L. A. L. REV. 711, 711–12 (1992).

84. The discussion here of Sniderman and Piazza's work, and of the views of racism skeptics, is drawn from PAUL N. SNIDERMAN & THOMAS PIAZZA, THE SCAR OF RACE 32–51, 66–86, 171 (1993). For a definition of institutional racism, *see* Roy L. Brooks and Mary Jo Newborn, *Critical Race Theory and Classical-Liberal Civil Rights Scholarship: A Distinction Without a Difference*, 82 CAL. L. REV. 787, 789 (1994).

85. Literally all the empirical research, whether surveys, experiments, or field studies, on attitudes toward rape is summarized and critiqued in COLLEEN A. WARD, ATTITUDES TOWARD RAPE: FEMINIST AND SOCIAL PSYCHO-LOGICAL PERSPECTIVES (1995). The discussion here draws on Ward, *supra*, at 44–45, 50–55, 64–65, 73–86, as well as David R. Holcomb et al., *Attitudes About Date Rape: Gender Differences Among College Students*, C. STUDENT J. 25, 434–39 (1991); R. F. Rich and R. J. Sampson, *Public Perceptions of Criminal Justice Policy: Does Victimization Make a Difference?, in* VIOLENCE AND VIC-TIMS 5, 109–18 (1990). Another important recent study consistent with the view defended here is IDA M. JOHNSON & ROBERT T. STIGLER, FORCED SEX-UAL INTERCOURSE IN INTIMATE RELATIONSHIPS 77–102 (1997).

86. MICHAEL ET AL., *supra* note 32, at 221.

87. *See, e.g.,* Karen L. Cipriani, *The Numbers Don't Add Up: Challenging the Premise of J.E.B. v. Alabama*, 31 AM. CRIM. L. REV. 1253, 1266 (1994) (study finding 63 percent of seated jurors female, 36 percent male, between January and June 1993 in the District of Columbia Circuit Court); Laura G. Dooley, *Our Juries, Ourselves: The Power, Perception, and Politics of the Civil Jury*, 80 COR-NELL L. REV. 325, 361 (1995) (summarizing study of federal courts in eight major cities finding that women constituted close to 53 percent of serving jurors, men just under 47 percent). To say that men are *more* likely than women to hold reactionary attitudes does *not* necessarily mean that women's attitudes are progressive. Moreover, some studies find women *more* willing than men to blame victims, especially where the victim has been careless. *See* WARD, *supra* note 85, at 80–82. To the extent that women's attitudes are the same as, or more reactionary than, men's under particular circumstances, my argument in text that patriarchal attitudes are alive and well is even stronger. Indeed, it may be the case that women blame careless victims and men blame seductive ones, the two sexes thus jointly creating powerful pressures for acquittal. *See idem.*

88. *See* WARD, *supra* note 85, at 47–48, 59 (impact of education on rape attitudes); STEPHEN J. ADLER, DISORDER IN THE COURT 50–63, 82–83, 219 (1994) (describing ways in which the well-educated escape jury duty). Race may complicate matters further. *See* WARD, *supra* note 85, at 49 (black and Hispanic minorities in the United States found in survey research to hold more stereotyped and victim-blaming attitudes, which may be significant in juries drawn from urban areas with large minority populations).

89. *See* WARD, *supra* note 85, at 63–64, 87–88, 95–110 (describing nature of rape attitude studies); Taslitz, *Myself Alone, supra* note 3, at 94–98 (when jurors draw on cultural stories).

90. *See* Taslitz, *Patriarchal Stories, supra* note 2, at 471 n. 549 (summarizing data on how a small male group can sometimes dominate jury deliberations).

91. *See* idem at 394–402 (discussing Denier assault on feminism in detail). *See generally* TANYA MELICH, THE REPUBLICAN WAR AGAINST WOMEN: AN INSIDER'S REPORT FROM BEHIND THE LINES (1996).

92. *See* FED. R. EVID. 413–15; JOSEPHINE DONOVAN, FEMINIST THEORY: THE INTELLECTUAL TRADITIONS OF AMERICAN FEMINISM 31–64 (1992) (defining philosophical school of "cultural feminism"); Dalhi Myers, *Feminism, the New Federal Rules of Evidence, and Me: An Unlikely Detractor* 4–6 (1995) (unpublished manuscript on file with author) (tracing political machinations that led to the new Federal Rules of Evidence 413–15); NANCY A. MATTHEWS, CONFRONTING RAPE: THE FEMINIST ANTI-RAPE MOVEMENT AND THE STATE 9–40 (1994) (tracing grassroots growth of rape law reform); *cf.* Andrew E. Taslitz, *Interpretive Method and the Federal Rules of Evidence: A Call for a Politically Realistic Hermeneutics,* 32 HARV. J. ON LEGIS. 329, 355–57, 379–81 (1995) (explaining economics and politics of how legislatures work, from which flows the "political feminism" distinction); NORMAN J. FINKEL, COMMONSENSE JUSTICE: JURORS' NOTIONS OF THE LAW 319–37 (1995) (jurors' notions of commonsense justice are more subjective, contextual, and character-based than the law's). The position that adoption of Rules 413–15 shows the widespread adoption of feminist attitudes was also articulated by numerous attendees at the First International Conference on Criminal Evidence Law, held in The Hague, Netherlands, December 1995.

93. *See* RICHARD DELGADO, THE RODRIGO CHRONICLES 48 (1995) (homeostatic function); GIRARDEAU SPANN, RACE AGAINST THE COURT (1993) (similar point about Supreme Court's constitutional decisions about race); Lisa C. Ikemoto, *Traces of the Master Narrative in the Story of African-American /Korean-American Conflict: How We Constructed Los Angeles,* 66 S. CAL. L. REV. 1581 (1993) (using a similar definition as a partial explanation for white supremacy).

94. *See* Taslitz, *Patriarchal Stories, supra* note 2, at 389–402.

NOTES TO CHAPTER 2

1. The facts of the Audrey Savage and David Forshile case and all relevant quotes concerning that case come from AUDREY SAVAGE, TWICE RAPED 4–13, 29–34, 50–65, 68–77, 80–81, 92–116, 119–23, 138–40 (1990).

2. *See, e.g.,* PETER LAUFER, A QUESTION OF CONSENT: INNOCENCE AND COMPLICITY IN THE GLEN RIDGE RAPE CASE 63 (1994).

3. *See* SAVAGE, *supra* note 1, at 67–70, 127–78.

4. The facts of the Mike Tyson case and all relevant quotations concerning that case are drawn from J. GREGORY GARRISON & RANDY ROBERTS, HEAVY JUSTICE: THE STATE OF INDIANA V. MIKE TYSON 1–53, 54, 78, 103, 125, 183–225, 213, 221–22, 234, 242, 246, 249–50, 254, 256, 295 (1994). *See also* L. Patrick Auld, Note, *State of Indiana v. Michael Tyson: Was the Fight Fair?* 31 CRIM. L. BULL. 113, 120–21 (1995). Some of Auld's arguments are rebutted in GARRISON & ROBERTS, *supra*, at 239–42.

5. GARRISON & ROBERTS, *supra* note 4, at 52–53.

6. *See* Auld, *supra* note 4.

7. The facts and quotations here are all taken from LAUFER, *supra* note 2, at xvi, xvii, 8–11, 37–46, 52–53, 63–67, 127–45. For a more thorough analysis of the sociological factors and cultural history of Glen Ridge involved in the rape, *see* BERNARD LEFKOWITZ, OUR GUYS: THE GLEN RIDGE RAPE AND THE SECRET LIFE OF THE PERFECT SUBURB (1997). The victim's name used by Laufer, "Betty Harris," is a pseudonym adopted to protect her true identity.

8. *See* VLADIMIR NABOKOV, LOLITA (1955).

NOTES TO CHAPTER 3

1. *See, e.g.,* Stevi Jackson, *The Social Context of Rape: Sexual Scripts And Motivation, in* RAPE AND SOCIETY: READINGS ON THE PROBLEM OF SEXUAL ASSAULT 277, 287 (Patricia Searles & Ronald J. Berger eds. 1995); Aviva Orenstein, *No Bad Men! A Feminist Analysis of Character Evidence in Rape Trials* (draft manuscript 1997).

2. *See* Andrew E. Taslitz, *Myself Alone: Individualizing Justice Through Psychological Character Evidence,* 52 MD. L. REV. 1, 14–24 (1993); *Patriarchal Stories,* 492 n. 660 (reviewing case law on rape trauma syndrome and addressing related tactical concerns). *See generally* JUDITH ROWLAND, RAPE: THE ULTIMATE VIOLATION (1985) (on rape trauma syndrome). For a detailed analysis of varied meanings of the term "rape trauma syndrome," and of the scientific support for various uses of the concept, *see* DAVID L. FAIGMAN ET AL., MODERN SCIENTIFIC EVIDENCE: THE LAW AND SCIENCE OF EXPERT TESTIMONY §§ 10–2 to 10–2.4.2, at 414–35. There may be admissibility problems in many jurisdictions with expressly raising the "bruising" argument regarding

rape trauma syndrome. *See* Taslitz, *Patriarchal Stories, supra,* at 492 n. 660 (also noting ways to address these problems).

3. *See, e.g.,* Model Rules of Professional Conduct Rule 3.8 cmt. (1983) ("A prosecutor has the responsibility of a minister of justice."); Taslitz, *Patriarchal Stories, supra* note 2, at 492 n. 61 (defending ethical argument made here).

4. It would also often be wrong for defense counsel to appeal to racism, for example, by feeding images of black victims as whores by definition. *See, e.g.,* Andrew E. Taslitz and Sharon Styles-Anderson, *Still Officers of the Court: Why the First Amendment Is No Bar to Challenging Racism, Sexism, and Ethnic Bias in the Legal Profession,* 9 GEO. J. LEG. ETHICS 781 (1996); GARY LAFREE, RAPE AND CRIMINAL JUSTICE: THE SOCIAL CONSTRUCTION OF SEX-UAL ASSAULT 133–40 (1989) (on intraracial rape).

5. *See* JEFFREY G. MURPHY & JULES L. COLEMAN, PHILOSOPHY OF LAW: AN INTRODUCTION TO JURISPRUDENCE, 120–24 (1990) (distinguishing between "vengeance" and "retribution"); Taslitz, *Myself Alone, supra* note 2, at 14–24 (criminal law embodies our deepest moral codes); LEE MADIGAN & NANCY C. GAMBLE, THE SECOND RAPE: SOCIETY'S CONTINUED BETRAYAL OF THE VICTIM 108–13 (1989); MARGARET T. GORDON & STEPHANIE RIGER, THE FEMALE FEAR 90–117 (1989).

6. *See* CASSIA SPOHN & JULIE HORNEY, RAPE LAW REFORM: A GRASSROOTS REVOLUTION AND ITS IMPACT 160, 166–70 (1992) (how early rape case dealt with pretrial process); PETER LAUFER, A QUESTION OF CONSENT: INNOCENCE AND COMPLICITY IN THE GLEN RIDGE RAPE CASE 80–82 (1994) (summarizing "rape myths"). For details on the question of the admissibility of a rape-trauma-based "bruise" argument, *see* FAIGMAN, *supra* note 2, at §§ 10–1 to 10–1.5, at 403–14.

7. *See* FED. R. EVID. 413–15; Act of Sept. 13, 1994, Pub. L. 103–322, 108 Stat. 2135; Richard Reuben, *Some Judges Oppose Evidence Amendment,* 81 A.B.A. J. 20 (1995) (quoting Professor Edward Imwinkelreid); Taslitz, *Myself Alone, supra* note 2, at 63–86; *see also* James Joseph Duane, *The New Federal Rules of Evidence on Prior Acts of Accused Offenders: A Poorly Drafted Version of a Very Bad Idea,* 157 F.R.D. 95 (1995).

8. *See* FED. R. EVID. 412 advisory committee's note (on why rape shield laws exclude evidence of prior sexual conduct). David F. Bryden & Roger Park, *"Other Crimes" Evidence in Sex Offense Cases,* 78 MINN. L. REV. 529, 531, 535 (1994) (suggesting that some asymmetry between prosecutors and defense counsel in sexual assault cases is necessary to a fair fight). For an argument that privacy concerns also justify this asymmetry, *see* Andrew E. Taslitz, *Race and Two Concepts of the Emotions in Date Rape* (draft manuscript).

9. *See* REPORT OF THE JUDICIAL CONFERENCE OF THE UNITED STATES ON THE ADMISSION OF CHARACTER EVIDENCE IN CERTAIN SEXUAL MISCONDUCT CASES (February 1995); Taslitz, *Myself Alone, supra*

note 2, at 63–86 (reviewing social science data regarding when character helps to predict conduct).

10. *See* Taslitz and Styles-Anderson, *supra* note 4, at 4; Appellant's Opening Brief at 25–33, *Reynolds v. Florida* (June 22, 1990) (No. 89–2668). The American Bar Association has adopted a resolution adding a comment to Rule 8.4 of the Model Rules of Professional Conduct that declares some racist or sexist conduct by lawyers to be unethical if "prejudicial to the administration of justice." But the Rules themselves have not yet been changed. *See* American Bar Association Standing Committee on Ethics and Professional Responsibility and Criminal Justice Section, *Resolution to Amend Comments to Rule 8.4* (adopted by the A.B.A. in August 1998).

11. *See Batson v. Kentucky,* 476 U.S. 79 (1986) (holding that purposeful racial discrimination in jury selection violates the equal protection clause of the United States Constitution); *J.E.B. v. Alabama* ex rel. T. B., 114 S. Ct. 1419 (1994) (extending *Batson* to gender); Julie A. Wright, *Using the Female Perspective in Prosecuting Rape Cases,* FED. PROSECUTOR 19 (1995) (discussing how to determine when and why individual women may be unfair to the state in a rape case and thus still subject to a peremptory strike consistent with *Batson*).

12. *See* COLLEEN A. WARD, ATTITUDES TOWARD RAPE: FEMINIST AND SOCIAL PSYCHOLOGICAL PERSPECTIVES 78–79, 144, 201 (1995); K. Paulsen, *Attribution of Fault to a Rape Victim as a Function of Locus of Control,* 107 J. SOC. PSYCH., 131, 132 (1979); Barry Thornton et al., *Social Perceptions of Rape Victims' Culpability: The Influence of Respondent's Person-Environmental Attribution Tendencies,* 35 HUM. REL., 225, 225–37 (1981).

13. For a detailed discussion of analogous procedures and how courts have addressed the problem of juror privacy, *see* Taslitz, *Patriarchal Stories, supra* note 2, at 498 n. 693.

14. *See Commonwealth v. Gibson,* 567 A. 2d, 724, 732–33 and n. 10 (1989) (noting jurisdictions split on whether the purposes of voir dire include the intelligent exercise of peremptories or are limited to the need to ensure a competent, fair, and impartial jury); JEFFREY ABRAHAMSON, WE, THE JURY: THE JURY SYSTEM AND THE IDEAL OF DEMOCRACY 131–39, 143–76 (1994) (going further than the proposal here in that he argues for the complete elimination of peremptories); FEDERAL JUDICIAL CENTER, REFERENCE MANUAL ON SCIENTIFIC EVIDENCE (1994).

NOTES TO CHAPTER 4

1. DEBORAH TANNEN, YOU JUST DON'T UNDERSTAND: WOMEN AND MEN IN CONVERSATION (1990) [hereinafter DON'T UNDERSTAND]. Another popular but far less scholarly version of a Tannen-like thesis is JOHN GRAY, MEN ARE FROM MARS, WOMEN ARE FROM VENUS (1992). *Cau-*

tionary note: There is a huge number of views on whether and to what extent male and female ways of speaking differ. Moreover, many researchers find methodological flaws in other researchers' work. Certainly more research is needed in many of the relevant areas. It would be impossible in a single brief chapter to address all the necessary views and qualifications. The absence of a deeper level of nuance and detail may trouble some readers trained in linguistics or experimental psychology. Nevertheless, my synthesis of the research is both accurate and fair, and a greater level of detail would ultimately not affect the validity of the arguments made here.

2. TANNEN, DON'T UNDERSTAND, *supra* note 1, at 26.

3. The "Way One" analysis here draws on, without precisely tracking, Tannen's own analysis in TANNEN, DON'T UNDERSTAND, *supra* note 1, at 15–43, 50–95, combined with the further development of her ideas in DEBORAH TANNEN, TALKING FROM 9 TO 5: HOW WOMEN'S AND MEN'S CONVERSATIONAL STYLE AFFECTS WHO GETS HEARD, WHO GETS CREDIT, AND WHAT GETS DONE AT WORK 119–22, 148–49, 300–301 (1994) [hereinafter 9 TO 5]. Tannen characterizes her own work as primarily describing patterns of difference rather than exploring their origins, for example, as rooted in biology or culture. *See* DEBORAH TANNEN, GENDER AND DISCOURSE 12–13 (1994). Nevertheless, she acknowledges that she has "been inclined to regard socialization (that is, cultural experience) as the main influence shaping patterns of behavior." *Id.* at 13. That is why, she explains, she "cites research on the role of childhood peer groups as the source of gendered patterns in ways of speaking." *Id.* at 13. That is why I describe as "Tannen's way" the idea that Josh and Linda were socialized into their different attitudes towards language use.

4. Tannen's critics see her views as "essentialist," meaning that she views gender as a fundamental set of personality traits, rooted in childhood socialization, rather than as a set of behaviors and attitudes caused by daily social and political contexts. *See* MARY CRAWFORD, TALKING DIFFERENCE: ON GENDER AND LANGUAGE 8–9, 91–93 (1995). There are essentialists who largely agree with Tannen's conclusions but root their essentialism in biology, not childhood socialization. *See* ROBERT L. NADEAU, S/HE BRAIN: SCIENCE, SEXUAL POLITICS, AND THE MYTHS OF FEMINISM (1996) (expressly linking biology with Tannen's theories); ROBERT POOL, EVE'S RIB: SEARCHING FOR THE BIOLOGICAL ROOTS OF SEX DIFFERENCES (1994) (summarizing the research on biological differences between the sexes, including regarding language use). Tannen herself rejects the "essentialist" label put on her work by her critics, viewing the term as an "ostracizing label . . . used as a sophisticated form of academic name-calling." TANNEN, GENDER AND DISCOURSE, *supra* note 3, at 14 n. 7. In a recent work, she indeed challenges the tendency of academics to divide themselves into "warring camps" that distort one another's views, seeing the "essentialist/non-essentialist" dichotomy as precisely such a distortion.

See DEBORAH TANNEN, THE ARGUMENT CULTURE: MOVING FROM DEBATE TO DIALOGUE 274–76 (1998). I agree with Tannen's concern about warring camps, but I do not see the "essentialist" label as derisive. *Cf.* ROBIN WEST, CARING FOR JUSTICE 1–20 (1997) (countering many of the critiques of essentialism). Many "essentialists" recognize the importance of childhood socialization in a way that some "social constructionists" do not, and essentialists identify roadblocks to change (to be overcome) that others may miss. Indeed, Tannen, while rejecting the essentialist label, notes that "cultural patterns are extremely resistant to change." *See* TANNEN, GENDER AND DISCOURSE, *supra* note 3, at 13. I summarize Tannen's critics' views of her work here in a style that approximates their own voice precisely because I want to show the foolishness of warring camps. First, even under Tannen's critics' dichotomy, similar solutions are often called for regardless of on which side you stand. Second, the purported dichotomy is false because socialization and current power imbalances both matter—what I have called the "middle way"—a way that Tannen might see as closer to her own vision than to her critics' characterization of her work. For those interested in detailed explanations of the process of childhood socialization underlying social essentialist theories, *see* DONNA EDER, SCHOOL TALK: GENDER AND ADOLESCENT CULTURE 32–36, 61–81, 84–91, 125–48 (1995); JUDY MANN, THE DIFFERENCE: GROWING UP FEMALE IN AMERICA 44 (1994); BARRIE THORNE, GENDER PLAY: GIRLS AND BOYS IN SCHOOL 34–37, 53–58, 73–76 (1994) (rejecting essentialism but with research that can easily be used to support essentialist arguments).

5. The "Way Two" analysis here stems from the numerous critiques of Tannen's work and the articulation of one social constructionist alternative. *See, e.g.,* CRAWFORD, *supra* note 4, at 14, 17–18, 33–34, 40–43, 98, 106–8, 127–28 (on Tannen's allegedly flawed reasoning, one social constructionist alternative, and Josh's freedom to act unilaterally); A. Freed, *We Understand Perfectly: A Critique of Tannen's View of Cross-Sex Communication* 4 (paper presented at the Berkeley Women and Language Conference 1992) (the sense of entitlement to act unilaterally is "part of the social empowerment that men enjoy."); S. Troemel-Plotz, *Review Essay: Selling the Apolitical,* 2 DISCOURSE & SOC'Y, 489, 497–98 (1991) (critiquing Tannen generally). These social constructionists also object to what they see as Tannen's essentializing women because it ignores the role of intersectionality, treating women as an undifferentiated mass, isolated from race, class, and religion. *See* CRAWFORD, *supra* note 4, at 16, 36, 46. On intersectionality *generally, see* Kimberlè Crenshaw, *Demarginalizing the Intersection of Race and Sex: A Black Feminist Critique of Anti-Discrimination Doctrine, Feminist Theory, and Anti-Racist Politics,* 1989 U. CHI. LEGAL F. 139. Certain social constructionists and similar theorists also object to what they consider to be Tannen's stress on personality because consciousness-raising then becomes more important than collective action. *See* JANET HOLMES, WOMEN, MEN, AND

POLITENESS 197 (1995). Furthermore, these social constructionists are irritated by their perception that Tannen has an extremely charitable view of male intentions and willingness to encourage traditional male-female stereotyping. *See* CRAWFORD, *supra* note 4, at 106–98, 127–28. Tannen rejects all these criticisms as unfairly mischaracterizing her work. *See, e.g.*, TANNEN, GENDER AND DISCOURSE, *supra* note 3, at 12–13, 14 n.7; Deborah Tannen, *Response to Senta-Troemel-Ploetz's "Selling the Apolitical,"* 3 DISCOURSE AND SOCIETY 249 (1992) (persuasive detailed response to Tannern's critics). Indeed, she is careful to point out that she is concerned with power imbalances, recognizes that ill intentions can sometimes play a role (though she stresses that no such intentions are necessary to account for differences), and favors institutional reform. *See* TANNEN, GENDER AND DISCOURSE, *supra* note 3, at 1–14; TANNEN, 9 TO 5, *supra* note 3, at 298–306. My "way two" analysis captures the critics' vision of the world, while my "way three" analysis seeks to reject their dichotomy between essentialism and social constructionism, articulating an approach that may be closer to Tannen's view of her own work. I say "may" because I am admittedly a bit uncertain about the extent to which Tannen would buy into my precise articulation of this third way. She certainly rejects the essentialist label and considers herself a social constructionist. *See* TANNEN, GENDER AND DISCOURSE, *supra* note 3, at 10–13, 14 n.7. She has, on the other hand, been inclined to regard socialization as an important influence shaping behavior but without articulating in detail the processes by which socialization does its work. This may be because she sees her task primarily as a descriptive one. *See id.* at 12–13, 14 n.7. The patterns that she describes indeed served as the impetus for this book.

   6. Troemel-Plotz, *supra* note 5, at 497–98.

   7. There is no single, coherent group of linguists—unlike the "two cultures" and "social constructionist" theorists—whose views constitute this "Third Way." But *see* CRAWFORD, *supra* note 4, at 97 ("There is no inherent limitation to the two-cultures approach that would prevent its development as a theory of difference and dominance."). Elizabeth Aries's survey of the research literature articulates a view, however, very close to this "Third Way." *See* ELIZABETH ARIES, MEN AND WOMEN IN INTERACTION: CONSIDERING THE DIFFERENCES (1996) (conceding, in synthesizing research literature, that socialization teaches us gendered roles and status, but arguing that power/status differences in particular contexts, not personality differences, explain male-female linguistic behavior). My major quarrel with Aries is that I think that she underestimates the power of socialization to impede change, an observation I believe supports the necessity for more radical reforms, not the conservative complacency that Aries fears. Aries also seems to view the low-status ("feminine") style as nothing but evidence of subordination. I think, however, that feminine communication styles can play a helpful role in creating a more caring, just society. *See, e.g.*, WEST, CARING FOR JUSTICE, *supra* note 5 (on the links between care and justice). My

phrase "The Third Way" concisely captures these two differences between my approach and Aries's. Deborah Tannen's view of her own work as a form of social constructionism in which socialization is an important determinant of behavior may also be consistent with my "third way." *See* TANNEN, GENDER AND DISCOURSE, *supra* note 3, at 10–13, 14 n.7.

8. Because Aries and I ultimately explain observed gender differences as stemming primarily from differences in context and relative male-female power, our approaches can be reconciled with a fourth school of thought that views linguistic behavior as too contextualized and gender dichotomies as too oversimplifying and likely to contribute to gender stereotyping for any sound gendered generalizations to be made. *See generally* RETHINKING LANGUAGE AND GENDER RESEARCH: THEORY AND PRACTICE (VICTORIA L. BERGVALL et al. eds. 1996). Indeed, because my bottom line is that both justice and fact-finding accuracy require trial procedures to account for linguistic differences that disadvantage a particular group (here, women), the reasons for the differences ultimately do not matter. I nevertheless spend time staking out my "Third Way" because there are those who disagree, viewing essentialism as a recipe for complacency. *See* CRAWFORD, *supra* note 4.

9. *See, e.g,* JENNIFER COATES, WOMEN, MEN AND LANGUAGE 33 (2d ed. 1993) (quoting this proverb: "Many women, many words; many geese, many turds."); Jonathan Swift, *Thoughts on Various Subjects, in* WORKS (1735) (explaining female volubility thus: "[W]hereas common speakers have only one set of ideas, and one set of words to clothe them in; and these are always ready at the mouth. So people come faster out of a church when it is almost empty than when a crowd is at the door.").

10. My own habit of watching *Bewitched* reruns on Nick-at-Nite is the source of this observation. For a more charitable view of the show's gendered messages, *see* SUSAN J. DOUGLAS, WHERE THE GIRLS ARE: GROWING UP FEMALE WITH THE MASS MEDIA 127 (1994).

11. Dale Spender, *Talking in Class, in* LEARNING TO LOSE: SEXISM AND EDUCATION 1489 (Dale Spender et al. eds., 1980) (discussing silence theme and quoting Sophocles' play *Ajax*). *See also* COATES, *supra* note 9, at 34–35.

12. *See, e.g.,* CRAWFORD, *supra* note 4, at 42; Deborah James and Janice Drakich, *Understanding Differences in Amount of Talk: A Critical Review of Research, in* GENDER AND CONVERSATIONAL INTERACTION 281, 297–99, 301–3.

13. Pamela Fishman, *Conversational Insecurity, in* LANGUAGE: SOCIAL PSYCHOLOGICAL PERSPECTIVES (H. Giles et al. eds. 1980). But *see* Jennifer Coates, *Gossip Revisited, in* JENNIFER COATES & DEBORAH CAMERON, WOMEN IN THEIR SPEECH COMMUNITIES: NEW PERSPECTIVES ON LANGUAGE AND SEX 94–122 (1989) (where gender hierarchy is not afoot, women's supportive linguistic behavior encourages other women to speak, rather than serving as "shitwork").

14. ARIES, *supra* note 7, at 107–8, 122–29, 138 (summarizing research but noting need for further work); HOLMES, *supra* note 5, at 30–71 (expressing greater confidence than Aries in the state of some of this research).

15. TANNEN, 9 TO 5, *supra* note 3, at 59.

16. *See* James and Drakich, *supra* note 12, at 289–90.

17. *See* idem at 293; TANNEN, DON'T UNDERSTAND, *supra* note 1, at 128, 235; TANNEN, 9 TO 5, *supra* note 3, at 119–22, 148–49, 300–301; *accord* DAVID GRADDOL & JOAN SWANN, GENDER VOICES 73–74 (1992).

18. Ann Cutler and Donna R. Scott, *Speaker Sex and Perceived Apportionment of Talk*, 11 APPLIED PSYCHOLINGUISTICS 253, 264 (1990).

19. *See* idem at 264–69; DALE SPENDER, THE WRITING OR THE SEX 9 (1989) *accord*; James and Drakich, *supra* note 12, at 302–3.

20. HOLMES, *supra* note 5, at 40–47 (on antagonistic elicitations); TANNEN, DON'T UNDERSTAND, *supra* note 1, at 149–87 (male perception of antagonism as bonding ritual, female perception of antagonism as a threat to group solidarity).

21. *See* CRAWFORD, *supra* note 4, at 42–44 (topic control); TANNEN, GENDER AND DISCOURSE, *supra* note 3, at 36–39 (taciturnity in some interactional contexts as an instrument of power); TANNEN, 9 TO 5, *supra* note 3, at 277–79 (example of a male at a business meeting getting credit for a woman's idea). These generalizations are always subject to context, for example, a relatively silent but highly-well-respected person sometimes exercises power though speaking little. *See* idem at 281–83; *see generally* Deborah Tannen, *The Relativity of Linguistic Strategies: Rethinking Power and Solidarity in Gender and Dominance, in* GENDER AND CONVERSATIONAL INTERACTION 165–89 (Deborah Tannen ed. 1993) (summarizing research literature on the importance of context in eliciting linguistic behaviors) [hereinafter *Relativity*]. Factors other than how we speak matter too. Thus, there is some evidence that women are ignored by men simply because they are women, regardless of speaking style. *See, e.g.,* TANNEN, 9 TO 5, *supra* note 3, at 286–89 (summarizing research).

22. Jack W. Sattel, *Men, Inexpressiveness and Power, in* LANGUAGE, GENDER AND SOCIETY 119–20 (Barrie Thorne et al. eds. 1983).

23. TANNEN, DON'T UNDERSTAND, *supra* note 1, at 189 (malevolent aggressor quotation); ARIES, *supra* note 7, at 84–86, 99 ("power-oriented" versus "collaborative" interruption terminology). Aries identifies topic-shifting alone as the hallmark of power-orientation. I have modified her definition slightly to meet Tannen's objection that some topic-shifting, for example, to offer a matching story to the speaker's tale, builds solidarity by sending the message "I've had troubles just like yours. I understand." TANNEN, DON'T UNDERSTAND, *supra* note 1, at 295. A topic change that shifts attention primarily to the original listener cannot, however, build solidarity. Although there are many complex divisions of interruption types classified by the interruption's function, and much

debate about what constitutes an interruption, in many schemes simply overlapping speech does not; those subtleties do not alter the basic argument here. *See, e.g.*, C. W. Kennedy and C. T. Camden, *A New Look at Interruptions*, 47 WESTERN J. SPEECH COMM. 45–58 (1983) (positing five uses of interruptions); Tannen, *Relativity, supra* note 21, at 175 (stressing supportive overlaps as satisfying speaking together). Both intentions and effects matter too in judging whether an interruption grants power. Thus, an interruption intended to seize the floor may fail, and one meant to promote solidarity might be misunderstood. *See* ARIES, *supra* note 7, at 99 (importance of speaker perception and reaction to interruption); *see* TANNEN, DON'T UNDERSTAND, *supra* note 1, at 199–201 (misunderstood solidarity-promoting overlap).

24. ARIES, *supra* note 7, at 82, 89, 91, 100 (summarizing literature); HOLMES, *supra* note 5, at 53 (on gaining the floor). *But see* Tannen, *Relativity, supra* note at 21, at 59, 62–73 (taking position that "in this as in all matters of conversational rights and obligations, there are individual and cultural differences. Some people would feel interrupted by an offer of salad; others would not.").

25. ARIES, *supra* note 7, at 80–81, 91–96, 100; HOLMES, *supra* note 5, at 52–53. Aries points out that subordinates do sometimes interrupt their superiors more than the reverse, but the subordinates do so to support the boss by expressing agreement, requesting elaboration, or completing the boss's thought. *See* ARIES, *supra* note 7, at 94–95.

26. DEBORAH CAMERON, FEMINISM AND LINGUISTIC THEORY 140–42 (2d ed. 1992) (summarizing "muted groups" theory that language reflects the reality of dominant groups, thus "muting" the free expression of alternative models of the world); Robin Lakoff, *The Silencing of Women, in* LOCATING POWER: PROCEEDINGS OF THE SECOND BERKELEY WOMEN AND LANGUAGE CONFERENCE 345, 348, 351 (1992); CATE POYNTON, LANGUAGE AND GENDER: MAKING THE DIFFERENCE iv (1989) (collecting quotations on the power of silencing voices); *accord*, ANDREW VOGEL ETTIN, SPEAKING SILENCES: STILLNESS AND VOICE IN MODERN THOUGHT AND JEWISH TRADITION 128 (1994) ("The silences of tales untold carry their own pain."). *See also* ARIES, *supra* note 7, at 180–82 (interrupters are viewed as more "driving," that is, in part, more confident.) My point is that silenced arguments are never heard, silenced tales never considered. In contexts of public deliberation, such as jury trials, such silence thus translates into power, even if silence in other contexts may not necessarily be a source of power.

27. Carol Edelsky, *Who's Got the Floor?, in* GENDER AND CONVERSATIONAL INTERACTION 189, 189–92, 230 (DEBORAH TANNEN ed. 1993) (articulating the "singly developed" versus "collaborative" floor model); James and Drakich, *supra* note 12, at 293–94 (favorably evaluating the model).

28. Edelsky, *supra* note 27, at 189.

29. *See, e.g.,* TANNEN, 9 TO 5, *supra* note 3, at 298–306 (recommending various institutional strategies to increase women's say in the workplace).

30. *See* ROBIN TOLMACH LAKOFF, LANGUAGE AND WOMAN'S PLACE (1975) (originating the "women's language" thesis); ARIES, *supra* note 7, at 102–46 (excellent summary and critique of Lakoff's thesis). More recently, Lakoff has shown a modestly greater sensitivity to context, recognizing that women sometimes "code-switch" from female to male speech patterns in certain contexts. *See* ROBIN TOLMACH LAKOFF, TALKING POWER: THE POLITICS OF LANGUAGE 202 (1990) (hereinafter TALKING POWER).

31. LAKOFF, TALKING POWER, *supra* note 30, at 205–6.

32. ARIES, *supra* note 7, at 104–29, 138–46 (on importance of context and state of research); CRAWFORD, *supra* note 4, at 28–40 (on lack of adequate confirming or disconfirming evidence of invariant women's speech).

33. *See* ARIES, *supra* note 7, at 163–94 (summarizing and evaluating research); *see* CAMERON, *supra* note 26, at 44, (describing Lakoff's theory as consistent with "folklinguistics"); JENNIFER COATES, WOMEN, MEN AND LANGUAGE, 16–37 (2d ed. 1993) (defining "folklinguistics").

34. *See* ARIES, *supra* note 7, at 184–88.

35. Idem at 186, 190–93, 203.

36. Idem at 178–84; TANNEN, 9 TO 5, *supra* note 3, at 70, 98, 117–20, 122, 177, 279–80; TANNEN, DON'T UNDERSTAND, *supra* note 1, at 91–92, 156–58. Importantly, we evaluate men and women differently even when they use the same speech "style." Thus women are evaluated more negatively when using "women's speech" than are men using the same speech. ARIES, *supra* note 7, at 181–82.

37. TANNEN, 9 TO 5, *supra* note 3, at 117 (source of quotation); ARIES, *supra* note 7, at 183–84 (the double-bind).

38. *See* ARIES, *supra* note 7, at 183–84 (negative male reactions); *see* TANNEN, DON'T UNDERSTAND, *supra* note 1, at 63–64 (listener versus lecturer).

39. SUZETTE HADEN ELGIN, NATIVE TONGUE 161 (1984). *See also* CASEY MILLER & KATE SWIFT, WORDS AND WOMEN: NEW LANGUAGE IN NEW TIMES 60 (updated ed. 1991) (on naming as aiding categorization); DALE SPENDER, MAN-MADE LANGUAGE 163–64 (1980) (on cognitive effects of categorization).

40. *See* BETTY FRIEDAN, THE FEMININE MYSTIQUE 37 (with a new introduction 1974) (originally published in 1963); SPENDER, *supra* note 39, at 184 (discussing women's naming "sexual harassment").

41. SUZETTE HADEN ELGIN, GENDERSPEAK: MEN, WOMEN, AND THE GENTLE ART OF VERBAL SELF-DEFENSE 40–41, 43, 47 (1993).

42. This discussion, and the quotations from the relevant Jewish texts, are drawn from JUDITH HAUPTMAN, REREADING THE RABBIS: A WOMAN'S VOICE 85–88 (1998) (brackets in original). Although the excerpts are unsettling

to many modern readers, they reflect views fully consistent with the more subtle effects of modern cultural rape narratives. On the other hand, a convincing case has been made that rabbinic Judaism was relatively progressive for its time, a "reformed patriarchy." *See* AVIVA CANTOR, JEWISH WOMEN, JEWISH MEN: THE LEGACY OF PATRIARCHY IN JEWISH LIFE 2–6 (1995).

43. *See* COLLEEN A. WARD, ATTITUDES TOWARD RAPE: FEMINIST AND SOCIAL PSYCHOLOGICAL PERSPECTIVES 78–82 (1995); ROBERT T. MICHAEL ET AL., SEX IN AMERICA: A DEFINITIVE SURVEY 221 (1995).

44. Mary M. Gergen, *Life Stories: Pieces of a Dream, in* STORIED LIVES (G. Rosenwald et al. eds. 1992); *see generally* CAROL TAVRIS, THE MISMEASURE OF WOMAN 302–3 (1992) (generally addressing male-female storytelling differences).

45. Barbara Johnstone, *Community and Contest: Midwestern Men and Women Creating Their Worlds in Conversational Storytelling, in* GENDER AND CONVERSATIONAL INTERACTION 62, 69–76 (1993).

46. Idem at 69–76.

47. *See* MARTIN J. MALONE, WORLDS OF TALK: THE PRESENTATION OF SELF IN EVERYDAY CONVERSATION 90–99 (1997), who argues that differences in the content of male and female stories do not necessarily translate into power differences. Even female narratives of community told to men can in certain contexts involve exchange of tales among equals. Malone is right that context and ideology interact (along with upbringing and individual personality) to determine behavior. My argument, however, is that rape trial context disempowers women, and there is at least some evidence to suggest that a female preference for community-based narratives may further disempower women under present rules of evidence and procedure.

48. On the treatment of rape victims at trial, *see generally* LEE MADIGAN & NANCY GAMBLE, THE SECOND RAPE: SOCIETY'S CONTINUED BETRAYAL OF THE VICTIM (1991); GREGORY MATOESIAN, REPRODUCING RAPE: DOMINATION THROUGH TALK IN THE COURTROOM (1993).

49. ARIES, *supra* note 7, at 13–15, 17, 38, 140–41, 190, 209 (white, middle-class nature of most samples); JOSHUA DRESSLER, UNDERSTANDING CRIMINAL LAW 633 (2d ed. 1995) ("Based on government survey data, an African-American woman is nearly twice as likely to be raped as a white woman, although in absolute terms, white women are victims more often than non-whites.") One-half of all rape victims are also poor (within the bottom one-third of the income distribution). Central-city residents are additionally much more likely to be victimized than residents of suburban or rural regions. Idem at 534.

50. *See* JAMES HASKINS & HUGH BUTTS, M.D., PSYCHOLOGY OF BLACK LANGUAGE 26 (1993) (on "soul"); THOMAS KOCHMAN, BLACK AND WHITE STYLES IN CONFLICT 18–41 (1981) (ethnographic and survey

study documenting the dynamic, oppositional, high-spirited, black speaking style); Geneva Smitherman, *Testifying, Sermonizin' and Signifying: Anita Hill, Clarence Thomas, and the African-American Verbal Tradition, in* AFRICAN-AMERICAN WOMEN SPEAK OUT ON ANITA HILL-CLARENCE THOMAS 224, 228–42 (Geneva Smitherman ed., 1995) (summarizing the AVT and its significance).

51. *See, e.g.,* Victoria Jackson Binion, *An Analysis of Factors Influencing the Development of Sex Role Identity and Sex Role Attitudes of Contemporary Black Women* 18–26, 108, 119 (Ph.D. diss. 1981) (finding greater androgyny among black than white women because of differing historical experience); CRAWFORD, *supra* note 4, at 76 (black and white women friends both agree that the black member is the more assertive of the two); Denise Troutman-Robinson, *The Tongue or the Sword: Which Is Master?, in* AFRICAN-AMERICAN WOMEN SPEAK OUT ON ANITA HILL-CLARENCE THOMAS 224, 228–42 (Geneva Smitherman ed. 1995) (arguing that Anita Hill, during the confirmation hearings for now-Justice Clarence Thomas, demonstrated that "African-American women have learned that only the strong survive; their language, in turn, contains social manifestations of strong language."). *But see* Smitherman, *supra* note 50, at 234–41 (arguing Hill was disbelieved because she was too "low-keyed, clinical, dispassionate, unemotional"). Other researchers have sometimes disagreed with the black female assertiveness thesis, instead finding adult black women "saccharin sweet" and black females' contest behavior brief relative to black men's. *See* ROGER D. ABRAHAMS, TALKING BLACK 77 (1976) (contest element); U. HANNERZ, SOULSIDE: INQUIRIES INTO GHETTO CULTURE AND COMMUNITY 96 (1969) (saccharin sweetness).

52. M. A. Gillespie, *We Speak in Tongues*, 2 M.S. 32, 41 (January-February 1992) (source of quotation); PAULA GIDDINGS, WHEN AND WHERE I ENTER: THE IMPACT OF BLACK WOMEN ON RACE AND SEX IN AMERICA 325–35 (1984) (on the Moynihan Report and its aftermath); Linda L. Ammons, *Mules, Madonnas, Babies, Bathwater, Racial Imagery and Stereotypes: The African-American Woman and the Battered Woman Syndrome*, 1995 WIS. L. REV. 1003 (on battered black women).

53. The leading study of African-American naturally occurring speech patterns is MARJORIE HARNESS GOODWIN, HE-SAID, SHE-SAID: TALK AS SOCIAL ORGANIZATION AMONG BLACK CHILDREN 136, 145, 188, 284–88 (1990) (stressing similarities among the speaking styles of working-class black and white boys and girls, despite also finding some differences). Harness did find, however, that girls move closer to, without completely adopting, male forms when girls are clearly placed in a relatively higher status than the norm. For example, when playing house, the "mommy" (higher status) would use more aggravated directives than the child (lower status). Unlike boys, however, the girls supported their aggravated directives with justifying explanations, such as the

need to protect the child. *See* idem. Other commentators have concluded that working-class and black girls are more likely to engage in direct confrontation than are middle-class white girls. *See* HOLMES, *supra* note 5, at 71 (citing sources). Nevertheless, I found the similarities to white behavior more striking than any differences. On black-white linguistic interaction, *see* MICHAEL J. HECHT & MARY JANE COLLIER, AFRICAN-AMERICAN COMMUNICATION 54, 61, 89–92 (1993).

54. *See* ARIES, *supra* note, at 224 n. 92: "The data are relevant to other minorities and disadvantaged groups in interaction. Race, like sex, serves as an external status characteristic, and blacks, like women, are assumed to have less task-ability. Studies of interracial groups of blacks and whites have found that when the greater competence of blacks has been demonstrated to both black and white group members, inequalities are reduced."

55. See HECHT & COLLIER, *supra* note 53, at 54, 61, 89–92 (blacks change speaking styles when they want to be perceived positively by whites); KOCHMAN, *supra* note 50, at 18–41 (whites see black dynamic speaking styles as indicative of lesser rationality, objectivity, and authority, but of greater hostility, emotionality, and rudeness); WARD, *supra* note 43, at 48–50 (on black attitudes toward rape and gendered sex roles, conclusions admittedly based on limited research).

56. ARIES, *supra* note 7, at 20, 140–44, 190–93; NADEAU, *supra* note 4, at 14–16, 81–86; Janet M. Bing and Victoria L. Bergvall, *The Question of Questions: Beyond Binary Thinking, in* RETHINKING LANGUAGE AND GENDER RESEARCH: THEORY AND PRACTICE 1–24 (1996).Bing and Bergvall urge linguists to ask questions other than "How do men and women differ?"; they argue that such questions dichotomize us into male-female stereotypes. Such stereotypes block opportunity and denigrate individual difference. *See* idem. Although I agree that these risks arise, ignoring difference where it exists (even though the differences are nonessential) can itself block opportunity and denigrate the individual. If rape trials operate pursuant to "male" rules, feminine-style women (and men) suffer. Furthermore, "feminine" styles, despite their resulting from power differentials, may normatively have much to teach us.

57. *See, e.g.,* ARIES, *supra* note 7, at 39–42, 136–44, 186–88, 198. Some feminists might object to my use of the terms *powerful* and *powerless* here as stereotyping women into weak victims. My intent, however, is simply to highlight by a useful shorthand the relative powerlessness of many women at a rape trial. *See* idem at 130 (discussing O'Barr's characterization of supportive styles as linked to "powerlessness," not gender). Logic suggests that many date rape victims will be the same social class as their assailants, thus making gender an even more important determinant of relative status at the rape trial. Moreover, I noted earlier in this chapter that even a higher-status woman has her status mitigated by her gender. On the other hand, a rape victim of lower social class than her assailant is

handicapped by both her gender *and* class. *See* PEGGY REEVES SANDAY, A WOMAN SCORNED: ACQUAINTANCE RAPE ON TRIAL 214–16 (1996) (making similar point in the context of the William Kennedy Smith trial). Remember too that women are more likely than men to be perceived as using powerless styles simply because they are women. Institutional linguistic reform must also focus on the rape victim's plight, even in the rare consent defense case in which her assailant is of lower social class, because the woman's gender as a mark of lower status combines with cultural rape narratives to make fair assessments of her credibility hard. On the question of the magnitude of observed male-female linguistic differences, *see* ARIES, *supra*, note 7, at 139, 186 (arguing the size of observed differences is often not noted or small, a point I have argued in text does not undermine the position defended here); *accord* JOHN M. CONLEY & WILLIAM O'BARR, JUST WORDS: LAW, LANGUAGE, AND POWER 65 (1998) ("[M]ost of the witnesses who used powerless language were women and . . . most men did not use it. This meant that most women, most of the time, were speaking a style that the legal system devalued; men, by and large, did not suffer this disadvantage.").

58. *See* NADEAU, *supra* note 4, at 16–19, 95–97, 125–38 (defending concept of "complementarity").

59. On the tension between individualized and group justice, *see* Doriane Lambelet Coleman, *Individualizing Justice Through Multiculturalism: The Liberals' Dilemma*, 96 COLUM. L. REV. 1093 (1996); CHARLES R. LAWRENCE III & MARI J. MATSUDA, WE WON'T GO BACK: MAKING THE CASE FOR AFFIRMATIVE ACTION 80–87, 96–111, 124–41, 191–92 (1997).

NOTES TO CHAPTER 5

1. The American Bar Association Project on Standards for Criminal Justice— Standards Relating to the Prosecution and the Defense Function 174 (American Bar Association 1971) (source of quote). On the nature of the adversarial system and its modern failings generally, *see* PATRICK M. GARRY, A NATION OF ADVERSARIES: HOW THE LITIGATION EXPLOSION IS RESHAPING AMERICA 48–49, 66 (1997); MARY ANN GLENDON, A NATION UNDER LAWYERS: HOW THE CRISIS IN THE LEGAL PROFESSION IS TRANSFORMING AMERICAN SOCIETY (1994); ANTHONY KRONMAN, THE LOST LAWYER (1995); SOL LINOWITZ, THE BETRAYED PROFESSION: LAWYERING AT THE END OF THE TWENTIETH CENTURY (1994); BENJAMIN SELLS, THE SOUL OF THE LAW (1994).

2. JENNIFER L. PIERCE, GENDER TRIALS: EMOTIONAL LIVES IN CONTEMPORARY LAW FIRMS 1–2 (1995).

3. On lawyer "civility," *see, e.g.,* Section of the American Bar Association, *Lawyer's Creed of Professionalism* (1988), *reprinted in* STEPHEN GILLERS &

ROY D. SIMON, JR., REGULATION OF LAWYERS: STATUTES AND STAN-
DARDS 662–65 (1995); Andrew E. Taslitz and Sharon Styles-Anderson, *Still Officers of the Court: Why the First Amendment Is No Bar to Challenging Racism,
Sexism, and Ethnic Bias in the Legal Profession*, 9 GEO. J. LEGAL ETHICS 781,
825 (1996) ("[T]he ABA's policy statement on civility in the profession has done
little to change the unnecessarily brutal warfare that continues in much of American litigation."). On lawyers' use of emotions as tactics, *see* PIERCE, *supra* note
2. On the metaphors governing legal practice, *see* PIERCE, *supra* note 2, at
50–80; FRANKLIN STRIER, RECONSTRUCTING JUSTICE: AN AGENDA
FOR TRIAL REFORM 7–30 (1996).

4. STRIER, *supra* note 3, at 27–28.

5. On the degree to which, and ways in which, women follow male litigators'
rules, *see, e.g.,* LANI GUINIER ET AL., BECOMING GENTLEMEN: WOMEN,
LAW SCHOOL, AND INSTITUTIONAL CHANGE (1997); DANA JACK &
RAND JACK, MORAL VISIONS AND PROFESSIONAL DECISIONS: THE
CHANGING VALUES OF WOMEN AND MEN LAWYERS (1989); PIERCE,
supra note 2, at 103–40.

6. For analyses of lawyers' evidentiary and linguistic rules and practices at
trial, *see* GREGORY MATOESIAN, REPRODUCING RAPE: DOMINATION
THROUGH TALK IN THE COURTROOM (1993); RICHARD RIEKE &
RANDALL K. STUTMAN, COMMUNICATION IN LEGAL ADVOCACY
(1990); WILLIAM O'BARR, LINGUISTIC EVIDENCE (1982).

7. This summary of the facts of the William Kennedy Smith case is drawn
from Gregory Matoesian, *"I'm sorry we had to meet under these circumstances":
Verbal Artistry (and Wizardry) in the Kennedy Smith Rape Trial, in* LAW IN AC-
TION: ETHNOMETHODOLOGICAL AND CONVERSATION ANALYTIC
APPROACHES TO LAW 142–43 (Max Travers & John Manzo, eds. 1997)
[hereinafter *Verbal Artistry*], and Gregory M. Matoesian, *Language, Law, and
Society: Policy Implications of the Kennedy Smith Trial*, 29 LAW & SOC. REV.
669, 670 n. 1 (1995) [hereinafter, *Policy Implications*]. Most of the trial testimony quoted in this chapter was transcribed in code that re-creates for language
specialists the precise sound of the witness's and lawyer's speech. That level of precision is unnecessary for my purposes, and the code is confusing to lay and law-
trained readers. Consequently, I have rewritten the testimony in ordinary words
in a way that seeks to retain some of the flavor of spoken speech while avoiding
any specialized codes, thus improving readability.

8. Matoesian, *"You Were Interested in Him as a Person?"*: *Rhythms of Domination in the Kennedy Smith Rape Trial*, 22 LAW AND SOCIAL INQUIRY, 55,
60–61 (1997) [hereinafter *Rhythms of Domination*].

9. This analysis of Bowman's testimony is drawn from idem at 62–65. The
trial examples in this chapter and much of the explanation of their significance are
drawn from Paul Drew, *Contested Evidence in Courtroom Cross-examination:*

The Case of a Trial for Rape, in, TALK AT WORK: INTERACTION IN INSTI-TUTIONAL SETTINGS 470–520 (Paul Drew and John Heritage eds., 1992); LYNDA LYTLE HOLMSTROM & ANN WOLBERT BURGESS, THE VICTIM OF RAPE 157–259 (new ed. 1983); Matoesian, *Verbal Artistry, supra* note 7, at 1–44; Matoesian, *Rhythms of Domination, supra* note 8, at 1–41; Matoesian, *Policy Implications, supra* note 7, at 669–701; MATOESIAN, REPRODUCING RAPE, *supra* note 6.

10. *See, e.g.,* FED. R. EVID. 412 and its accompanying Advisory Committee Note.

11. For a discussion and examples of general character assaults and repeating questions despite sustained objections, *see* HOLMSTROM & BURGESS, *supra* note 9, at 178–89; MATOESIAN, REPRODUCING RAPE, *supra* note 6, at 179. For an analysis of clothing as indicating "trampishness," *see* DUNCAN KENNEDY, SEXY DRESSING, ETC.: ESSAYS ON THE POWER AND POLI-TICS OF CULTURAL IDENTITY 126–213 (1993), with illustrative trial examples at MATOESIAN, REPRODUCING RAPE, *supra* note 6, at 179 (T-shirt emblazoned with "Don't Touch"). *See also* Advisory Committee Note, 1994, FED. R. EVID. 412 (explaining reasons for Congress's amending the federal rape shield law to prohibit "sexy dressing"-like inquiries.)

12. Matoesian, *Policy Implications, supra* note 7, at 678–83 (discussing the pantyhose removal and the "sweet little kiss" exchanges between Bowman and Black).

13. MATOESIAN, REPRODUCING RAPE, *supra* note 6, at 117.

14. *See* HOLMSTROM & BURGESS, *supra* note 9, at 117.

15. RIEKE & STUTMAN, *supra* note 6 (defining "semantic contagion").

16. On the power of words to create categories that shape thinking, *see, e.g.,* VIRGINIA VALIAN, WHY SO SLOW? THE ADVANCEMENT OF WOMEN (1998).

17. MATOESIAN, REPRODUCING RAPE, *supra* note 6, at 166–67.

18. Matoesian, *Policy Implications, supra* note 7, at 695.

19. Matoesian, *Rhythms of Domination, supra* note 8, at 61.

20. HOLMSTROM & BURGESS, *supra* note 9, at 203.

21. *See* RIEKE & STUTMAN, *supra* note 6, at 158–59, 176–77 (on persua-sive effect of vivid, detailed answers and juror assumptions of bases for questions).

22. *See* Matoesian, *Verbal Artistry, supra* note 7, at 139–42 (defining "poet-ics").

23. Idem at 143–49.

24. Idem at 150.

25. *See* idem at 140–42 (making similar points).

26. RIEKE & STUTMAN, *supra* note 6, at 182–85.

27. There is some dispute over the persuasive power of implied conclusions.

Tactically, lawyers generally agree that it is best not to ask the "one question too many," which seeks the witness's agreement with the lawyer's conclusion. That inquiry gives the witness a chance to suggest an alternative interpretation of her testimony. *See* THOMAS MAUET, FUNDAMENTALS OF TRIAL TECHNIQUES 218 (2d ed. 1988). Furthermore, rhetorical questions—those that pose a question without answering it—can be effective if well placed, where the desired answer is strongly suggested by the evidence. *See* JEFFREY T. FREDERICK, THE PSYCHOLOGY OF THE AMERICAN JURY 179–81 (1987). On the other hand, there is some disputed empirical data supporting the explicit statement of conclusions as most effective, but those data should mean only that the lawyer must state his conclusions at some point, perhaps during closing argument, not that it is wise to do so during cross. *See* idem at 187–88, 238 & n. 131.

28. MATOESIAN, REPRODUCING RAPE, *supra* note 6, at 170–72 (source of quote, definition of the three noted poetic devices, and explanation of their application to these illustrations.)

29. Idem at 176.

30. Idem at 172–73.

31. Idem at 175–76.

32. Idem at 177.

33. Idem at 173 (recounting degree and method by which poetic devices achieve an impact).

34. *See generally* HOLMSTROM & BURGESS, *supra* note 9, at 204–12 (rapid-fire questioning and needling); Matoesian, *Verbal Artistry, supra* note 7, at 137–38, 170–71 (detailing to death and pursuing an answer); MATOESIAN, REPRODUCING RAPE, *supra* note 6; Kim Lane Scheppele, *Just the Facts, Ma'am: Sexualized Violence, Evidentiary Habits, and the Revision of Truth,* 37 N.Y. L. SCHOOL L. REV. 123, at 163–66, 180–82, 186 (inconsistency, pursuing a response, and preemptive interruption).

35. *See, e.g.,* RIEKE & STUTMAN, *supra* note 6, at 130–31.

36. MATOESIAN, REPRODUCING RAPE, *supra* note 6, at 179–80.

37. Idem at 150.

38. The discussion of silence here is largely drawn from MATOESIAN, REPRODUCING RAPE, *supra* note 6, at 135–57, and Scheppele, *supra* note 34.

39. MATOESIAN, REPRODUCING RAPE, *supra* note 6, at 145.

40. Drew, *supra* note 9, is the source of this discussion of victim resistance, except where otherwise noted.

41. Idem at 478–79, 482–83.

42. Idem at 478–79.

43. Idem at 486.

44. *See* idem at 495–502 (defining "maximal" descriptors).

45. Idem at 489.

46. Idem at 487–88.

47. *See, e.g.* RIEKE & STUTMAN, *supra* note 6, at 130–31.

48. HARVEY SACKS, LECTURES ON CONVERSATION 1964–72 (G. JEF-FERSON ed., 1992).

49. RIEKE & STUTMAN, *supra* note 6, at 156, 184, 188–94 (uninterrupted narratives are more persuasive); MATOESIAN, REPRODUCING RAPE, *supra* note 6, at 110–33 (reviewing ways in which objections reduce a witness's credibility).

50. *See* MATOESIAN, REPRODUCING RAPE, *supra* note 6, at 110–34 (on linguistic functions of objections); MAUET, *supra* note 27, at 331–64 (summarizing various bases for objections).

51. MATOESIAN, REPRODUCING RAPE, *supra* note 6, at 95; RIEKE & STUTMAN, *supra* note 6, at 58, 191–94 (persuasive effect of objections is complex but often benefits objector).

52. MURRAY EDELMAN, FROM ART TO POLITICS: HOW ARTISTIC CREATIONS SHAPE POLITICAL CONCEPTIONS 93 (1995).

53. Idem.

54. Idem at 95.

55. *See* STRIER, *supra* note 3, at 75–82.

NOTES TO CHAPTER 6

1. For critiques of the adversary system implicitly, if not explicitly, based on its unique brand of market individualism, *see* MIRJAN R. DAMASKA, EVIDENCE LAW ADRIFT 74–124 (1997) (especially regarding cognitive flaws); PATRICK M. GARRY, A NATION OF ADVERSARIES: HOW THE LITIGATION EXPLOSION IS RESHAPING AMERICA 43–73 (1997) (sports analogy and the culture of selfish individualism); PAUL G. HASKELL, WHY LAWYERS BEHAVE AS THEY DO 1–26, 85–105 (1998) (minimal ethical limits on unbridled competition in slavish devotion to the client's cause).

2. David Luban, *The Adversary System Excuse, in* LAWYERS: A CRITICAL READER 6–7 (Richard Abel ed. 1997)(claim that adversary system at best turns on "a question-begging analogy to eighteenth-century economic theories of the Invisible Hand, theories that are themselves myth rather than fact. . . ."); *see* HASKELL, *supra* note 1, at 77–78 (on discovery as a game).

3. *See* Carrie Menkel-Meadow, *The Trouble with the Adversary System in a Post-Modern, Multicultural World*, 1 J. INST. STUDY OF LEGAL ETHICS 49 (1996) (zero-sum game analogy); *accord* GARRY, *supra* note 1, at 64–65 (adversary system is rooted in the "win-lose, opponent-trashing mind-set of sports. . . ."). *See also* HASKELL, *supra* note 1 (on pernicious influence of ethical codes' requiring absolute allegiance to client interests over justice); Andrew E. Taslitz and Sharon Styles-Anderson, *Still Officers of the Court: Why the First Amendment Is No Bar to Challenging Racism, Sexism, and Ethnic Bias in the*

Legal Profession, 9 GEO. J. LEGAL ETHICS 781 (1996) (urging amendment of ethics codes to take the lawyer's duty as an officer of the court more seriously).

4. 2 TRIAL OF QUEEN CAROLINE 5 (Shackell and Arrowsmith 1821).

5. *See* HASKELL, *supra* note 1, at 76–80 (on civil discovery reform); STEPHEN L. CARTER, CIVILITY: MANNERS, MORALS, AND THE ETIQUETTE OF DEMOCRACY 286 (1998) (on lawyer civility codes). The type of discovery reform discussed here is limited to civil litigation, but civility codes may, in theory, reach both civil and criminal litigators. In practice, I know of few criminal (or civil) litigators who believe that civility codes have significantly changed their professional lives. For a discussion of the systemic and emotional reasons for continuing lawyer incivility, despite ethics and civility codes, *see generally* MARK PERLMUTTER, WHY LAWYERS (AND THE REST OF US) LIE & ENGAGE IN OTHER REPUGNANT BEHAVIOR (1998). Despite these failures, further efforts at encouraging civility are worth a try. Some local bars, for example, are creating "implementation committees" to try to bring practice in line with theory. *See, e.g.,* Andrew H. Marks, *Civility: A Hallmark of Professional Excellence, in* THE WASHINGTON LAWYER 8 (September/October 1998).

6. *See* HASKELL, *supra* note 1, at 1–24. These observations are contextual ones, for there are also situations in which lawyers may not engage in many of these sorts of behavior. *See* idem at 1–24. On the degree to which lawyers' ethical codes depart from ordinary standards of morality, *see generally* WILLIAM H. SIMON, THE PRACTICE OF JUSTICE: A THEORY OF LAWYERS' ETHICS (1998).

7. 115 S. Ct. 797 (1995).

8. Idem at 805. *See also* FED. R. EVID. 410, Advisory Committee Note. Rule 410 does permit use of plea negotiations at trial in two narrow circumstances not relevant here. *See* idem.

9. *See* Malinda L. Seymore, *Isn't It a Crime: Feminist Perspectives on Spousal Immunity and Spousal Violence*, 90 N.W.U.L. REV. 1032 (1996). Seymore's article demonstrates that the many commentators who claim that "No jurisdiction permits the accused to assert the adverse testimony privilege when the crime charged is against the spouse or a child of one or both of the spouses" are wrong. *See* GRAHAM LILLY, AN INTRODUCTION TO THE LAW OF EVIDENCE 448 (3d ed. 1996). Five states and the District of Columbia have no spousal crime exception to spousal immunity. Seymore, *supra,* at 1059. More important, the many states that have a spousal violence or spousal crime exception often interpret it narrowly. For example, disorderly conduct arising from a husband's threats to kill his wife; a husband's murder of his wife's alleged lover; and a husband's "torching" his wife's belongings to stop her from leaving him have all been held in various states to fall outside the exception. *See* idem at 1050–59. While the law "on the books" thus might require battered wives to testify against their hus-

bands, the law in practice often leaves that decision to the wives' free market choices.

10. The description here of traditional economic views and the critique of both markets and the adversary system as reinforcing gender bias fuse ideas drawn from RICHARD DELGADO & JEAN STEFANCIC, MUST WE DEFEND NAZIS? HATE SPEECH, PORNOGRAPHY, AND THE NEW FIRST AMENDMENT 70–92 (1997) (neutral rules, inability to see present racism, microtransactions); Menkel-Meadow, *supra* note 3 (cognitive flaws of the adversary system); Janice Moulton, *A Paradigm of Philosophy: The Adversarial Method*, in WOMEN, KNOWLEDGE, AND REALITY: EXPLORATIONS IN FEMINIST PHILOSOPHY 11–23 (Ann Gary and Marilyn Pearsall eds., 2d ed. 1996) (more cognitive flaws of the adversary system); CASS SUNSTEIN, FREE MARKETS AND SOCIAL JUSTICE 151–166 (1997) (third-party or "buyer" discrimination).

11. *See* Taslitz and Styles-Anderson, *supra* note 3, at 787–95 (cataloguing lawyers' often successful appeals to racial and gender bias and discrimination). In Styles-Anderson and my efforts to persuade the ABA to bar certain racist and sexist conduct by lawyers, we frequently encountered this "zealous representation" or "legitimate advocacy" objection. *See also* MODEL RULES OF PROFESSIONAL CONDUCT Preamble cmt. 2 ("As advocate, a lawyer asserts zealously the client's position under the rules of the adversary system.").

12. *See also* JODI DAVID ARMOUR, NEGROPHOBIA AND REASONABLE RACISM: THE HIDDEN COSTS OF BEING BLACK IN AMERICA (1997) (on cognitive factors causing unconscious racism, even in many whites who abhor it).

13. *See* VIRGINIA VALIAN, WHY SO SLOW? THE ADVANCEMENT OF WOMEN (1998) (explaining cognitive causes of cumulative minor disadvantages for women in a wide range of social, economic, and political activities); *accord* LANI GUINIER ET AL., BECOMING GENTLEMEN: WOMEN, LAW SCHOOL, AND INSTITUTIONAL CHANGE (1997) (describing a similar process at work in law schools).

14. *See* Andrew E. Taslitz, *Abuse Excuses and the Logic and Politics of Expert Relevance*, 49 HASTINGS L. J. 1039 (forthcoming 1998) (on relevance); Andrew E. Taslitz, *Myself Alone: Individualizing Justice Through Psychological Character Evidence*, 52 MD. L. REV. 1, 14–24 (1993) (on pressures for judges to consider a narrow definition of relevant circumstances).

15. *See* Andrew E. Taslitz, *A Feminist Approach to Social Scientific Evidence: Foundations*, 5 MICH. J. GENDER & L. 1 (1998) (on emotion and reason in evidence law).

16. *See, e.g.,* KIM LANE SCHEPPELE, LEGAL SECRETS: EQUALITY AND EFFICIENCY IN THE COMMON LAW 96–98 (1988) (describing how lawyers' categories shape trial narratives).

17. For a discussion of externalities, *see* MARK SEIDENFELD, MICRO-ECONOMIC PREDICATES TO LAW AND ECONOMICS 63–64, 92–93 (1996); CHARLES WOLF, JR., MARKETS OR GOVERNMENT: CHOOSING BETWEEN IMPERFECT ALTERNATIVES 21–23, 39–40, 109–10 (2d ed. 1994). The market will, under certain conditions not present in rape trials (for example, where transaction costs are zero), self-correct, "internalizing" the externalities. For a discussion of the role of externalities in evidence law, as illustrated by "identity impacts," *see* Peter Margulies, *Adjudicating Identity: Subordination, Social Science Evidence, and Criminal Defense*, 1–21 & n. 31, 39–45 (draft manuscript 1998).

18. 511 U.S. 127 (1994).

19. Idem at 141–42 (emphasis added).

20. Idem at 140.

21. Idem.

22. Idem at 146.

23. Idem at 193–94 (footnotes omitted). I discuss *J.E.B.*'s majority opinion here, including its reliance on *Ballard v. United States*, 392 U.S. 187 (1946), to stress the Court's recognition of the importance of trial-generated externalities. When concurring and dissenting opinions in *J.E.B.* are considered, however, the Court's vision of the jury as a communal, deliberative body is more confused than the majority opinion and my analysis of it here suggest. *See* Taslitz, *Feminist Approach, supra* note 15, at 92 n. 233.

24. *See, e.g.*, Luban, *supra* note 2, at 11–12; Menkel-Meadow, *supra* note 3. *J.E.B.* is the progeny of *Batson v. Kentucky*, 476 U.S. 79 (1986), a criminal case. *See also Edmonson v. Leesville Concrete Co.*, 500 U.S. 614 (1991) (*Batson* applies to civil and criminal trials).

25. *See* AKIL REED AMAR & ALAN HIRSCH, FOR THE PEOPLE: WHAT THE CONSTITUTION REALLY SAYS ABOUT YOUR RIGHTS 52–54 (1998) (on jury's restraining state power); GODFREY D. LEHMAN, WE THE JURY: THE IMPACT OF JURORS ON OUR BASIC FREEDOMS 224–48 (1997) (illustrating jury's role in fighting both private and governmental racism in the case of Dr. Ossian Sweet). *See also* SIMON, *supra* note 6, at 170–94 (explaining flaws in the argument that the civil and criminal justice systems are ethically distinct).

26. Ronald Goldstock et al., Justice That Makes Sense, *in* CRIMINAL JUSTICE 61 (ABA Winter 1998).

27. *See* Andrew E. Taslitz, *Patriarchal Stories I: Cultural Rape Narratives in the Courtroom*, 5 S. CAL. REV. L. & WOM.'S ST. 387, 402–4 (1996).

28. *See* LEE MADIGAN & NANCY GAMBLE, THE SECOND RAPE: SOCIETY'S CONTINUED BETRAYAL OF THE VICTIM (1991); *accord* JOHN M. CONLEY & WILLIAM O'BARR, JUST WORDS: LAW, LANGUAGE AND POWER 32 (1998) ("[W]hile . . . [adversarial] strategies may not be unique to

rape trials, they have a poignancy in the rape context that is unmatched elsewhere. A woman telling a story of physical domination by one man is subjected to linguistic domination by another. In this sense, revictimization is real, and its mechanism is linguistic.").

29. The source of the quote is Paul Brest and Ann Vandenberg, *Politics, Feminism, and the Constitution: The Anti-pornography Movement in Minneapolis,* 39 STAN. L. REV. 607, 659 (1987). For arguments that language constitutes our world, *see* John Darnton, *Accepting Nobel, Morrison Proves Power of Words,* N.Y. TIMES C, at 17, 20. (December 8, 1993) ("[O]ppressive language does more than represent . . . the limits of knowledge; it limits knowledge"); JOHN STEWART, LANGUAGE AS ARTICULATE CONTACT: TOWARD A POST-SEMIOTIC PHILOSOPHY OF COMMUNICATION 2–32, 103–30 (1995) ("worlding" theory); *accord* Martin Heidegger, *Letter on Humanism,* in BASIC WRITINGS 193 (David F. Krell ed. 1977) ("Language is the house of Being. In its home [the hu]man dwells."). For an argument that language constitutes much, but not all, of our world, *see* JOHN R. SEARLE, THE SOCIAL CONSTRUCTION OF REALITY 1–70, 95–145 (1995).

30. *See* KENNETH KARST, LAW'S PROMISE, LAW'S EXPRESSION: VISIONS OF POWER IN THE POLITICS OF RACE, GENDER AND RELIGION 1–32 (1993) (law's expressive function affects group status; speech of Unreason); Taslitz, *Feminist Approach, supra* note 15 (group politics and evidence law).

31. 511 U.S. at 141–42. *See* KARST, *supra* note 30, at 10–13, 32–43.

32. *See* AMAR & HIRSCH, *supra* note 25, at 51–58, 93–114 (jury is a deliberative body central to republican self-government); Taslitz, *Feminist Approach, supra,* note 15, at 83–99 (analogous vision of jury based upon feminist theory).

33. *See* JUDITH WAGNER DECEW, IN PURSUIT OF PRIVACY: LAW, ETHICS, AND THE RISE OF TECHNOLOGY 61–81 (1997) (on privacy's value); GARRY, *supra* note 1, at 62–65 (one-up, one-down nature adversary system); FRANKLIN STRIER, RECONSTRUCTING JUSTICE: AN AGENDA FOR TRIAL REFORM 1–51 (1996) (similar); Menkel-Meadow, *supra* note 3 (effect of adversary system on human relationships); JENNIFER L. PIERCE, GENDER TRIALS: EMOTIONAL LIVES IN CONTEMPORARY LAW FIRMS (1995) (similar); Taslitz, *Myself Alone, supra* note 14 (on deindividualizing justice).

34. *See* SUNSTEIN, *supra* note 10, at 32–70 (social norms/law connection); Taslitz, *Patriarchal Stories, supra* note 27, at 394–424 (on gendered norms and rape trials).

35. The analyses here of "separate," "connected," and "constructed" knowing are primarily drawn from Blythe McVicker Clinchy, *Connected and Separate Knowing: Toward a Marriage of Two Minds,* in KNOWLEDGE, DIFFERENCE AND POWER: ESSAYS INSPIRED BY WOMEN'S WAYS OF KNOWING 206–240 (Nancy Rule Goldenberger et al. eds. 1996); MARY FIELD BELENKY

ET AL., WOMEN'S WAYS OF KNOWING: THE DEVELOPMENT OF SELF, VOICE, AND MIND (1986).

36. Clinchy, *supra* note 35, at 207 (quoting interview subject).

37. Idem at 208 (quoting interview subject).

38. Idem at 217.

39. CHARLES HORTON COOLEY, SOCIAL ORGANIZATION: A STUDY OF THE LARGER MIND 156 (1909).

40. *See* ALFIE KOHN, THE BRIGHTER SIDE OF HUMAN NATURE: ALTRUISM AND EMPATHY IN EVERYDAY LIFE 98–262 (1990) (perspective taking); MARTHA NUSSBAUM, POETIC JUSTICE: THE LITERARY IMAGINATION AND PUBLIC LIFE 53–78 (1995) (explaining Adam Smith's "judicious spectator" and its role in legal life, a role consistent with connected knowing).

41. *See* Taslitz, *Feminist Approach, supra* note 15, at 63–71 (judicious spectator and expert evidence); Andrew E. Taslitz, *A Feminist Approach to Social Scientific Evidence Revisited: On Markets, Dualisms and Historical Method* (forthcoming 1999) (connected knowing's role in analyzing scientific evidence).

42. *See* Ann Stanton, *Reconfiguring Teaching and Knowing in the College Classroom*, in KNOWLEDGE, DIFFERENCE, AND POWER: ESSAYS INSPIRED BY WOMEN'S WAYS OF KNOWING 31 (1996) (defining "constructed knowing"); BELENKY ET AL., *supra* note 35, at 131–52 (similar).

43. MIRJAN DAMASKA, EVIDENCE LAW ADRIFT 92–94, 99–103 (1997) (Anglo-American adversarial systems create fragmented direct examinations and filter out evidence not clearly favorable to one side or the other); THOMAS MAUET, FUNDAMENTALS OF TRIAL TECHNIQUES 347–48 (2d ed. 1988) (the objection, the "question calls for a narrative answer").

44. RICHARD D. RIEKE & RANDALL K. STUTMAN, COMMUNICATION IN LEGAL ADVOCACY 156, 184, 188–94 (1990).

45. DAMASKA, *supra* note 43, at 92–94, 99–103 (on "staccato effect" of objections and fragmentary nature testimony); GREGORY M. MATOESIAN, REPRODUCING RAPE: DOMINATION THROUGH TALK IN THE COURTROOM 110–33 (1993) (on objections).

46. *See* FED. R. EVID. 611; MCCORMICK ON EVIDENCE 9–10 (3d ed. 1984).

47. *See* HASKELL, *supra* note 1, at 22; CHARLES W. WOLFRAM, MODERN LEGAL ETHICS 647–48 (1986) (witness preparation to aid truthful testimony is ethical).

48. *See* FED. R. EVID. 103 (generally requires prompt objections to preserve appellate rights).

49. *See* DAMASKA, *supra* note 1, at 86, 89–90, 99–100 (on trial judge's limited ability to control adversarialism). C. F. S. Van Der Merwe, *Cross Examination of the (Sexually Abused) Child Witness in a Constitutionalized Adversarial Trial System: Is the South African Intermediary the Solution?, in* PROCEEDINGS

OF THE FIRST WORLD CONFERENCE ON NEW TRENDS IN CRIMINAL INVESTIGATION AND EVIDENCE 242–43, 248 (1997) (specially trained laypersons "have professional skills and practical experiences in examining witnesses" that lawyers lack).

50. *See* Van Der Merwe, *supra* note 49. I limit the intermediary procedure to consent defense cases because they are the ones where cultural rape narratives matter. Where the victim's nonconsent is instead conceded, the only question is who did the crime, not whether there was a rape in the first place.

51. *See generally* MADIGAN & GAMBLE, *supra* note 28.

52. AMEND. V., U.S. CONST. ("No person shall . . . be subject for the same offense to be twice put in jeopardy of life or limb. . . ."); STEPHEN A. SALTZBURG, AMERICAN CRIMINAL PROCEDURE: CASES AND COMMENTARY 1249–61 (5th ed. 1996) (The double jeopardy clause bars a prosecutor from appealing an acquittal).

53. *See, e.g.*, FEDERAL JUDICIAL CENTER, REFERENCE MANUAL ON SCIENTIFIC EVIDENCE (1994).

54. JOSEPHINE DONOVAN, FEMINIST THEORY: THE INTELLECTUAL TRADITIONS OF AMERICAN FEMINISM 1–30 (1992) (describing liberal feminist position that women are as rational and competent as men); CAROL HYMOWITZ & MICHAELE WEISSMAN, A HISTORY OF WOMEN IN AMERICA (1978) (surveying history of feminism in the United States as often involving a struggle for recognition of male-female equality of reason and ability); Wendy W. Williams, *Equality's Riddle: Pregnancy and the Equal Treatment/Special Treatment Debate*, FEMINIST LEGAL THEORY: FOUNDATIONS 128–30 (1993) (discussing feminist debate about whether to recognize pregnant women as meriting "special treatment").

55. 5 JOHN HENRY WIGMORE, A TREATISE ON THE ANGLO-AMERICAN SYSTEM OF EVIDENCE TRIALS AT COMMON LAW ¶1367, at 32 (1961). The failure of cross-examination to promote truth in rape cases stems from the combined effects of "feminine" language styles and cultural rape narratives. Consequently, although some rape and other defendants may use "less powerful" speaking styles than many middle-class white males, that does not justify the defendants' use of intermediaries too, for they, unlike rape victims, do not face the further handicap of patriarchal cultural rape tales. Nor do men suffer from the perceptual biases that lead jurors to hear women as speaking in a "feminine" style when they are not. Additionally, most consent defense cases are likely to involve men and women from similar social classes so that gender will magnify for women more than men the degree of real and perceived subordinate language style. The salience of gender at rape trials also increases women's subordinate roles, and gender mitigates the linguistic benefits enjoyed by more powerful women even in less threatening settings. On the other hand, future research may support the extension of the intermediary procedure to criminal defendants in

some cases. It is thus plausible that cultural narratives about spousal abuse combine with feminine language styles in a way that would justify using intermediaries in cases of battered women charged with killing their abusers.

56. *See* idem; STRIER, *supra* note 33, at 32–36 (on purported benefits of adversarial examination).

57. *See* DAMASKA, *supra* note 1, at 74–124 (comparing Continental with Anglo-American adversarial systems).

58. *See generally* GARRY, *supra* note 1, at 43–57 (adversarial culture is rooted in individualism); JAMES P. LEVINE, JURIES AND POLITICS (1992) (juries are a political institution); LLOYD E. MOORE, THE JURY: TOOL OF KINGS, PALLADIUM OF LIBERTY (2d ed. 1988) (tracing historical forces molding the modern jury).

59. DAMASKA, *supra* note 1, at 101. Much of the analysis here of the flaws in adversarial "truth-finding" procedures is drawn from DAMASKA's text. *See* idem at 74–124.

60. Idem at 81.

61. *See* idem at 74–124 (on Continental theory); Moulton, *supra* note 10 (on feminist theory).

62. DAMASKA, *supra* note 1, at 86.

63. Idem at 90 (quoting Marvin Frankel, *The Search for the Truth: An Umpireal View*, 123 U. PA. L. REV. 1031, 1042 (1975)).

64. DAMASKA, *supra* note 1, at 101.

65. Idem.

66. *See* Taslitz, *Patriarchal Stories, supra* note 27, at 405–39. The political role of the jury is discussed in chapter 7.

67. AMEND. VI, U.S. CONST.

68. Much of the argument here on face-to-face confrontation is similar to that made in Van Der Merwe, *supra* note 49, at 239–52, which also summarizes much of the relevant law supporting propositions I make in text. On meaningful cross-examination and confrontation, *see* Andrew E. Taslitz, *Catharsis, the Confrontation Clause, and Expert Testimony*, 22 CAP. U. L. REV. 103–44 (1993) [hereinafter *Catharsis*].

69. *See Coy v. Iowa*, 487 U.S. 1012 (1998) (holding that placement of a screen between the defendant and two sexual assault complainants violated the confrontation clause where the Iowa statute authorizing the procedure created a generalized, legislatively imposed presumption of trauma, rather than individualized findings that the particular witness needed special protection).

70. 497 U.S. 836 (1990).

71. Idem at 851.

72. *See* idem at 845, 850, 853.

73. *See* LUCY S. MCGOUGH, CHILD WITNESSES: FRAGILE VOICES IN THE AMERICAN LEGAL SYSTEM 228 (1994).

74. 497 U.S. at 855.

75. *See, e.g.,* NANCY A. MATTHEWS, CONFRONTING RAPE, THE FEMINIST ANTI-RAPE MOVEMENT AND THE STATE (1994); CASSIA SPOHN & JULIE HORNEY, RAPE LAW REFORM: A GRASSROOTS REVOLUTION AND ITS IMPACT 15–48 (1992).

76. *See* MCGOUGH, *supra* note 73, at 164–69 (making precisely this argument and reviewing lower court cases on the point).

77. 497 U.S. at 856–57 (emphasis added).

78. *See* idem at 842, 858–61. The "trauma" in *Craig* was shown by expert testimony, without the victim's ever being examined in the defendant's presence. Idem at 842. The Court rejected the defendant's argument that this procedure was necessarily flawed. *See* idem at 858–61.

79. On the need for a careful inquiry into psychological and related experts' abilities to make individualized judgments, *see* Taslitz, *Myself Alone, supra* note 14, at 72–85.

80. *White v. Illinois*, 502 U.S. 346, 356–57 (1992); *Ohio v. Roberts*, 448 U.S. 56, 66 (1980).

81. *See Craig*, 497 U.S. at 844–45, 855–58; *White*, 502 U.S. at 358.

82. 487 U.S. 1012 (1988).

83. Idem at 1033.

84. Idem.

85. *Ohio v. Roberts*, 448 U.S. 56, 65 (1980).

86. Idem at 73 (citations omitted). *See* Taslitz, *Catharsis, supra* note 68, at 104–13 (reading confrontation clause precedent as establishing something less than actual effectiveness in cross-examination); *Delaware v. Fensterer*, 474 U.S. 15 (1985) (per curiam) (similar); *United States v. Owens*, 484 U.S. 554, 560 (1988) (confrontation clause requires only "realistic weapons" for cross-examination).

87. *Pennsylvania v. Richie*, 480 U.S. 39 (1987) (plurality opinion). Nevertheless, the Court did remand the case under the due process clause to enable the trial judge to determine whether the records contained any information that may have affected the outcome of the trial. See idem at 58.

88. *See Fensterer*, 474 U.S. 15.

89. *Owens*, 484 U.S. 554.

90. *See, e.g., White*, 502 U.S. at 356 & n. 8–358.

91. *See, e.g., Rock v. Arkansas*, 483 U.S. 44 (1987) (per se exclusion of defense's hypnotically-refreshed-recall expert violated Sixth Amendment's compulsory process clause where procedural safeguards were available to protect against an excessive risk of error); Taslitz, *Catharsis, supra* note 68 at 113–22 (explaining how *Rock*-based approach of creating procedural safeguards for the admissibility of expert techniques is consistent with the Court's confrontation clause jurisprudence).

92. *See* DAMASKA, *supra* note 1, at 74–124 (nature and justifications for adversary system); SIMON, *supra* note 6, at 63–64, 138–69 (similar, but also proposes more contextual and less abusive system of legal ethics as fully consistent with the adversary system).

93. *Craig*, 497 U.S. at 846.

94. *See* idem at 845 (emphasis added) ("The word 'confront' means a clashing of forces or ideas. . . .").

95. Idem at 847 (emphasis added) (quoting *Fensterer*, 474 U.S. at 22).

96. *See* MCGOUGH, *supra* note 73, at 189–232 (detailing her proposal).

97. Idem at 216.

98. *See* idem at 219–20, 269–76 for a summary of the proposed safeguards and procedures, and a model statute.

99. Idem at 227 (quoting in part 5 JOHN HENRY WIGMORE, WIGMORE ON EVIDENCE ¶1420, at 252 (J. Chadbourn rev. 1974)).

100. *See, e.g.*, Margaret Berger, *The Deconstitutionalization of the Confrontation Clause*, 76 MINN. L. REV. 557 (1992) (one central concern of the confrontation clause is "restraining the capricious use of government power."); Randolph J. Jonakait, *The Origins of the Confrontation Clase: An Alternative History*, 27 RUTGERS L. J. 77 (1995) (confrontation clause operates with other Sixth Amendment rights to empower defense counsel and challenge information the government relies on); Robert P. Mosteller, *Remaking Confrontation Clause and Hearsay Doctrine Under the Challenge of Child Sexual Abuse Prosecutions*, 1993 U. Ill. L. Rev. 691, 717, 736–62 (1993) (confrontation clause was designed to protect the defendant against the introduction of evidence produced by the government under *ex parte* inquisitorial techniques). The only leading commentator not focusing on trustworthiness or governmental-constraint justifications for the confrontation clause is Professor Scallen, who stresses the cathartic and social values of face-to-face confrontation. *See* Eileen A. Scallen, *Constitutional Dimensions of Hearsay Reform: Toward a Three-Dimensional Confrontation Clause*, 76 MINN. L. REV. 623 (1992). Even she concedes, however, that traditional procedures must sometimes be altered for "compelling need." Idem at 651.

101. The modeling of what I have called "empathic experts" here partly tracks, then builds on, Aviva Orenstein, *No Bad Men!: A Feminist Analysis of Character Evidence in Rape Trials*, 49 HASTINGS L. J. 45–61 (1998) (draft manuscript). *See* idem at 45–51, for an analysis of rape trauma syndrome testimony.

102. Because these proposed experts offer educational background and are offered ultimately to prove mental state ("non-consent") rather than acts or identity, the experts should not run afoul of prohibitions against using character evidence to prove conduct under Federal Rule of Evidence 404 and its analogues. *See* Taslitz, *Myself Alone*, *supra* note 14, at 44–48 (404 prohibition probably does not extend to proving mental state under existing case law); *cf.* Myrna Raeder, *Proving the Case: Battered Woman and Batterer Syndrome: The Double-Edged*

Sword: Admissibility of Battered Woman Syndrome by and against Batterers in Cases Implicating Domestic Violence, 67 U. COLO. L. REV. 789 (1996) (arguing for an analogous educational approach in domestic violence cases).

103. Orenstein, *supra* note 101, at 53 (summarizing and quoting *Key v. State*, 765 S.W. 2d 848,850 (1989)).

104. *Key*, 765 S.W. 2d at 850–51.

105. *Cf.* Taslitz, *Feminist Approach, supra* note 15, at 44–46, 57–58 (summarizing feminist literature on the importance of experts concerning the batterer-battered relationship in battered woman prosecutions).

106. *See* Morrison Torrey, *When Will We Be Believed? Rape Myths and the Idea of a Fair Trial in Rape Prosecutions*, 24 U. C. DAVIS L. REV. 1013 (1991) (subjects exposed to sexually violent depictions of rape, which ordinarily increases rape-myth acceptance, showed reduced myth acceptance, even weeks after exposure, when also educated about rape myth inaccuracy and rape trauma). *But see* Scott Sundby, *The Jury as Critic: An Empirical Look at How Capital Juries Perceive Expert and Lay Testimony*, 6 VA. L. REV. 1109, 1178–84 (1997) (for social science experts to be persuasive, they must integrate their testimony into the case's specific facts in a way that provides a coherent narrative consistent with, and that makes sense of, the lay testimony; moreover, jurors are skeptical of much social science).

107. ARMOUR, *supra* note 12, at 122. Armour's summary of habitual cognitive reasoning processes about race informs the discussion here about rape. *See* idem at 115–53. *See also* Taslitz, *Patriarchal Stories, supra* note 27, at 404–33 (explaining how juror cognitive processes give cultural narratives a grip on jurors' evidentiary imaginations). The efficacy of this proposed reform, like that of the intermediary procedure, will, of course, need to be further assessed empirically as it is implemented.

NOTES TO CHAPTER 7

1. 343 U.S. 250 (1952).

2. Idem at 252.

3. Idem at 262–63. The current precedential value of *Beauharnais* has been called into question. ROBERT C. POST, CONSTITUTIONAL DOMAINS: DEMOCRACY, COMMUNITY, MANAGEMENT 104–5, 112–13, 308–9 (1995). Other scholars have argued either that *Beauharnais* is, or at least should still be, good law, especially in light of the enormous harm done by group defamation. *See generally* GROUP DEFAMATION AND FREEDOM OF SPEECH (MONROE H. FREEDMAN & ERIC M. FREEDMAN ed. (1995)) (collecting articles on these and related subjects).

4. *See, e.g.*, RUPERT BROWN, PREJUDICE: ITS SOCIAL PSYCHOLOGY 147–49, 176–85, 242–45 (1995); LARRY MAY, THE MORALITY OF

GROUPS: COLLECTIVE RESPONSIBILITY, GROUP-BASED HARM, AND CORPORATE RIGHTS 2–4, 112–20, 135–44 (1987) (philosophers' argument, drawing on social science data); *accord* KENNETH L. KARST, LAW'S PROMISE, LAW'S EXPRESSION: VISIONS OF POWER IN THE POLITICS OF RACE, GENDER, AND RELIGION 1–30, 67–111 (1993) [hereinafter LAW'S PROMISE] (similar argument, drawing on history and political theory).

5. *See* MAY, *supra* note 4, at 136–41 (on the importance of gender identity); *see also* Andrew E. Taslitz, *A Feminist Approach to Social Scientific Evidence: Foundations*, 5 MICH. J. GENDER & L. 1, 18–23 (1998) (on group identity as central to our sense of self).

6. Much of the analysis here of group definition and the relationship between harm to individuals and harm to groups is drawn from MAY, *supra* note 4, at 2–30, 73–81, 112–45.

7. Idem at 39.

8. MAY, *supra* note 4, at 139–40 (source of quotation and explanation why women are a coherent group); DEBORAH L. RHODE, SPEAKING OF SEX: THE DENIAL OF GENDER INEQUALITY 66–94 (1997) (how media images confirm traditional gender stereotypes); Andrew E. Taslitz, *Patriarchal Stories I: Cultural Rape Narratives in the Courtroom*, 5 S. CAL. REV. L. & WOM.'S ST. 387, 389 (1996) (on how gender roles limit women's freedom); Iris Marion Young, *Polity and Group Difference: A Critique of the Ideal of Universal Citizenship*, *in* FEMINISM AND POLITICAL THEORY (Cass Sunstein ed. 1990) (on why women constitute an oppressed group).

9. *See, e.g.*, DEBORAH TANNEN, TALKING FROM 9 TO 5: HOW WOMEN'S AND MEN'S CONVERSATIONAL STYLES AFFECT WHO GETS HEARD, WHO GETS CREDIT AND WHAT GETS DONE AT WORK (1994) (explaining how language, demeanor, and related gendered stylistic differences affect female advancement in the workplace).

10. For definitions of "the personal is political," *see* KENT GREENAWALT, FIGHTING WORDS: INDIVIDUALS, COMMUNITIES, AND LIBERTIES OF SPEECH 126–27 (1995); Martha Nussbaum, *Preface*, SEX, PREFERENCE, AND FAMILY: ESSAYS ON LAW AND NATURE v–viii (David M. Estlund & Martha C. Nussbaum eds. 1997).

11. *See* Taslitz, *Patriarchal Stories, supra* note 8, at 394–433 (effects of rape law and gendered ideology in molding female behavior and autonomy).

12. STEPHEN L. CARTER, THE DISSENT OF THE GOVERNED: A MEDITATION ON LAW, RELIGION, AND LOYALTY 5 (1998) (quoting Declaration of Independence).

13. Idem at 5–6.

14. LAWRENCE E. MITCHELL, STACKED DECK: A STORY OF SELFISHNESS IN AMERICA 1–2 (1998). For Professor Carter's analysis of how citizen "disallegiance" to the sovereign is promoted when it fails to hear citizen com-

plaints, *see* CARTER, *supra* note 12, at 3–49. For an analysis of the importance of encouraging dissent, and hearing dissenters, as First Amendment free speech values, *see* STEVEN H. SHIFFRIN, THE FIRST AMENDMENT, DEMOCRACY, AND ROMANCE (1990), whose views I have relied on but modified in light of other sources noted in this chapter.

15. *See* SHIFFRIN, *supra* note 14, at 96 ("[D]issent and the threat of dissent make hierarchy less oppressive. Dissent communicates the fears, hopes, and aspirations of the less powerful to those in power. It sometimes chills the abuse of power. . . .").

16. I here build on the concept of "effective voice" articulated in Victoria Smith, *Effective Voice Rights in the Workplace, in* FREEING THE FIRST AMENDMENT: CRITICAL PERSPECTIVES ON FREEDOM OF SPEECH 114–24 (David S. Allen and Robert Jensen eds. 1995).

17. *Stromberg v. California*, 283 U.S. 359, 363 (1931). My analysis of self-rule, collective autonomy, and responsive democracy fuses ideas developed in Hanna Pitkin, *Justice: On Relating Private and Public*, 9 POLITICAL THEORY 327, 343, 346 (1981); POST, *supra* note 3, at 119–96; John A. Powell, *Worlds Apart: Reconciling Freedom of Speech and Equality*, 85 KY. L. J. 9, 49–74 (1997). I also draw generally on various themes in KARST, *supra* note 4. On trial "fact-finding" as law creation, *see* Darryl K. Brown, *Plain Meaning, Practical Reason, and Culpability: Toward a Theory of Jury Interpretation of Criminal Statutes*, 96 MICH. L. REV. 1199 (1998); Taslitz, *Patriarchal Stories, supra* note 8, at 419–24.

18. Pitkin, *supra* note 17, at 327, 343, 346. POST, *supra* note 3, and Powell, *supra* note 17, also inform my observations about the social and constitutive nature of self-rule.

19. This analysis of individual autonomy builds on, and is largely a fusion of ideas in, GRACE CLEMENT, CARE, AUTONOMY, AND JUSTICE: FEMINISM AND THE ETHIC OF CARE 21–25 (1996); Christine Di Stefano, *Autonomy in the Light of Difference, in* REVISIONING THE POLITICAL: FEMINIST RECONSTRUCTIONS OF TRADITIONAL CONCEPTS IN WESTERN POLITICAL THOUGHT 95–111 (Nancy J. Hirschmann and Christine Di Stefano eds. 1996); WILLARD GAYLIN & BRUCE JENNINGS, THE PERVERSION OF AUTONOMY: THE PROPER USES OF COERCION AND CONSTRAINT IN A LIBERAL SOCIETY (1990); POST, *supra* note 3, at 7–15, 63–64, 74, 184–96, 268–89, 329–31. *See also* Lorraine Code, *Second Persons, in* SCIENCE, MORALITY AND FEMINIST THEORY 361 (Marsha Hanen and Kai Nielsen eds. 1987).

20. CLEMENT, *supra* note 19, at 25.

21. Thomas Emerson, in a now-classic article, clearly articulated a largely realist notion of truth as attained by the clash of individuals' ideas to improve individuals' judgment. *See* Thomas Emerson, *Toward a General Theory of the First Amendment*, 72 YALE L. J. 877 (1963). Yet even Emerson recognized two social

aspects of truth. First, the discovery of truth benefits society as a whole. Second, social institutions must make decisions about what constitutes truth in order to guide collective action. Nevertheless, Emerson sees social judgment as "vitally conditioned by the quality of the individual judgments which compose it." Idem at 882. Other theorists have recognized, however, that some truths are social in the sense that "truths" consist of whatever the relevant social collectivity agrees they are. *See, e.g.,* S. Ingner, *The Marketplace of Ideas: A Legitimizing Myth,* 1984 DUKE L. J. 1, 25 ("the assumption of the existence of objective truth is crucial to classic marketplace theory, [and] almost no one believes in objective truth today. . . ."); KENT GREENAWALT, SPEECH, CRIME, AND THE USES OF LANGUAGE 16–18 (1989) (arguing for the relevance of "truth-discovery" to First Amendment reasoning, even if notions of "objective" reality are questioned). *See also* Taslitz, *Feminist Approach, supra* note 5 (on truth creation at trials). On the theory that in a world of socially constructed truths, only truths determined by a truly representative process deserve allegiance, *see* SEYLA BENHABIB, CRITIQUE, NORM, AND UTOPIA (1986); THOMAS MCCARTHY, THE CRITICAL THEORY OF JÜRGEN HABERMAS 59, 334 (1978); Powell, *supra* note 17, at 70–74.

22. *See* Thomas Streeter, *Some Thoughts on Free Speech, Language, and the Rule of Law, in* FREEING THE FIRST AMENDMENT, *supra* note 16, at 31–40 (linguistic-style differences communicate social relations of power, hierarchy, solidarity, and intimacy, giving the lie to the marketplace of ideas metaphor).

23. John Powell has persuasively argued in similar but not identical fashion that meaningful participation in society's critical institutions is a common value underlying *both* free speech and equal protection. *See* Powell, *supra* note 17, at 72–76. Powell, like me, roots his theory in the work of Kenneth Karst. *See* KENNETH L. KARST, BELONGING TO AMERICA (1989).

24. *See* Powell, *supra* note 17, at 74.

25. Civil Rights Act of 1866; *see* KARST, BELONGING TO AMERICA, *supra* note 23, at 49–51.

26. *See* KARST, BELONGING TO AMERICA, *supra* note 23, at 49–51.

27. U.S. CONST., Amend. XIV (emphasis added).

28. *See* WILLIAM E. NELSON, THE FOURTEENTH AMENDMENT: FROM POLITICAL PRINCIPLE TO JUDICIAL DOCTRINE 104 (1988) ("[T]he Fourteenth Amendment . . . [and] the Civil Rights Act of 1866 . . . were inextricably linked in the spring of 1866, since section one was added to the Amendment at least in part to remove doubts about the constitutionality of the 1866 Act.").

29. *Dred Scott v. Sandford,* 60 U.S. (19 How.) 393 (1857). *See generally* DON E. FEHRENBACHER, THE DRED SCOTT CASE: ITS SIGNIFICANCE IN AMERICAN LAW (1978).

30. *Dred Scott,* 60 U.S. (19 How.) at 416.

31. *See* KARST, BELONGING TO AMERICA, *supra* note 23, at 43–49 (analyzing *Dred Scott*).

32. *See* idem at 15–27.

33. *See* KARST, LAW'S PROMISE, *supra*, note 4, at 106–11, 125–46 (making similar point).

34. *See, e.g.*, KARST, BELONGING TO AMERICA, *supra* note 23; Powell, *supra* note 17; Young, *supra* note 8.

35. *See* MICHAEL WALZER, SPHERES OF JUSTICE 31–40, 78–79 (1983).

36. Powell, *supra* note 17, at 74–79.

37. KARST, BELONGING TO AMERICA, *supra* note 23, at 4.

38. Powell, *supra* note 17, at 74–78 (defining "critical institutions"); *cf.* POST, *supra* note 3, at 183–84 (explaining social, cultural, and political functions of the courts).

39. *See* Young, *supra* note 8 (defining and critiquing the modern notion of "universal" citizenship).

40. Idem at 124–25. Young also explains that groups can transcend their own self-interest. *See* idem at 130–31. For an illustration of differences in group perceptions of reality, *see* Andrew E. Taslitz, *An African-American Sense of Fact: O.J. and Black Judges on Justice*, 7 B. U. PUB. INT. L. J. 219 (1998).

41. *See* Young, *supra* note 8, at 118, 135–36; Herma Hill Kay, *Equality and Difference: The Case of Pregnancy*, 1 BERKELEY WOM.'S L. J. 1–38 (1985). On the current status of the law concerning differential treatment of pregnant women, *see* Candace Saari Kovacic-Fleischer, *United States v. Virginia's New Gender Equal Protection Analysis with Ramifications for Pregnancy, Parenting, and Title VII*, 50 VAND. L. REV. 845 (1997).

42. AMY GUTMANN, LIBERAL EQUALITY 191–202 (1980) (discussing the study of community control of schools); JANE MANSBRIDGE, BEYOND ADVERSARIAL DEMOCRACY (1980) (on white middle-class male comfort with authority); Young, *supra* note 8, at 125 (interpreting Gutmann's and Mansbridge's works).

43. MANSBRIDGE, *supra* note 42.

44. Young, *supra* note 8, at 126.

45. *See* idem at 128–29.

46. That some men are harmed too by our evidentiary policies and some women are not does not alter the equal protection analysis. In *United States v. Virginia*, 116 S. Ct. 2264 (1996), for example, the Court held that Virginia Military Institute's (VMI) exclusion of women violated equal protection. Unchallenged experts had testified that most women prefer cooperative learning and would not, therefore, want to be exposed to VMI's "adversative" educational methods. The Court held, however, that it was sufficient to implicate equal protection that only "some" women suffered from VMI's exclusionary policy. *See* idem at 2279–80. Moreover, although the Court condemned differential policies

excluding women, it noted, "Sex classifications may be used to compensate women 'for particular economic disabilities [they have] suffered' . . . 'to promote equal employment opportunity'. . . [and] advance full development of the talent and capacities of our Nation's people." Idem at 2276. The new evidentiary policies proposed in this book seek to "advance full development of the . . . capacities of our Nation's people" by giving equal access to a fair hearing for the many rape victims and by giving them "standing" to raise the constitutional claims discussed here. I do not address the mechanics by which they would do so, however, because I see my arguments as directed toward the constitutional obligations of the federal and state legislatures rather than the courts. *Cf.* Doriane Lambelet Coleman, *Individualizing Justice Through Multiculturalism: The Liberals' Dilemma*, 96 COL. L. Rev. 1093, 1129–35 & nn. 202–5 (1996) (conceding that victims of criminal acts generally lack standing to challenge, under the equal protection clause, a prosecutor's decision to forgo pursuing criminal charges in a particular case; however, some courts do recognize a right of communities and their members offended by selective nonprosecution to attack discriminatory prosecutorial practices and policies in the courts; furthermore, the primary or initial constitutional obligation to prevent such discrimination lies with the legislature and the executive, not the judiciary); *Georgia v. McCollum*, 505 U.S. 42, 55–57 (1992) ("[T]he State has standing to assert the excluded jurors' rights" to equal protection against their being barred from jury service because of their race by a criminal defendant who exercises his peremptory challenges [a party's right to bar a limited number of potential jurors from service without stating a reason]). *See also* Laurie L. Levenson, *Change of Venue and the Role of the Criminal Jury*, 66 S. CAL. L. REV. 1533, 1557–11 (1993) (California Constitution amended to give "the people," and not just criminal defendants, a right to due process of law); Karyn Ellen Polito, Note, *The Rights of Crime Victims in the Criminal Justice System: Is Justice Blind to the Victims of Crime?*, 16 NEW ENG. J. CRIM. & CIV. CONFINEMENT 242 (1990) (summarizing current obstacles to, and potential ways to improve, victim participation in the justice system). That I endorse reforms to benefit rape victims does not mean, however, that I embrace all of the victims' rights movement, which includes many proposals dangerous to sound conceptions of a fair trial. *See, e.g.*, Robert P. Mosteller, *Victims' Rights and the United States Constitution: An Effort to Recast the Battle in Criminal Litigation*, 85 GEO. L. J. 1691 (1997) (summarizing these dangers).

47. AKHIL REED AMAR & ALAN HIRSCH, FOR THE PEOPLE: WHAT THE CONSTITUTION REALLY SAYS ABOUT YOUR RIGHTS 52 (1998). The jury has sometimes failed in its role as guardian against governmental abuses. My argument is only that the Framers saw it in part as serving such a role and that we should design our laws and practices to improve the jury's ability to serve a checking function.

48. Idem at 52. The U.S. Supreme Court has, however, sometimes wrongly

failed to appreciate the analogy between a bicameral judiciary and a bicameral legislature. *See* AKHIL REED AMAR, THE BILL OF RIGHTS: CREATION AND RECONSTRUCTION 104–9 (1998) (debunking the flaws in the Court's reasoning).

49. *See* AMAR & HIRSCH, *supra* note 47, at 53, 57*; GODFREY D. LEHMAN, WE, THE JURY: THE IMPACT OF JURORS ON OUR BASIC FREEDOMS 151–73 (1997) (summarizing juries' historical role as defender of free speech). The Framers' faith in the jury as a guardian of free speech rights was likely rooted partly in a jury's acquittal of John Peter Zenger on a charge of libeling colonial authorities. *See, e.g.,* LEHMAN, *supra,* at 151–73. Nevertheless, the Framers' free speech concepts at the time of the Bill of Rights' ratification were arguably narrow by modern standards, and the jury failed to protect dissident speakers prosecuted under the Alien and Sedition Acts. *See* idem at 175–204. That failure may have been due more to prosecutorial and judicial abuses of the trial process than to any inherent failure of the jury system. *See* idem at 175–204. Views of free speech became much more generous, however, with the repeal of the Alien and Sedition Acts in the wake of the election of 1800. *See* Craig R. Smith, *The Hamiltonian Federalists, in* SILENCING THE OPPOSITION: GOVERNMENT STRATEGIES OF SUPPRESSION OF FREEDOM OF EXPRESSION 1–20 (Craig R. Smith ed. 1996). But the concept of free speech was then more majoritarian than libertarian, the primary concern being to protect popular speakers from unrepresentative government officials. *See* AMAR, *supra* note 48, at 20–26. With growing Southern repression of abolitionist speech, greater concern was later placed on protecting unpopular minorities from majority tyranny. *See* idem at 231–42. That led the Reconstruction Congress to have mixed feelings toward juries. On the one hand, Northerners fought for Northern jury trials as a way to protect blacks in the North from summary return to their purported slave masters under the Fugitive Slave Act of 1850. On the other hand, the Reconstruction Congress understood that Southern juries could not reasonably be expected to protect the free speech rights of newly freed slaves. *See* idem at 231–42; Andrew E. Taslitz, *Discovery, the Fourth Amendment, and the Informed Citizen* (draft manuscript 1998). That concern may help justify doctrines in modern free speech case law showing some measure of distrust in the jury. *See* AMAR, *supra* note 48, at 231–42. But this history merely demonstrates that judges and juries each have roles to play in protecting free speech. Because the criminal defendant has a constitutional right to a jury trial, U.S. CONST., Amend. VI, I have stressed the jury's role. But for either judge or jury to serve as an effective guardian of free speech and equality rights, each much be fully informed in the ways that I have here suggested.

50. *See* AMAR & HIRSCH, *supra* note 47, at 53.

51. ALEXIS DE TOCQUEVILLE, DEMOCRACY IN AMERICA 250 (J. P. Mayer and Max Lerner eds. 1966).

52. *See* AMAR & HIRSCH, *supra* note 47, at 54 (citizenship breeding ground); JEFFREY ABRAMSON, WE THE JURY: THE JURY SYSTEM AND THE IDEAL OF DEMOCRACY 89 (1994) ("The lawmaking jury [envisioned by the Framers] . . . served as a hands-on school where citizens learned the virtues of self-government by actively participating in their community's laws.").

53. AMAR & HIRSCH, *supra* note 47, at 54.

54. *See* idem at 93–114; ABRAMSON, *supra* note 52, at 90–95; Brown, *supra* note 17, at 21–27.

55. *See* RICHARD D. BROWN, THE STRENGTH OF A PEOPLE: THE IDEA OF AN INFORMED CITIZENRY IN AMERICA, 1650–1870 (1996).

56. The view of the Fourteenth Amendment articulated here is drawn from ROBIN WEST, PROGRESSIVE CONSTITUTIONALISM 1–44 (1994), which carefully describes the history and philosophy supporting this interpretation.

57. Idem at 24.

58. WILLIAM E. NELSON, THE FOURTEENTH AMENDMENT: FROM POLITICAL PRINCIPLE TO JUDICIAL DOCTRINE 78–79 (1988).

59. *See* WEST, *supra* note 56, at 30–44.

60. *See* JOAN HOFF, LAW, GENDER AND JUSTICE: A LEGAL HISTORY OF U.S. WOMEN 248–49 (1991) (explaining "middle scrutiny"); *Craig v. Boren*, 429 U.S. 190 (1976) (early case clearly stating that middle scrutiny governs gender classifications).

61. WEST, *supra* note 56, at 39.

62. *See* SANDRA LIPSITZ BEM, THE LENSES OF GENDER: TRANS-FORMING THE DEBATE ON SEXUAL INEQUALITY 133–64 (1993) (arguing that our culture makes gender central to our identity).

63. *See* ALLAN H. JOHNSON, THE GENDER KNOT: UNRAVELING OUR PATRIARCHAL LEGACY 5, 14, 26–27, 84–88 (1997) (making this argument in slightly different terms).

64. WEST, *supra* note 56, at 36.

65. JODY DAVID ARMOUR, NEGROPHOBIA AND REASONABLE RACISM: THE HIDDEN COST OF BEING BLACK IN AMERICA 81 (1997). *See also* Taslitz, *Feminist Approach, supra* note 5, at 39–40 (evidentiary narratives as "pitched conflict").

66. WEST, *supra* note 56, at 41.

67. 198 U.S. 45 (1905).

68. *See* WAYNE D. MOORE, CONSTITUTIONAL RIGHTS AND POWERS OF THE PEOPLE 196–214 (1996). That some of the Court's decisions involved state, and some federal, legislation does not alter the fundamental point that the Constitution may authorize, even mandate, legislative action even where the judiciary may not so act. *See* idem 196–238.

69. Idem at 211–12. For a summary and analysis of the "switch in time that saved nine," *see* idem at 197–214.

70. Idem at 212 (emphasis in original).

71. Idem at 159 (quoting Essays of Brutus, no. II, November 1, 1787, in 2 THE COMPLETE ANTI-FEDERALIST 372 (1981) (Herbert Storing ed.)).

72. Letters of Agrippa, no. XVI, February 5, 1788, in 4 THE COMPLETE ANTI-FEDERALIST at 111.

73. MOORE, *supra* note 68, at 159.

74. *See* idem at 165–66.

75. 11 PAPERS OF JAMES MADISON 298–99 (Julian P. Boyd ed.). *See also* MOORE, *supra* note 68, at 166.

76. 11 PAPERS OF JAMES MADISON *supra* note 75, at 298–99.

77. WEST, *supra* note 56, at 43. *See also* JOHN J. DINAN, KEEPING THE PEOPLE'S LIBERTIES: LEGISLATORS, CITIZENS, AND JUDGES AS GUARDIANS OF RIGHTS 1–60 (1998) (pre-twentieth-century republican conception of government relied primarily on legislative action and citizen virtue, not courts, to protect individual liberties).

78. U.S. CONST., Amend. XIV.

79. *See* MOORE, *supra* note 68, at 269–74.

80. Idem at 273.

81. U.S. CONST., Amend. XIV (emphasis added). *Cf.* JAMES E. BOND, NO EASY WALK TO FREEDOM: RECONSTRUCTION AND RATIFICATION OF THE FOURTEENTH AMENDMENT 251–67 (1997) (offering a generally flawed analysis of the Fourteenth Amendment but properly recognizing a continuing role for state governments in defining privileges and immunities and ensuring equal protection); DINAN, *supra* note 77, at 1–60 (*state* legislatures in particular long viewed as having the first obligation to protect individual liberties).

82. *See* JOSHUA DRESSLER, UNDERSTANDING CRIMINAL LAW 531–56 (2d ed. 1995) (largely relying on state cases as central to understanding the law of rape).

NOTES TO THE CONCLUSION

1. 2 SIR MATTHEW HALE, THE HISTORY OF THE PLEAS OF THE CROWN 634 (1847) [1678]. For histories of the rape law reform movement, *see* NANCY A. MATTHEWS, CONFRONTING RAPE: THE FEMINIST ANTI-RAPE MOVEMENT AND THE STATE 1–15 (1994); PEGGY REEVES SANDAY, A WOMAN SCORNED: ACQUAINTANCE RAPE ON TRIAL 161–207 (1996); CASSIA SPOHN & JULIE HORNEY, RAPE LAW REFORM: A GRASS-ROOTS REVOLUTION AND ITS IMPACT 15–48 (1992).

2. On perceived motives for women to lie and the ideology of early rape law, *see* SANDAY *supra* note 1, at 50–65, 82–140, 180. On the content and significance of early rape law, *see* SPOHN & HORNEY, *supra* note 1, at 15–48.

3. PAUL H. GEBHARD, JOHN H. GAGNON, WARDELL P. POMEROY,

& CORNELIA V. CHRISTENSON, SEX OFFENDERS: AN ANALYSIS OF TYPES 108–9 (1965); SANDAY, *supra* note 1, at 163 (summarizing the Kinsey study).

4. SPOHN & HORNEY, *supra* note 1, at 17. A claim of self-defense in an assault or homicide trial is one of the few areas other than sexual assault where the criminal law made (and still makes) the victim's conduct explicitly relevant. *See* JOSHUA DRESSLER, UNDERSTANDING CRIMINAL LAW 199–230 (2d ed. 1995).

5. *People v. Abbott,* 19 Wend. 192, 195–96 (N.Y. 1838).

6. Margaret A. Clemens, *Elimination of the Resistance Requirement and Other Rape Law Reforms,* 47 ALBANY L. REV. 871, 871 (1983).

7. Idem.

8. *See, e.g.,* SANDAY, *supra* note 1, at 161–83; SPOHN & HORNEY, *supra* note 1, at 15–48; Andrew E. Taslitz, *Patriarchal Stories I: Cultural Rape Narratives in the Courtroom,* 5 S. CAL. REV. L. & WOM.'S ST. 387, 389–402 (1996).

9. *See* Taslitz, *supra* note 8, at 389–402 (on rape law reformers' failures, backlash, and Camille Paglia); TRANSFORMING A RAPE CULTURE (Emilie Buchwald et al. eds. 1993).

10. *See* Taslitz, *supra* note 8, at 396–99, 404–10 (collecting empirical data).

11. SUSAN BROWNMILLER, AGAINST OUR WILL: MEN, WOMEN AND RAPE 229 (1975).

12. *Cf.* D. Brereton, *How Different Are Rape Trials? A Comparison of the Cross-Examination of Complainants in Rape and Assault Trials,* 37 BRITISH J. CRIM. 242 (1997) (comparative study of transcripts of assault and rape trials in an Australian county revealed both strong similarities between the two types of proceedings and features unique to rape trials).

13. Whether a woman consented, and thus whether an acquittal was wise, is partly a matter of interpretation. *See* Taslitz, *Patriarchal Stories, supra* note 8, at 394–433. To say that acquittals are too "high" in some apolitical, objective way is thus difficult. Nevertheless, an acquittal is "unjustified" if based on biased or incomplete information, or if the jury relied on patriarchal values.

Index

Abolitionism, 146–48
Accumulation of disadvantage, 108–9
Acquaintance rape, 28
Adversary system: alternatives to, 111; and binary thinking, 107–8; as clash of ideas, 129–30; as combat and sport, 81; compared to Continental systems, 120–23; and emotions, 108–9; and equal resources, 81; and externalities, 109–11; flaws in, 105–15; gender bias in, 105–9; and interruptions, 108; and intimidation, 129; and male communication styles, 81–82; not a sporting contest; 129–30; as party-controlled, 121–23; as rigorous testing, 129; and spousal immunity, 186–87; and truth-discovery, 120–21
African American: communication styles, 77–80, 178–80; illustrating plight of, 1–11; images of females, 31–33; images of males, 28–31; males as wolf pack, 31; as rape victims, 31–33; and tonal semantics, 78; verbal tradition, 78; women as welfare queens, 31
Agonistic language, 70
Alternative description, 96–97
Amount of talk, 69–73
"Asking for it," 21–22

Bavli (sacred Jewish text), 76–77
Beaching. *See* Fraternities
Beauharnais v. Illinois: and group-individual justice connection, 134–37; and group harm, 134–35
Bewitched, 69
Bowman, Patricia, cross-examination of, 82–83. *See also* Smith, William Kennedy
Brown v. Board of Education, 142
Brownmiller, Susan, 154

Bullying: and psychopaths, 28; and *Rambo*, 26; rules for, 25–26; and Audrey Savage case, 29; and *The Terminator*, 26–27; and Mike Tyson, 52. *See also* Central Park jogger case

Carter, Stephen, 137–38
Caste, 113
Categorization, 86–87
Central Park jogger case, 28; compared with similar black victim, 32; and race, 30–31; and Mike Tyson, 52
Character: as cross-situational, 27; expert witnesses about, 16; of victims, 6–7
Citizenship, 142–47; evidence rules can degrade, 144–45; and group difference, 144; as informed, 145; the jury as breeding ground for, 145–47; and "paradox of democracy," 144; universal, 143–44
Civil codes, 104
Civil Rights Act of 1866: equal protection and degradation, 142; and the fourteenth amendment, 142; and meaningful participation, 142; and universal citizenship, 143–44
Clients, 103
Clockwork Orange, A (Burgess), 28
Closed circuit television, 123–28; and child abuse victims, 130–31; and communication styles, 79–80; and race, 77–80. *See also* Confrontation clause
"Complementarity," notion of, 80
Confrontation clause: and case-specific rules, 126–27; and closed circuit television, 123–28; and ex parte affidavits, 131; and gender translation, 128–31; and general rules, 127–28; and hearsay, 127–28; and interest-balancing, 124–27; and intermediary, 128–31; and internal

205

About the Author

Andrew E. Taslitz is a professor of law at the Howard University School of Law, where he teaches criminal law, criminal procedure, evidence, and professional responsibility. Professor Taslitz is a former prosecutor in Philadelphia, Pennsylvania, where, for a time, he specialized in prosecuting, and later trained others to prosecute, juvenile sexual assault cases. He is the author of numerous articles in the areas in which he teaches, most recently focusing his work on feminist evidence law and sexual assault. He is the immediate past Co-Chair of the American Bar Association (ABA) Criminal Justice Section's Committee on Race and Racism, where he helped to spearhead an ultimately successful effort to have the ABA amend its Comments to the Model Rules of Professional Conduct to prohibit certain racist or sexist behavior by lawyers in the course of representing clients.

Professor Taslitz is the co-author of the Foundation Press text, CONSTITUTIONAL CRIMINAL PROCEDURE (1997), and of a monograph-length Legal Appendix to CONTAINING THE THREAT FROM ILLEGAL BOMBINGS: AN INTEGRATED NATIONAL STRATEGY FOR MARKING, TAGGING, RENDERING INERT, AND LICENSING EXPLOSIVES AND THEIR PRECURSORS (1998), published by the National Research Council. He is a member of the Editorial Board of the ABA periodical, CRIMINAL JUSTICE, and a member of the Executive Committee of the Association of American Law Schools Section on Criminal Justice. He received his J.D. in 1981 from the University of Pennsylvania Law School.